921   Lewis, Paul
Burgoyne   The man who lost America; a biography of
           Gentleman Johnny Burgoyne.   Dial, 1973.

           1. Burgoyne, John 2. U.S. - Hist. -
           Revolution I. T.

THE MAN WHO LOST AMERICA

A Biography of Gentleman Johnny Burgoyne

The Dial Press
New York
1973

THE MAN WHO

A Biography of Gentleman Johnny Burgoyne

LOST AMERICA

by PAUL LEWIS

Excerpt from George Bernard Shaw's notes for *The Devil's Disciple* is reprinted by permission of The Society of Authors, on behalf of the Bernard Shaw Estate.

Library of Congress Cataloging in Publication Data

The man who lost america.

Bibliography: p.
1. Burgoyne, John, 1722–1792.   I.   Title.

DA67.1.B8G47   973.3′41′0924 [B]   72–10285

Printed in the United States of America
First Printing
Design by Lynn Braswell

for Jo and Bob Williams

Should the American colonists rebel against the treatment accorded them by His Majesty's Government, I, for one, would not blame them. As for myself, I can but hope I shall never be required to take the field against them, as they would fight like men possessed by demons.

—John Burgoyne, Member of Parliament,
in an address delivered in the
House of Commons, October 23, 1774.

One

Environment and heredity guaranteed that John Burgoyne would be a gentleman, a fashionable product of the eighteenth century endowed with a keen appreciation of fine food and wine, a rival in dress of the great beaux of the era, a man with a penchant for gambling and a sharp eye for attractive ladies. His own talents combined to make him the most prominent of the Burgoynes, a noted soldier, a distinguished Member of Parliament, and a playwright who, in his own Age of Enlightenment, was regarded as the peer of Richard Brinsley Sheridan.

Some historians tried to account for his unexpected genius by claiming he was the illegitimate son of Lord Bingley, a wealthy bachelor diplomat, and the legend was so persistent that it lasted into the early years of the present century, but the truth of the matter is that Bingley was his godfather, nothing more. It is typical of Gentleman Johnny, however, that a hint of scandal should be attached to his good name for more than one hundred years after his own lifetime.

The Burgoynes were members of the minor aristocracy, tracing their lineage to 1387, when the founder of the line, Roger Burgoyne, was granted extensive estates by John of Gaunt. His father was the second son of a baronet, Sir John Burgoyne, who inherited neither a title nor riches of consequence, but who made a career of being a man about town. He was known in the first quarter of the eighteenth century as a fop who could distinguish good claret from inferior merely by sniffing the cork, and who sent meals back to the kitchen when a dish was not cooked to his precise taste. He was also an inveterate and exceptionally lucky gambler, a man who spent most of his afternoons playing cards, and developed such skill that he was usually ahead of the game.

The elder Burgoyne could afford his expensive tastes because his wife, the former Anna Maria Burnestone, was an heiress who brought a handsome dowry into their marriage. Relatively little is known about her, but she appears to have been something of a paragon, a beautiful girl who matured with grace and was still lovely in middle age. She was vivacious and articulate, qualities her son inherited, and it was from her that he acquired his interest in the theater.

John Burgoyne, tactfully named for his wealthy grandfather, was born in the London town house of his parents on January 11, 1722, and his mother had good cause to rejoice. Not only was he a healthy infant who came into the world in a year when the plague was prevalent in the city, but his appearance had an immediate, salutary effect on his father. Giving up his gambling, in which he rarely indulged thereafter, the elder Burgoyne used family influence to obtain an appointment as a King's Magistrate on the London bench, a post he held for the rest of his life, serving assiduously if not with any particular distinction.

A friend and later a fellow magistrate was Henry Fielding, known to posterity as the author of *Tom Jones*, as the creator of Tom Thumb, and as a successful dramatist. Anna Maria's love of the theater made her an admirer of Fielding, who was a frequent dinner guest, and it has been argued that John Burgoyne decided early in life to emulate the author. Unfortunately, this logical thesis is speculative, since no hard facts are available to substantiate it. In fact, it is doubtful that John dined with his parents when guests were present, and if the usual practice of the period was followed, he caught only an occasional glimpse of Fielding, being called into the drawing room to greet the visitor, then being banished again to his own playroom.

But his mother's influence on him was profound, and at the age of seventy, shortly before his own death, he continued to refer to her in glowing terms. He also enjoyed a solid, stable relationship with his father, who insisted he obtain a sound foundation in the classics. "I was made to read Latin even before I learned to read English. The first book I read from beginning to end was Caesar's *Gallic Wars*," John Burgoyne wrote many years later. Some of his early biographers used this comment as the basis for the claim that Burgoyne was inspired by the example of Julius Caesar to follow a military career, but this romantic notion cannot be validated by anything that the future general himself ever indicated.

Educated at home by tutors until the age of ten, as was the custom of the day, John was then sent off to one of the better and more aristocratic of England's great public schools, Westminster. He showed a consistent enthusiasm for the classics and became proficient in Latin and Greek, thereby forming the basis for his lifelong penchant of quoting from both ancient tongues. But he did not otherwise distinguish himself as a scholar, a leader, or an athlete.

He formed a close friendship with a classmate, Lord Strange, the eldest son and heir of the eleventh Earl of Derby, a relationship that would be maintained for the rest of their lives. The friendship exerted a major influence on John, who visited various of the Derby homes and estates and saw at first hand how England's greatest aristocrats lived. In due time he also became acquainted with the sixth of Lord Strange's sisters, Charlotte Stanley, with whom he would elope in the culmination of a romance that created one of the more sensational scandals of its day.

A military career loomed as inevitable when John, at the

age of fifteen, in 1737, received an honorary appointment as sub-brigadier of the Third Troop of Horse Guards, such appointments being a usual practice in families of substance when a boy showed future promise as an officer. John was already an accomplished horseman, and on visits to the Derby estates he delighted in riding bareback, disconcerting the grooms who entertained justifiable fears that he might break his neck. He also took up fencing as a sport, and in his late teens took instructions from a professional swordsman. He was an apt pupil, and soon demonstrated great proficiency with the saber, the heaviest of the weapons used by duelists.

The life of a soldier was a natural outlet for an untitled aristocrat who would not inherit a great fortune, and on April 23, 1744, when young Burgoyne was twenty-two, his parents advanced him the funds to purchase a commission as a cornet, the equivalent of the present-day second lieutenant, in the First Dragoons, one of the most elite of British cavalry regiments. One year later the young officer received a normal promotion to the rank of first lieutenant, and the following January, thanks to his family's influence and that of Lord Strange, he was made a captain. In 1747 his need for money made it necessary for him to sell his commission, and he formally retired from the Royal Army in the autumn of 1751, for all ostensible intents and purposes terminating his military career. He did not resume it until five years later, in the summer of 1756, when he returned to duty as a captain of the Eleventh Dragoons.

Cornet Burgoyne was one of the more dashing of London's young men about town. He was five feet, ten inches tall, and stood a half-head above most of his contemporaries. His hair was brown, his eyes were a deep shade of blue and he had acquired his father's liking for clothes, which he wore with an air that called him to the attention of gentlemen and ladies alike. His military duties were light, he was rarely required to wear his uniform, and he soon developed the habit of visiting various salons, often in the company of Lord Strange and other blue-bloods. Conversation was a high art that required dexterity and a nimble wit, and young Burgoyne became as expert in verbal fencing as he was able in the handling of a sword, his small talk usually peppered with classical citations, which he first quoted in Greek or Latin and then translated for the benefit of listeners whose education might have been deficient.

It is small wonder that, as a drawing-room veteran, the dialogue he wrote in his plays forty years later had a ring of authenticity lacking in the works of his rival, Sheridan. When Burgoyne portrayed high-society ladies and gentlemen dueling with words, he was writing about his peers, and within the limitations of theatrical artifice currently being employed, he never sounded a false note.

An energetic youth in his early twenties could not be satisfied with mere talk, to be sure, and Burgoyne found an outlet for his craving for action in cards, his father's one-time favorite pastime. He became an expert whist player, and Lord Strange wrote that Burgoyne had a professional gambler's sixth sense in games of twenty-and-one, a French import that English aristocrats were adopting with enthusiasm.

If John Burgoyne had already developed intellectual depth, much less the liberal convictions that became evident in his maturity, he succeeded in concealing these traits from his contemporaries. He was facile, but there is no evidence available that even hints at the substance of the future Burgoyne.

By the time Burgoyne bought his commission he was already a confirmed ladies' man, and it would not be long before the Earl of Derby, quoting his eldest son and heir, would complain that the young officer's unerring eye for beauty had already made him notorious. As a theater buff who rarely missed a performance of a new comedy, Burgoyne made the acquaintance of several attractive actresses, women who, according to the custom of the time, were amenable to the granting of favors to gentlemen who presented them with substantial gifts or, preferably, hard cash.

Even at this early age, however, John Burgoyne displayed a taste and reticence unusual in the eighteenth-century London boulevardier. Most young men took their women wherever they found them, more often than not in the taverns and streets of a city where the impoverishment of the poor left no career other than prostitution open to a pretty girl of the lower classes. Lord Strange and other friends were impressed by Burgoyne's fastidiousness: he refused to associate with low women, no matter how comely, unless they were clean, fashionably attired, and could converse with him. Strange is the authority for the Burgoyne creed to the effect that the time a man and woman spent in bed together accounted for only a portion of a successful affair, and that the full enjoyment of the relationship depended as much on their mutual ability to exchange ideas and thoughts.

At the age of twenty-three Lieutenant Burgoyne fell in love for the first time, amusing his friends and relieving his mother, who had worried about his associations with actresses. The lady was the twenty-two-year-old Frances Poole, a black-haired beauty who was one of the most popular young members of the aristocracy. Burgoyne, who later tried to intimate that the relationship had been only a flirtation, faced stiff competition from four or five other gallants, but the competition whetted his appetite, and he launched a determined pursuit of the delectable Frances.

He lost. The winner was Lord Palmerston, whom Frances' family preferred because of his title and wealth, and she married him in one of the season's more important weddings. On the night prior to the ceremony Palmerston's friends tendered him a bachelor dinner, and Lieutenant Burgoyne proved he was a good loser by reading aloud a poem he had just written and was dedicating to the bridegroom. The verse indicated that the poet possessed a modest talent, even though he repeated the final word of his first line at the end of the second line:

" 'Twas mine to see each opening charm,
    New beauties rise—new graces charm;
        'Twas mine to feel their power;
Nature and morals just and pure,
    For that has made the fruit mature
        Since I adored the flower.

"After hard conflict passion cool'd;
    Discretion, honor, reason ruled

O'er the subsiding flame;
Till Charlotte to my vacant breast,
With kindred charms and virtues blest,
A sweet successor came."

Self-assumed poetic license enabled the author to twist the facts somewhat, but those who knew him were not fooled. He had wooed Frances and another had won her. The rest of his verse was accurate: he quickly found a successor in the Earl of Derby's youngest daughter, seventeen-year-old Lady Charlotte Stanley, who was six years his junior. He had known her ever since she had been a little girl, but had paid no attention to her in her adolescence; and then, one day, he discovered he was smitten.

Charlotte was a blue-eyed blonde with a matchless complexion, somewhat more slender than the standard of the period considered perfect. The most widely read of the Stanley clan, she was at home in French, Spanish, and Portuguese, as well as in Greek and Latin. A true intellectual who harbored liberal sentiments far removed from the views of her tradition-bound class, she had been destined, like her older sisters, for an alliance of state with another of the nation's leading families.

Instead she fell in love with Lieutenant John Burgoyne, who, his charm and his friendship with her eldest brother notwithstanding, was not regarded by the Earl of Derby as an eligible suitor. Only men who had titles, vast wealth and the prospect of rising still higher in the aristocratic hierarchy were encouraged to apply for her hand.

Burgoyne was welcome enough at the various Derby homes, provided he accompanied Lord Strange there, but the Earl soon made it plain to him that when he came alone for the obvious purpose of courting Charlotte he was received with reservations. Strange became a willing partner in a conspiracy, and Charlotte soon was paying protracted visits to her brother's new London town house, where she and Burgoyne could meet without the knowledge of her parents.

By early 1747, when Burgoyne was twenty-five and Charlotte had just passed her nineteenth birthday, the impasse became serious. Lord Derby was urging her to make a choice between two suitors, members of the nobility who had his approval, and had forbidden Burgoyne the privilege of visiting any of his homes. Although the love of John and Charlotte was genuine, Lord Strange, who understood his father, warned them that no power on earth could persuade the Earl to change his mind.

Under the circumstances the young couple were forced to elope, and the rector of St. James's Church in Piccadilly performed the marriage ceremony, braving the Earl of Derby's wrath. Lord Strange gave his sister to his best friend, and a few other young people were in attendance. Immediately after the ceremony the newlyweds vanished, reappearing the following day in Bath, at that time England's most fashionable resort, where they spent the next ten days. It did not occur to either the bride or groom to go to a place where they would be less conspicuous; after all, Bath was the spa where aristocrats always gathered.

The Earl of Derby's reaction was predictable: he cursed his son and heir, damned his new son-in-law, whom he refused to receive, and disinherited Lady Charlotte Burgoyne. Anna Maria Burgoyne, who had been widowed the previous year, took the newlyweds under her roof, but could offer them little other than moral support. Her own estate had diminished, and she could give them financial assistance only by making sacrifices her gallant son would not permit.

Like the protagonist of a comedy in the period when John Burgoyne would be writing his plays, the dashing young officer faced the problem of augmenting his meager Army pay so he could afford to support a wife in some small measure of the style to which she had been accustomed since birth. He thought of writing poetry, but knew no one would pay him for his efforts, so he was reduced to gambling at twenty-and-one. For the only time in his life his luck deserted him, and he lost his entire purse, nervous tension contributing to his downfall, according to a letter Charlotte wrote to her mother.

The situation required drastic remedial action, and John

Burgoyne, recently promoted to the rank of captain, was equal to the first emergency of his adult life. He sold his commission for a lump sum of cash, and now had no other funds except the small annual stipend his father had left him. Lady Derby, who did not share the Earl's wrath, did what she could for her youngest daughter and son-in-law by giving them a gift of five hundred pounds.

The young couple promptly left England for France, where, they said, the cost of living would be less. Their mothers were horrified, since it appeared that England and France soon would renew their perennial warfare. Lord Strange disapproved, too, claiming that France was a land inhabited by barbarians, but his brother-in-law countered with the riposte that "the French are the most civilized of people, which is the reason we take such pains to learn their language."

Charlotte and John, pinching ha'pennies for the first time in their young lives, did not engage a suite on their cross-Channel voyage, but traveled in steerage with the peasants.

Two

The seven and one-half years that John Burgoyne and his wife spent on the Continent gave them an outlook, an approach to life, and a philosophy that left a permanent stamp on them, removing them from the insular, inward-looking Englishmen of their era. They not only became more cosmopolitan on the surface, even developing a liking for foreign foods and wines, but they learned the ultimate secret of all civilized men and women, that alien people were not inferior because they observed different customs and entertained different aspirations.

Lady Charlotte's liberalism was confirmed by her long sojourn abroad, and her husband, who had never bothered to think of such things, became so tolerant that some of his closest friends in England were uncomfortable in his presence and turned away from him. It was not accidental that of all senior officers in the

British Army, Burgoyne—even more than his colleague, Sir William Howe—sympathized with the American rebels, understood their position and their reasons for insurrection, and secretly rejoiced when they won their independence.

After staying for short periods in several places, the young Burgoynes finally rented a small house in the village of Pacy, on the River Seine, approximately halfway between Rouen and Paris, and this dwelling was their permanent home for about six years. No members of the gentry did their own housework or cooking in the eighteenth century, so they were attended by two housemaids, and their living standard cannot be described as anything other than opulent. After what they had known in England, however, they were living in hardship. Charlotte did her own marketing, often accompanied by her husband, and John did his own gardening, being unable to afford yet another servant. He grew a number of vegetables in order to cut down on food bills, and Charlotte announced that cabbages were lovelier and had a sweeter scent than roses. Funds were lacking for a carriage, so the couple walked everywhere in the village, and on their occasional trips into Paris they traveled by public coach.

Living in France posed no terrors for Charlotte, who knew the language, but John could neither speak the tongue nor understand it. He struggled valiantly in an attempt to learn it, but the facility he had displayed in the classical languages deserted him. Eventually he could get along well enough in French, but his accent was execrable, and years later, when he was fond of quoting proverbs in French in House of Commons speeches, he mangled French so badly that his colleagues laughed aloud at him.

Gardening and long walks kept Burgoyne fit, and after a period of about three years he began to pay twice-monthly visits to Paris. The state of the couple's finances improved at once, and Burgoyne was forced to confess to his wife, from whom he was unable to keep any secrets, that he was picking up impressive sums by playing twenty-and-one with several wealthy gentlemen in the British community there.

This dramatic change, to which Charlotte made no objection,

enabled the pair to choose between renting a larger house or traveling on the Continent. They elected the latter, and at various times visited the Low Countries, a number of German principalities, the Italian states, and Spain, making them among the most widely traveled English aristocrats of their generation. They enjoyed new places, they were dutiful in seeing museums, churches, and historical sites, but they found their greatest pleasure in observing local customs, noting native modes of dress, and gaining an appreciation of foreign foods. Years later, when the Burgoynes discussed menus with fellow Englishmen, they knew whereof they spoke.

Only the German states failed to impress them, and Burgoyne wrote to his mother that he found the German temperament "too blunt and cruel," even though he admired the boundless energies of the people he met. This basic dislike, which he never lost, was destined to hamper his relations with the German mercenary troops who formed a portion of his command during the most important military campaign of his life, which culminated in the Battle of Saratoga.

The large English colony in Rome gave the young couple a royal welcome late in 1754, and the Burgoynes stayed there for six months, almost but not quite succumbing to the temptation to give up their house in Pacy and move to Rome. They finally opted for France because of Burgoyne's success at twenty-and-one on his bi-weekly visits to Paris, which made travel possible.

Early in 1755, during the visit to Rome, Burgoyne's first known portrait was done by Allan Ramsay, the Scottish portraitist who, after his own return to England, would become the Royal Family's official painter-in-residence. Ramsay was something of a flatterer, and portrayed Burgoyne as he liked to see himself, a remarkably handsome man of thirty-three who wore his stylish clothes with a flair, a man whose features were regular, whose physique was supple and slender, and whose eyes were little short of magnetic.

In the early spring of 1755 the Burgoynes finally returned to Pacy, and soon thereafter John's mother paid them a visit there. She stayed with them for three months, taking care not to reveal to them that she was fatally ill, and a short time after her return to London she died. John was forced to go to England to settle her estate, which brought him a small additional income, so he and Charlotte gave up the house in Pacy and went home.

Lord Strange, who met their ship when it dropped anchor at Dover, was pleased to report to his father that the Burgoynes were devoted to each other, and he told the literal truth. John, who in his bachelor days had unfailingly spotted a pretty face and a trim ankle, had literally forsaken all others, and was completely faithful to Charlotte, no mean accomplishment in a time when aristocratic husbands were expected to stray. Charlotte returned her husband's love, and their marriage was clouded only by her inability to bear children, a condition that physicians in France, Italy, and Holland had pronounced chronic.

The Earl of Derby, under pressure from his Countess and his eldest son, agreed to receive the returned runaways at his London town house. John charmed him, Charlotte instinctively knew how to behave, and before the visit ended they were restored to his good graces. Soon thereafter he returned Charlotte to his will, and the couple enjoyed the full protection of the powerful Stanley family. Using a portion of John's inheritance they bought a house in Belgravia, then as later one of the most fashionable of London neighborhoods, and their dinner parties, replete with exotic foreign dishes, wines, and brandy, became the talk of the town.

In January, 1756, John Burgoyne celebrated his thirty-fourth birthday, and appeared satisfied with his life of amiable pleasure. He had achieved nothing, but displayed no ambition, he and his wife loved each other, and they had enough money for their immediate needs. If they required more, John could probably provide it by playing cards with some of his wealthy friends.

The approach of the conflagration that would be known to posterity as the Seven Years' War stirred John Burgoyne's latent yearning to perform great deeds, become famous and acquire a fortune. The only profession he knew, other than card-playing, was that of the soldier, and the time seemed ripe for someone who could ride and handle a sword, and who wanted to test his mettle as a leader of men. The Earl of Derby and Lord Strange quietly used their influence, and in 1756 John Burgoyne was restored to active duty as a cavalry officer. He was given a new commission as a captain, and was assigned to the eighteenth-century equivalent of a commando regiment, the Eleventh Dragoons.

The principal theater of war was located in the German states, but the War Office in London developed a new theory which the generals were eager to test. Hand-picked brigades, each made up of one regiment of cavalry, one of infantry, and a battalion of sappers, or engineers, would be sent to France on hit-and-run raids to be conducted on the coasts of Normandy and Brittany. According to the theoreticians, these diversions would force the French to withdraw troops from Germany, where they were badly needed, in order to protect native soil.

Captain Burgoyne's troop received special training for such operations, and the commanding officer of the unit demonstrated an attitude toward his men that was revolutionary. The common soldiers of the eighteenth century were regarded by virtually all of their superiors as little better than cattle. They were fed and watered regularly, given enough rest to perform the tasks required of them, and were considered dumb beasts who had to be punished, severely and cruelly, for even the slightest infraction of military regulations.

But John Burgoyne thought of his men as human beings, a novel and startling concept. He supported them in dealings with higher authority, he was fair in his own treatment of them, and their personal welfare was as important to him as his own. He asked them to perform no exercises in their training program in which he himself was unwilling to participate, and he adopted the extraordinary policy of explaining the reasons for the difficult maneuvers in which they engaged.

This approach made Burgoyne's superiors uneasy, but they were compelled to admit that the morale of his troop was higher than that of any other unit. His men were fiercely loyal to him, and never complained of hardships. To be sure, it did not occur to the generals and colonels that his humanitarian methods should be tried elsewhere; the most they would concede was that he was endowed with an unusual gift of leadership that placed him high on the list of those eligible for a senior command.

John Burgoyne had shown no such tendencies when he had sold his previous commission in 1747, and the difference in his approach nine years later was so marked that it demonstrates to perfection the changes in the man himself. His wife's correspondence with him and her family indicates that his more compassionate and understanding attitude was partly a reflection of her own. One additional factor probably played an important part in his maturation process: he and Lady Charlotte had spent much of their time abroad with the peasants of Pacy, and gained an understanding of ordinary people that was denied most aristocrats of the era, who lived in splendid isolation.

The first test of Burgoyne's theories came in 1758, when his troop was one of the units that participated in a surprise attack on the French port of Cherbourg. Royal Navy sloops-of-war carried the assault troops across the English Channel, landing a force of approximately fifteen hundred men shortly before dawn. The cavalrymen and their mounts, who had been crowded together on the decks of the swift, graceful ships that had not been intended for such a purpose, swam ashore from the inner side of the vast Cherbourg harbor.

Unit commanders were ordered to inflict as much damage on the town as possible, while at the same time sparing civilians. Thanks to unbelievably bad planning, no specific targets were named, so the commanders of regiments, battalions, and cavalry troops were left to their own devices. Captain Burgoyne's men formed their ranks on the docks, and the commanding officer's familiarity with the town gave him an advantage that others lacked. He led his troop to the munitions arsenal located about a half-mile from the waterfront, and succeeded in blowing it up. Returning to the harbor, he noted that no other unit had as yet bothered to attack the small French garrison stationed in an ancient fort overlooking the harbor, so he hastily rectified this gross oversight. The confused French defenders surrendered to him when he posted men at each of the fort's three entrances, blocking their means of escape, and he astonished his regimental commander by returning to the sloop with two hundred prisoners of war. The feat was all the more remarkable because his command numbered only one hundred and forty men.

Commended in the dispatches of every senior officer who took part in the raid, Captain Burgoyne was hailed on his return to England as a minor hero. The Stanley family at long last had reason to be proud of him, and he was received in a private audience by the Prince of Wales, later King George III, thus inaugurating a personal relationship that would grow deeper and increasingly significant through the years. When the Prince invited the young cavalry officer to accompany him on a morning canter for the purpose of "exercising the horses," it was evident that the Earl of Derby's son-in-law was a marked man.

The Cherbourg expedition was followed, later in 1758, by a similar hit-and-run assault on the old Norman fortress town of St. Malo. The commander was a major-general named Bligh, subsequently described by Horace Walpole as "an old General routed out of some horse armoury in Ireland." Totally incompetent for the task he had been given, Bligh and his immediate subordinates did not bother to check on the strength of the St. Malo garrison, which was considerable, nor did they plan a co-ordinated attack. In fact, it did not cross their minds that the defenders of the port were protected by several batteries of cannon manned by first-rate gunners.

Officially labelled a "misfortune," the assault was actually a disaster. The British invaders were driven back to the beaches, suffering heavy casualties, and the behavior of the senior officers was little short of disgraceful. Several of them, according to official accounts which the embarrassed War Office tried in vain to suppress, spent the better part of their brief sojourn in France reading London newspapers they had brought with them. Had the French displayed competence of their own, they could have killed or captured every Englishman who landed on their soil,

but they were guilty of dilatory conduct, too, and the Duc d'Ai-
guillon, the French commander of the port, shared the fate of
General Bligh and was censured.

Only Captain Burgoyne of the Dragoons emerged from the
fiasco with his reputation actually enhanced. Rallying several
other junior officers, he assumed command of enough troops
to form a regiment. Then he led these men in a spirited coun-
terattack against the French infantry, who were pursuing the
fleeing Englishmen to the beaches, and not only held off the defenders long enough for the routed assault troops to embark on
their transports, but delivered such savage blows that the de-
moralized French were unable to prevent the ultimate escape of
his own units.

Burgoyne was candid in his description of the incident,
writing to Lord Strange:

> C. and myself, who were upon the right, perceived
> a very large body of the enemy pushing with great ex-
> pedition upon the hill on our right in the intention to
> flank us. Of this we immediately informed the Generals,
> but received no order how to act, and were obliged to
> determine upon our own authority to wheel the troops
> we commanded so as to front the enemy.

There was an uproar in the House of Commons when news
of the debacle was received, and only the personal intervention
of King George II prevented the court-martial of General Bligh,
who was sent into immediate retirement. The newspapers picked
up the cry, and demands for a thorough investigation were
pressed, but the War Office took no action. Then a number of
pamphlets, long the Englishman's escape valve for frustrated
emotions, began to flood the country, demanding the punishment of others responsible, regardless of their rank or position.

The government was reluctant to make a formal inquiry.
The war was still being waged, and it was feared that the reputations of prominent men who were needed in the continuing effort would be sullied beyond repair if all the facts of the situation

became known. So the protests were ignored, the government hoping the tumult would subside.

No attempt was made, however, to keep secret the reward given to John Burgoyne. He received a double promotion to the rank of lieutenant-colonel, and was transferred to the Coldstream Guards, then and subsequently the most prestige-laden regiment in the Army. It was taken for granted—by Burgoyne himself, as well as by the entire aristocracy—that this was only the first of several promotions that would carry him to the top of the ladder. There were few officers with a real talent for military conduct who captured the public imagination in the Seven Years' War, and a man endowed with those qualities was certain to play a prominent role in the prosecution of the conflict.

Three

Lieutenant-Colonel John Burgoyne was second in command of the Coldstream Guards, and custom dictated that he take charge of the regiment in the field, the colonelcy being one of the personal adornments of the Prince of Wales. It was difficult, even dangerous, to tamper with custom, and not even the influence of the Earl of Derby could protect his son-in-law from royal wrath if Burgoyne went too far in his attempts to mold the Guards into his notion of a fighting unit. But the lieutenant-colonel, at last able to promote his ideas on a fairly large scale, felt secure in the support given him by the Prince of Wales, and instituted a program of reform that improved the spirit of the regiment within a short time.

There were rumors at Whitehall that King George II, tradition-bound and a harsh disciplinarian, would be displeased, and that Burgoyne soon would be transferred to an obscure post in the provinces. But the gossips had forgotten that their monarch was not a complete fool, and that he appreciated concrete results, even if the methods used to achieve them were not his own. In 1759, only six months after Burgoyne had received his promotion, the War Office decided to raise two new regiments of light horse, and at the personal instigation of George II the command of the first of them, the Sixteenth Hussars, was offered to Burgoyne, who received a full colonelcy.

Following the custom of the period, Colonel Burgoyne inserted advertisements in the newspapers and also ordered a large number of recruiting posters printed. His offers to members of his new command were so generous they created a sensation:

> You will be mounted on the finest horses in the world, with superb clothing and the richest accoutrements; your pay and privileges will be equal to two guineas per week; you will be everywhere respected; your society will be courted; you will be admired by the Fair, which, together with the chance of getting switched to a buxom widow, or of brushing with a rich heiress, renders the situation truly enviable and desirable.
>
> Young men out of employment or uncomfortable, "There is a tide in the affairs of men, which, taken at the flood, leads on to fortune"; nick in instantly and enlist.

Burgoyne, the poet, who did not hesitate to quote Shakespeare when recruiting cavalrymen, shrewdly appealed to young men other than plodding farm boys, and the response to his effort was overwhelming. So many volunteered for duty in the Sixteenth Hussars that the colonel commanding the regiment could pick and choose, and Burgoyne demanded that every potential member of the regiment demonstrate his ability to ride, handle a saber, and fire a pistol. The dregs were not for him.

He took particular care in the selection of his officers, all of them veterans with combat experience, and he issued a *Code of Instructions* for them, not only writing it himself but ruthlessly eschewing the flowery style in which he delighted. Officers, he declared, should not curse in the presence of their men, and he reminded them that, as educated men, they had gained a sufficiently large vocabulary to express themselves without swearing. He recommended that his officers tell occasional jokes "as an encouragement to the well-disposed and at the same time a tacit reproof to others."

He also listed the punishments that were forbidden, and he directed that no member of the regiment be subjected to them:

1. Bloodybacking, or flogging.

2. The Scavenger's Daughter, the tying of neck and heels, one of the oldest forms of torture known in England, and long practiced on political prisoners in the Tower of London and elsewhere.

3. Gantlope, or running the gauntlet.

4. Riding the wooden horse, a form of torture that was especially painful when iron spikes protruded from the wood.

5. Clubbing.

6. Striking a soldier with one's riding crop.

7. Kicking, with or without spurs attached to boots.

The worst of all punishments was also ended under the directions imposed by the *Code.* Under no circumstances would even the most incorrigible offenders be made to suffer R.N., or "Removal to the Navy," life before the mast being considered completely inhuman by the newly promoted colonel who had civilized notions far in advance of his century.

He deplored the German method, which he called "training men like spaniels by the stick." Instead, he emphasized, "The point of honor should be substituted in the place of severity." Therein lay the key to his thinking, even to the essence of his character. Honor was a man's first responsibility, Burgoyne believed; he who lived honorably was a gentleman, he who lacked honor was a cipher. "An Englishman will not bear beating so well as the foreigners," he observed in his *Code*, and he asked his officers to remember that even the newest recruits were "thinking beings."

The officers of the Sixteenth Hussars accepted their commander's edicts without question, as befitted soldiers, but their astounded colleagues in other regiments began to call the new colonel by a new name, which he would bear for the rest of his days. Within a short time he was known throughout the Army as Gentleman Johnny.

Most full colonels were distinguished men who paid no attention to the regiments they nominally commanded, and wore their uniforms on the one day each year when they held a formal review of their troops. But the commander of the Sixteenth Hussars had no intention of allowing others to do his work for him, and spent his days on the training field, returning to London and the patient Lady Charlotte only on weekends. The men were drilled incessantly, a practice unknown in England at the time; their boots were shined, their uniforms were clean, and their brass gleamed. From the outset they were taught pride in themselves and their regiment, and they worshiped their colonel.

In 1760, just as the regiment was rounding into shape, George II died, and was succeeded by his grandson, who became George III, so the new monarch had the privilege of taking the first salute of the Sixteenth Hussars, who were already known as Burgoyne's Light Horse. Never had an English regiment drilled with such precision, and the King was so pleased he attended an informal, weekly review thereafter, appearing in civilian attire rather than uniform so that a red carpet would not have to be laid on the parade ground for him. It might be noted that in 1763 King George himself gave the regiment a new name, calling it The Queen's Light Dragoons, as it has been known ever since.

In 1761 Burgoyne's Light Horse was ready for battle, and the regiment was assigned a place in another hit-and-run raid on the French coast, this time against the fortress of Belle Isle. Colonel Burgoyne played a major part in planning the operation, but he realized, as did several of his colleagues, that the attack could accomplish little of significance. The regiment behaved commendably, withdrawing after suffering only a few minor casualties, but the colonel shared the view of those who held that such operations were a waste of time, effort, and manpower.

A drastic deterioration of the international situation in the next year gave Colonel Burgoyne an opportunity to prove what he and his troops could achieve in an active theater of combat, and he happily seized the chance. Ever since his promotion to full colonel he had abandoned his usual reading, mostly drama and poetry, to study military tactics and strategy, and he was eager to try some of the theories he had developed.

Spain, which had entered the war on the side of France, was menacing Britain's oldest ally, Portugal, so London wasted no time, in 1762, and declared war on Madrid. The War Office asked regimental commanders to volunteer for duty in the Spanish-Portuguese Peninsula, and the first to come forward was Colonel Burgoyne, whose wife protested against the prospect of his prolonged absence from home. Burgoyne, the poet, tried to console Lady Charlotte by writing a verse for her. It began:

> Still does my Obstinate repine
> And reason's voice reprove;
> Still think him cold who would combine
> Philosophy with Love.

Charlotte, who had a logical mind of her own, was not impressed by her husband's arguments. She saw no reason for him to suffer discomforts and risk his life on foreign soil when his friendship with George III, combined with her family's influence, could win him the general's baton he coveted.

One of the rare major disputes in the married life of John and Lady Charlotte Burgoyne lowered the temperature in the Belgravia house. In vain the colonel pointed out that the expeditionary force being sent to Portugal would be made up of only seven thousand men, so his chances of winning a promotion would be enhanced. He had made the Army his permanent career, and would never win a truly high rank unless he proved himself in the field. His regiment was ready for combat, and he refused to let someone else win glory with his troops. He was forty years old, he had never done anything of consequence on behalf of his country, the inconveniences he would suffer were minor, and his career would be ruined if he withdrew.

Lady Charlotte withdrew into a silence she refused to break. John informed his brother-in-law that he was married to an "infernal bitch," and Lord Strange duly made a notation in his diary, but avoided the domestic conflict.

The commander of the expedition was a distant relative of King George's, General Wilhelm Schaumberg, Count of Lippe-Buckeburg and a field marshal in the army of Prince Ferdinand of Brunswick. He was an elderly martinet, stubborn and short-sighted, but he was the personal selection of King George, so the Army was forced to accept him. The blow of his appointment was softened somewhat for John Burgoyne, who was awarded a brevet, or temporary, commission as a brigadier, and he was given over-all command of the expedition's cavalry.

At the age of thirty-six he had been an elderly captain, but at forty he was Britain's youngest general, and Lady Charlotte was so proud of him that her reserve melted. She and her husband were reconciled, and Gentleman Johnny wrote her another, far more intimate poem before his departure. Eventually Lady Charlotte showed the verse to two of her sisters, but would not permit its publication; her husband respected her desire for privacy, and she carried it with her to her grave.

The voyage to Lisbon passed without incident, although the troops, who were crowded into small vessels with their horses, had little opportunity to enjoy the sea air. Initially Brigadier Burgoyne fared somewhat better, as he was given a suite of four cabins, including his own kitchen, for himself and his two aides-de-camp. But he ordered his aides to share a cabin, opened the space that had been vacated as a reading room for the men of the Sixteenth Hussars, and directed his personal cook to prepare meals of bread and cold meat for the regiment. He ate with the troops, shocking several conservative colonels, and was informed by the regimental sergeant-major that the men were ready to follow him to hell.

"To the best of my knowledge," Gentleman Johnny replied,

making one of the little jokes he had recommended in his *Code*, "we are only going to the Peninsula, sergeant-major."

General Schaumberg noted the deplorable condition of the Portuguese army in Lisbon, and well may have thought that he had arrived in hell. Brigadier Burgoyne's letters to his wife and brother-in-law indicate that he shared his superior's horror. The Portuguese troops were paid so little that guards on duty at the royal palace begged passersby for alms, high-ranking officers could not afford to pay the wages of their personal servants and gave them commissions as lieutenants instead, and even captains and majors were so poor their wives took in washing. Discipline was almost unknown, and the Portuguese infantrymen were sullen and lazy, and openly expressed their indifference to the outcome of the war.

On paper, at least, Brigadier Burgoyne's command was impressive. It included one thousand English light horse, made up of his own regiment and another, and to these units were added two thousand local horsemen, allegedly the cream of the Portuguese army. "I know not how to dispose of our gallant allies in a line of battle," the perplexed Gentleman Johnny confided in a letter to Lord Strange. "If I place them in the van they will impede our advance, if stationed in the center they will create confusion, and if ordered to hold the rear they will run away." He solved the problem by creating what he called a "mobile reserve," and assigned the Portuguese cavalry to it.

The first assignment given the brigade by General Schaumberg was a test of Burgoyne's ingenuity and skill, but he accepted the challenge. A large Spanish garrison, said by spies to number more than twelve thousand men, had gathered in the town of Valencia d'Alcantara, located on the Tagus River, a short distance across the Spanish border. That corps menaced all of central Portugal, and if it swept across the border it could isolate Lisbon from her interior provinces. It was essential that the fortress at Valencia d'Alcantara be captured, and the garrison either forced to withdraw or compelled to surrender, the latter goal being no more than a remote wish.

Brigadier Burgoyne was given command of the assault force,

which included one thousand English foot soldiers and three thousand Portuguese infantry, as well as his cavalry brigade. He gathered his force on the Portuguese side of the border, then began his march at midnight, fording the rain-swollen Tagus at low spots in the river. His guides were unfamiliar with the Spanish terrain and misled him, but he nevertheless managed to reach his destination shortly before dawn.

He paused to consider his situation, which was difficult. The garrison had not yet discovered his presence nearby, so his best hope of achieving a victory lay in launching a surprise attack. The Spaniards were veterans, his Portuguese were unreliable, and the enemy badly outnumbered his small corps. In addition, the cavalry had outpaced the infantry, which might not reach the site before mid-morning.

He decided not to wait, and gave the order for an immediate attack. The Sixteenth Hussars were given the place of honor in the vanguard, and the brigadier ignored the unwritten military rule to the effect that the commander-in-chief of a major operation should direct his troops from a command post located in the rear. Instead he rode with his standard-bearer and trumpeter at the head of the column, waving his sword as he silently urged his men forward.

The first rays of light were appearing overhead as the Sixteenth Hussars opened the main gate and rode into the town. The sleepy Spanish commander was awakened by an urbane English gentleman who apologized for disturbing his slumbers, but demanded his sword. The garrison surrendered without the firing of a single shot, and by the time the Portuguese cavalry rode in at the rear of the column, the capture of Valencia d'Alcantara was complete.

Brigadier Burgoyne demonstrated his wisdom by sending responsible British officers to the townspeople to take up a collection of cash on behalf of the victorious troops. It was the custom in the most civilized of centuries to sack a captured town, and the grandees paid heavily for the privilege of sparing their community the horrors of war. The ransom was paid, the invaders were satisfied, and by the time the infantry arrived on the scene the troops of the Spanish garrison were lined up outside the walls, their arms neatly stacked, waiting to be marched to the rear as prisoners.

King Joseph of Portugal was so delighted he presented Burgoyne with a diamond ring, and left him a bequest of one thousand pounds in his will. Gifts were given to virtually all British cavalry officers, the one exception being a brash member of Burgoyne's staff, a Captain Charles Lee, whose sharp tongue had offended the King. Lee was destined to migrate to the American colonies a few years later after becoming disenchanted with his prospects in the British Army. King Joseph also gave Burgoyne permission to send the captured flags to England if he wished, and the brigadier tactfully forwarded half to King George III in England, but presented the rest to King Joseph.

Burgoyne's official dispatch to the War Office was a model of rectitude, beginning, "I am conscious that the chief merit of the success was due to the admirable though not uncommon valor and activity of the troops I had the honor to command."

A victory-hungry England hailed Burgoyne's achievement in terms so lavish that a stranger unfamiliar with the details would have assumed he had won a major campaign rather than a battle of limited strategic importance. The Commons awarded him a gold medal and ordered him a sword with a gold hilt, which he was destined to lose a decade and a half later to a former military subordinate who commanded the American troops in the decisive Battle of Saratoga.

In October, 1762, Burgoyne's brigade won another surprise victory which was due, in the main, to the enterprise and daring of Charles Lee, now a temporary lieutenant-colonel. According to Burgoyne's account to the War Office, Lee sneaked a battalion of cavalry into the Spanish camp outside the little town of Villa Velha, and led his men in such a vigorous charge when the enemy tried to rally that the Spaniards fled. Burgoyne took care not to criticize his subordinate for his failure to pursue and capture the disorganized foe. Lee had been responsible for a victory, and it was typical of Gentleman Johnny not to shame a man who had won glory.

It was one of the ironies of the age that, fourteen years later, in December, 1776, Charles Lee, by then a major-general in the Continental Army and at that time second only to George Washington in rank, was surprised at breakfast in a farmhouse near Trenton, New Jersey, and captured by British dragoons commanded by officers who had been his own direct subordinates at Villa Velha. It is probable that Lee and the officer to whom he surrendered, a Lieutenant-Colonel Harcourt, were equally surprised.

The Seven Years' War came to an end in 1763, and John Burgoyne led his victorious cavalrymen back to England. He was received as a hero, but his joy was somewhat tempered when the War Office rescinded his temporary promotion to the rank of brigadier, and he reverted to the rank of colonel. He complained in writing to the War Office, but received no official reply, bureaucrats having decided to save themselves the embarrassment of justifying their position.

An indignant Lord Strange busied himself on his brother-in-law's behalf, and before 1763 came to an end John Burgoyne received consolation of a sort. He received permanent command of the Sixteenth Hussars, regardless of whether he remained on active duty, and the regiment became "his," an honor he kept until 1779. Nevertheless, he would have to wait another nine years before he received a permanent promotion to the rank of major-general.

In the meantime, however, his ambitions expanded, and realizing there was no immediate future in a soldier's life, he forcibly directed his career into other channels.

Four

Lady Charlotte Burgoyne was delighted that her husband had returned home in good health, his military reputation insured by the Peninsular campaign. But Gentleman Johnny did not share her joy. The Army was being reduced, officers were sent into involuntary retirement on meager half-pay, and a vigorous man of forty-one who had grown accustomed to the limelight was compelled to seek new outlets for his ambitions and energies.

It was typical of Burgoyne that he did not brood. He considered his situation calmly, discussing it with Charlotte and her brother, and he gave thought to several new careers. One was that of a playwright, and he tried his hand at writing a comedy, but the results failed to satisfy him, so he put his manuscript aside, showing it to no one.

Politics offered the involuntarily retired soldier a natural outlet for his energies through his desire to help the lot of the human race in the same way he had tried to improve the situation of the common soldier in the British Army. This also would give him an opportunity to retain a prominent place in the eyes of his countrymen. The Stanley family held a council of war, and the elderly Earl of Derby, who believed his son-in-law could do no wrong since his military triumphs in Portugal, demonstrated that a nobleman of his standing possessed almost unlimited power.

Among the many Stanley estates was a relatively small country house outside the village of Midhurst. Derby transferred it to his son-in-law's name—Burgoyne privately agreeing in writing to return the property to the Earl or his heir after it had served his purposes—and Gentleman Johnny, accompanied by Lady Charlotte, began to spend weekends at the house. Soon thereafter the Member of Parliament for Midhurst, who happened to be associated with Lord Strange in several real estate ventures, decided that private business was occupying so much of his time that he could no longer do justice to his constituents in Parliament.

His resignation made a by-election for the seat necessary, and Colonel John Burgoyne, whose honor prevented him from using the courtesy title of brigadier, announced his candidacy. His family tie to the house of Stanley being no secret, others who were interested decided to curb their ambitions, and he ran unopposed for the seat.

He appeared before the Speaker of the House in late November, 1763, and was applauded by both Tories and Whigs when he took his seat, the applause diminishing somewhat on the right side of the chamber when the Tories, who had assumed he would join them, discovered that he preferred to sit as an Independent. He was told that a lack of party affiliation would prevent him from being offered meaningful assignments, but he refused to give in to pressure, insisting he would be beholden to no one.

For more than a year the budding politician listened, observed, and learned, preparing for his career in Parliament with the same meticulous concern he had shown when studying military strategy and tactics. His attendance record was one of the best in the Commons, and he appeared daily to take his seat in that small section of back benches reserved for Independents. His manner was affable, his attire was flamboyant and he made it his business to become acquainted with all of his colleagues. He timed his arrival with care, usually making his appearance only a minute or two before a session was scheduled to begin, and a number of his amused fellow Members of Parliament likened his stroll to his seat to an actor's triumphal procession. He waved, smiled, bowed and shook hands; he exchanged hearty greetings with the convivial, but was dignified with the reserved.

When debate began in the Commons, the honorable Member for Midhurst fell silent, never challenging and never taking part in discussions of civilian affairs, either foreign or domestic. He voted according to the dictates of his conscience, and neither side could count on his support, with the result that both parties wooed him, a situation he enjoyed.

He was a changed man when military matters were debated, however, and when he was not making impassioned speeches himself he leaped to his feet frequently, asking sharp questions and demanding precise replies. He was the Army's most loyal defender, fought to prevent cuts in military appropriations, became an overnight leader in attempts to procure more modern armaments, and sometimes annoyed the War Office when he made strenuous objections to the promotion of incompetent officers who had supporters in high places.

To the dismay of his father-in-law and other confirmed Tories Burgoyne's closest friendships were made with men of more liberal persuasion. He became something of a protégé of the great Earl of Chatham, the former William Pitt the elder, one of Britain's greatest statesmen, whose power had declined somewhat since his removal to the House of Lords, but who still wielded more indirect influence than any other man in the country. Chatham appreciated Burgoyne's wit, and Gentleman Johnny stood in awe of Pitt's intellectual prowess.

Over the years Burgoyne formed two other significant personal relations. He became a friend of Edmund Burke, the great orator and champion of personal liberties, who was a few years his junior, and he formed an intimate friendship with a mercurial younger man, Charles James Fox, who became head of the Admiralty and then of the Treasury in the years immediately preceding the American Revolution.

It is significant that Chatham, Burke, and Fox were the acknowledged leaders of those who advocated the granting of greater freedom to the American colonists and eventually favored the cause of independence for the overseas possession, although Chatham believed that all ties with the mother country should not be severed. John Burgoyne shared the sympathies of these men, and as early as 1764 he could be relied upon to cast his vote in favor of giving the Americans greater self-government.

It would be a mistake, however, to conclude that Gentleman Johnny was a true liberal. Most of his views were orthodox, and he shared a majority of his father-in-law's thick-crusted opinions. His over-all political posture might most accurately be described as similar to that of Burke: Burgoyne was the champion of Americans and of civil liberties for all Englishman, but in other matters he was a supporter of the status quo. It was his unalterable conviction that the eighteenth century, the Age of Enlightenment, was the greatest period man had ever known, and that, in an imperfect world, Great Britain was the most civilized and glorious of nations. She had a few faults, to be sure, but he loved her and therefore was willing to overlook them.

In 1765 the M.P. for Midhurst decided to take advantage of a Parliamentary recess to engage in a project that, he believed, would be of great value to the country. He planned to inspect the armies of those nations on the Continent that would permit such a study, and would report his findings to the Commons and to the War Office. He would travel alone for the sake of convenience and speed, leaving a protesting Lady Charlotte at home.

What he conceived as a private matter soon became a semi-official tour. Both major political parties gave the project their blessing, and Lord Chatham, who knew more highly placed men abroad than any other Englishman, gave him letters of introduction to kings, prime ministers, and field marshals in order to smooth his path.

Burgoyne traveled with a wardrobe that filled eight leather boxes, and was accompanied by his valet, who looked after his clothes. Until a short time before his departure he planned to carry his own wines with him, but changed his mind when the government of France agreed to receive him. French wines were the best on earth, so he saw no need to protect his refined palate by taking treasures from his own cellar.

He made his whirlwind journey in civilian attire, and nowhere did he stress that he was a colonel on half-pay, an officer who had held the brevet rank of brigadier. He was a Member of Parliament engaged in a fact-finding expedition, and everywhere he asked seemingly innocent questions, not wanting his hosts to think he was a peacetime spy.

The Austrian army, he said in his report, was first-rate; the Imperial infantry was the world's finest, superbly trained and capable of making long marches without rest. The cavalry was somewhat less effective, both officers and men being inclined to make bravura displays of their horsemanship that contributed nothing to their efficiency as soldiers. The Austrian generals were "very knowing," he declared, but he criticized them:

> There are 338 general officers in the Imperial Austrian Army, and their cost cannot be justified in any military sense. Some are superannuated; others owe their preferment (and have no pretensions to it) to family rank and court intrigue; many have risen by gradual seniority, without faults, and without merits, whom it would be unjust to put by, yet whom the state can never employ for great purposes.
>
> In the Austrian service many of the most distinguished officers will be found among men of Irish extraction; and in the lower ranks the army swarms with the offspring of the best Roman Catholic families of that country. I cannot but regret that present policies

37

prohibit the employment of such splendid soldiers by the British Army.

He expressed great enthusiasm for the Hungarian cavalry, and wrote at length about the renowned Hungarian studs. He also advocated changes in the British uniform to incorporate features he found admirable in the clothing worn by Hungarian troops, including "the caps made so as to let down and cover the ears and neck in inclement weather, and the Hungarian trousers and lined half-boots without stockings." The over-all purpose of this uniform was to "unite as much as possible lightness, warmth and ease," and in his report he severely criticized the British uniform, which he called clumsy and "unfit for wear."

He also admired the uniform worn in the German principality of Brunswick, but found the Prussian uniform as cumbersome as the British. He recommended that the Prussian infantry drill, which was simple and effective, be adopted by Britain. The Prussian infantry was splendidly trained, he declared, but the Prussian cavalry was inferior, largely because good horsemen had to be granted a measure of freedom for individual initiative, and the Prussians were not permitted to think for themselves.

He had little respect for the common Prussian soldiers, saying that their ranks were filled with "strangers, deserters, prisoners and enemies of various countries, languages and religions. Their army," he added, "is more harassed with precautionary guards against their own soldiers deserting than against the enemy, and after an unsuccessful action, the number missing usually trebles the number to be accounted for by death or capture." He was even more scornful in his comments on the king of Prussia:

> He is jealous of prying eyes in all his employments. If he means to maneuver ten thousand men in private, he shuts up his country as effectually as his palace. But none dare complain or even think of making such complaint, liberty as the British know it being alien to the disposition and temperament of the Prussian.

Burgoyne lost some measure of his objectivity only in writing about the French, against whom he had fought three times. He thought the French cavalry were competent, although he noted their horses were inferior to those utilized by the British. Praising the valor of the individual French infantryman, he called the foot soldier sloppy and indifferent, a negative attitude that the factual record of French infantry did not justify. One notation was far-seeing, however: he said the French system of corporal punishment was reminiscent of Prussia and disgraceful; Frenchmen were proud, and the use of the stick not only robbed the French infantryman of his initiative but degraded him, making him sullen and rebellious. Unless there was change for the better in the system, he declared, the day was not far distant when companies, battalions and even regiments of French infantry would rebel.

The tour lasted for more than two months, and Burgoyne spent another month writing his report, which he called *Reflections and Observations*. Although given scant credit in his own time, it was hailed, a half-century later, as an exceptionally astute and perceptive document. The author made three copies, sending one to the War Office, presenting a second to Lord Chatham, and holding the third to read aloud in the House of Commons.

Chatham sent him a warm letter of thanks, praising the report and calling it valuable. The War Office scarcely bothered to acknowledge its receipt, however, and it disappeared in the bureaucratic maze. At Chatham's unofficial request Burgoyne did not read the report aloud in the Commons because it might have offended some of the nations he had visited. Instead he had additional copies made and gave them to Members of Parliament who were interested in military affairs.

None of the recommendations made by the author of *Reflections and Observations* were adopted in his own lifetime by the British Army. Burgoyne was disappointed, but admitted he was not surprised, having had too much experience as a soldier to expect the high command to perform overnight miracles.

His efforts were not wasted, however. In due time most of his suggestions were followed, and at the very least he enhanced his own reputation. He was regarded as the leading expert in the Commons on military affairs, making his promotion to the rank of major-general almost inevitable in the event that he should be recalled to active duty. Late in 1767 King George was persuaded to read the report, and was impressed by it, a fact which in itself lacked significance. The monarch liked to think of himself as a military expert, an opinion which no professional soldier in His Majesty's service shared.

The Crown had many gifts at its disposal for favorites, however, and early in 1768 Burgoyne was awarded one of these plums, the honorary governorship of Fort William, an old military base in the northern part of Great Britain where a token garrison was maintained. The prize paid an annual salary of three hundred pounds, and Burgoyne kept the post for ten years, until circumstances caused him to become so disillusioned with the king that he resigned the post.

After his return from his tour, Gentleman Johnny resumed his place in London society. He and Lady Charlotte entertained frequently, and often were seen at the theater and the salons of friends. Following the custom of the age, Burgoyne did his serious drinking in the company of other men, usually at a tavern on Richmond Hill called the Star and Garter, which he and his companions utilized almost as a private club.

In 1765 or thereabouts Gentleman Johnny, always interested in the arts and partial to artists, formed a close friendship with the greatest British painter of the time, Sir Joshua Reynolds, who frequently dined at the Burgoyne town house in Belgravia. There are numerous references in the correspondence of Lady Charlotte and in some of Burgoyne's own letters to a portrait of him done by Reynolds. The good colonel could not decide whether to pose in uniform or civilian attire, finally choosing the latter. But the portrait vanished at the time of Burgoyne's death late in the century, and has never been found, thus depriving posterity of a valuable work of art.

The generosity of King George made it possible for Burgoyne to gamble again, but he was a cautious player now, wagering small sums and finding his pleasure in "small victories," as

Lady Charlotte wrote to one of her sisters. Of all the joys sought by the gentry of the eighteenth century, only one was missing in Burgoyne's life. Still handsome in his mid-forties, with no sign of the double chin that would begin to appear a decade later, he was attentive to the ladies and flirted mildly at dinner parties and other functions, but he remained stubbornly loyal to his wife. Charlotte's health was beginning to decline, and she looked older than her years, but her husband refused to take advantage of the offers of romance that came his way, and there were many. Some of his friends found it difficult to believe that any gentleman would practice monogamy, and a number of them suspected that he engaged in dalliances on the sly. But the attempts made by enemies in the late 1770s to prove he had cheated on his wife were total failures. Burgoyne believed a man of honor kept his marriage vows, no matter what the behavior of his contemporaries.

A general election took place in 1768, making it necessary for Burgoyne to run for office if he wanted to keep his seat in the Commons. The Earl of Derby proposed another candidate for Midhurst, and had to find a new constituency for his son-in-law, a relatively simple matter since two seats were open in Preston, where one of the many Derby estates was located. Burgoyne ran for one of them, in partnership with Sir Henry Hoghton, who was also related to the Stanley family by marriage. They were opposed by two energetic candidates, Sir Frank Standish and Sir Peter Leicester, both of whom conducted vigorous campaigns.

Forced to work for their seats, Burgoyne and Hoghton matched the zeal of their opponents, and Gentleman Johnny became involved in an incident that left a permanent blemish on his otherwise spotless record. Each side accused the other of trying to intimidate voters, and all four of the candidates were guilty, although it was impossible to determine, through the maze of claims and countercharges, which side struck first.

Riots broke out in Preston on the day of the election, in March, and the contestants roamed through the town with bodyguards, each of them trying to drum up votes. The candidates accused the opposition of falsifying returns in various districts, and the officials breathed a sigh of relief when the polls finally closed. But that was not the end of the matter.

Colonel Burgoyne's attendants were three of his former sergeants, and these burly men may have believed they were sacking a Spanish town. Whatever their reason, a draper named Jackson went to court the next day, claiming that Burgoyne and the veterans had forced their way into his house, compelled him to swear on his knees that he would vote for the good colonel—and then had robbed him.

The embarrassed Burgoyne and his followers admitted all of the charges except robbery, which they denied. In the excitement over the narrow victory won by Burgoyne and Hoghton the affair was almost forgotten, but not even the influence of the Stanleys could prevent the outraged draper from pressing his case. Lord Strange intervened on behalf of his brother-in-law, and there were so many postponements that the case was put off until the following year. Jackson persisted, however, and on March 24, 1769, a full year after the incident, the court delivered its verdict.

Burgoyne and the former sergeants were found guilty of intimidation but not guilty on the charge of robbery. The colonel was forced to pay a stiff fine of one thousand pounds, and each of the sergeants was fined three hundred pounds, Burgoyne presumably paying on their behalf. All four could have been sent to prison, too, but the draper had won his victory, which included fifty per cent of the fines, the court wanted no further dispute with the Stanleys and a Member of Parliament, so the prison sentences that would have been meted out had justice followed its usual course were conveniently forgotten.

Burgoyne made it his business to call on the draper at home and place a substantial order with him. Then he returned to London, where the drawing-room wits made a number of feeble jokes at his expense, and thereafter the unfortunate matter was forgotten. Only a few of the more sensitive observers, including Gentleman Johnny's friend, Fox, noted that for some time he made no mention of honor in his House of Commons speeches.

Five

April 20, 1770, was an extraordinary day in the life of the urbane Gentleman Johnny Burgoyne, marking the only occasion on which he ever lost his temper in the House of Commons. A debate on the subject of Spain, a nation he continued to despise, was responsible, and the direct cause was an incident that took place in the remote Falkland Islands. According to a report that had reached London several months earlier, a squadron of ships belonging to the Spanish navy had invaded the Falklands, driven out the tiny British garrison, and "stolen the rudder" of the only British vessel in the harbor. The reasons Parliament waited so long to discuss the matter are obscure.

One Captain Walsingham, a retired officer in the Royal Navy, opened the debate with a pungent comment: "If any damned Spanish admiral had tried to remove the rudder from a ship of mine, I would have thought it my duty to knock his head off."

The Tories were placed on the defensive, and the Prime Minister, together with several members of his cabinet, tried to offer excuses. They wanted no war with Spain. The affair had been a tragic misunderstanding, but no lives had been lost, Spain had offered apologies, and the incident was considered closed. Confident they commanded a solid majority in the House, the Tories attempted to move on to other matters.

At that moment Burgoyne's temper exploded. He obtained the floor, and immediately launched into a furious tirade that brought members on both sides of the aisle to their feet, applauding and cheering:

> Spain gave fifteen minutes to a British officer to evacuate his garrison. Great Britain slept four months after this gratuitous insult. It has been the fashion to maintain—I have seen it in print and I have heard it in conversation—that military men are prejudiced judges in questions of this nature.
>
> Sir, I disdain the idea, and denounce it in the name of my profession. The man who would wantonly promote bloodshed, who upon private views of advantage or ambition would involve Europe in war, would be a promoter of ferocity—a disgrace to his profession, to his country and to human nature.
>
> But there are motives for which a soldier may wish for war. These are a sense of satisfaction due for an injury inflicted, a desire to make a return to our country for the honors and rewards we receive at her hands, a zeal to be the forward instrument to battle for the honor of the Crown, and the rights of the people of Great Britain. Sir, on behalf of those people and for the satisfaction of His Majesty's honor, I demand that Spain offer more than mere words as reparations to His Majesty's Government, and in order to translate these sentiments into appropriate action, I lay before this House a motion to that effect!

The House was swept up in a tide of emotionalism, and the Tory backbenchers joined the Whigs in voting for reparations. The Spanish government was frightened by this surge of nationalism, and afraid that Great Britain might declare war, paid two hundred and fifty thousand pounds in compensation, this enormous sum more than compensating the ship owner for the loss of his rudder and the members of the British garrison for their ruffled dignity.

John Burgoyne was the Parliamentary hero of the day, jingles were coined in his honor, and when he and Lady Charlotte attended a performance of *Hamlet* at Drury Lane, the great star of the age, David Garrick, interrupted a curtain speech to introduce the defender of British honor, who was rendered an ovation as he stood in his box, bowing to the audience.

Fresh from this triumph, Burgoyne launched an even more ambitious campaign the following year. This time his foe was the single most potent force in the economy of Great Britain, the East India Company. The directors of this mammoth organization were multi-millionaires who, on behalf of a private concern, were the rulers of the better part of the sub-continent of India, holding the natives in check by force of arms. The irregularities, financial and otherwise, in the affairs of the company were legion, but for decades they had been regarded as an evil similar to British weather, about which everyone complained but could do nothing.

John Burgoyne felt otherwise, and wanted a special committee, to be made up of select members of both Houses of Parliament, to conduct a full-scale investigation of the East India Company's entire operation. It was known that the concern was in immediate need of funds, which it was trying to raise, but this situation was only the tip of the iceberg. Huge fortunes were still being made, various practices in the conduct of the company's affairs were questionable, and the people of India were being oppressed by foreign masters who paid no more than token attention to their human needs.

Lord North, the Prime Minister, was opposed to an investigation, and let it be known that King George supported his stand. Some men, Burgoyne among them, doubted that the monarch took this position, inasmuch as George III was never reticent in telling others what he thought, believed, or wanted. In any event, Gentleman Johnny commanded powerful support. Charles James Fox made several of his more brilliant speeches in the Commons, attacking the East India Company, and then Edmund Burke launched his heavy oratorical artillery in a series of scathing assaults on an organization that, he declared, "conducts its business in private and thinks itself more powerful than the Crown."

The ultimate blow against the East India Company was struck when the Earl of Chatham arose in the House of Lords and announced that he, too, questioned the practices, business methods, and goals of the notorious company. Behind all these maneuvers was the guiding hand of John Burgoyne, who conducted the attack like a general moving his troops in a military campaign. Gentleman Johnny sought neither personal glory nor credit, but was motivated solely by his fear that the East India Company was using underhanded methods that would impugn the honor of Great Britain. He built his barrage with care, setting the dates when speaker after speaker in both the Commons and the Lords joined in the attack.

Public interest in the matter was lethargic at the outset, but the debate gradually stirred interest, and the newspapers, which had been reluctant to oppose some of Britain's wealthiest men, finally raised their voices, too. Lord North, a mild-mannered Parliamentarian who had no real zest for political combat, was powerless to stem the tide, and his own opposition faded when he became convinced that King George was among those who had been swayed by the oratory of the East India Company's foes and was beginning to favor the holding of an investigation. If the company had nothing to conceal, the monarch felt, the inquiry could do it no harm, but if there was chicanery in high places, the government and people had a right to know it.

By now Gentleman Johnny thoroughly understood both politics and the moods of the public. Displaying remarkable patience, he waited until April, 1772, by which time the entire nation was demanding an investigation. Then, but not until then, he arose in the Commons and made a spirited speech, at the end of which he moved the formation of Select Committee to Inquire into the Affairs of the East India Company. His address was one of the best he ever made in the House, and was written with all of the care that could be bestowed upon it by a man who was destined to make his mark, in the immediate future, as a professional playwright.

Referring to the "rapacity of their servants abroad and the knavery of their directors at home," Burgoyne delivered a thinly veiled warning to the Prime Minister: "A Minister who would be concerned in a business of this sort would deserve to be hanged. . . ."

At the climax of his speech Gentleman Johnny once again stressed honor; the honor of the country demanded a full-scale investigation because the servants of the company were guilty of misconduct, the directors were venal, and the business of the organization was "huddled together in one promiscuous tumult and confusion." His final words offered a convincing display of his own humanitarian feelings:

> The fate of a great portion of the globe, the fate of great States in which your own is involved, the distress of fifteen millions of people are involved in this question.
>
> Fifteen millions! Good God! What a call! The native of Hindustan, born a slave—his neck bent from the very cradle by the yoke—by birth, by education, by climate, by religion a patient, submissive, willing subject to Eastern despotism, first begins to feel, first shakes his chains, for the first time complains under the pre-eminence of British tyranny!

The debate was short and half-hearted, and Parliament voted almost unanimously in favor of making the inquiry. Burgoyne was made a member of the Select Committee, and worked diligently to gather evidence. In 1773 the matter came to a head with the questioning of Lord Clive, the head of the East India

Company, who had been the ruler of Bengal in all but name and had returned home as one of England's wealthiest and most prominent men.

Burgoyne and Clive clashed repeatedly, and the latter, himself a great soldier who knew the value of an attack, complained that he was being treated like a sheep-stealer. Clive spent several days on the witness stand, and Burgoyne was relentless, cross-examining him with the zeal and cunning of an experienced barrister.

The Commons conducted a final debate on the subject of the East India Company that lasted from noon of one day until mid-morning of the next. It was almost impossible to convict Robert Clive without condemning the entire system that had permitted him and his fellow directors to attain such power and gain such wealth. Clive was officially exonerated, with Burgoyne among those who voted against him.

The East India Company's victory was hollow, and no one knew it better than Clive, who the next year committed suicide. A new Parliamentary campaign was launched by Burke and Fox, guided behind the scenes by Lord Chatham, that changed and severely limited the authority and influence of the East India Company. Strict government controls were established, and the company gradually lost its power, which was assimilated by the Crown.

The inquiry was John Burgoyne's greatest single achievement in the Commons, and he was regarded as the equal of such men as Burke. King George was deeply impressed by his accomplishments, and a short time after the investigation was concluded, in the spring of 1773, Gentleman Johnny received word from the War Office that he had been promoted to the rank of major-general.

His star was still rising, and looking for fresh fields to conquer, he decided the time had come for him to attain distinction in yet another arena. The theater still beckoned, and he desperately wanted recognition as a dramatist. He was encouraged in this aim by David Garrick, who promised to produce and direct a play written by Gentleman Johnny, and to act in it as well if it contained a suitable role for him.

The wedding of a young relative in 1774 provided him with his inspiration. Lord Stanley, the nephew of the childless Lord Strange as well as of Lady Charlotte Burgoyne, was married at an estate of the Earl of Derby, whom he was destined to succeed two years later. The bride was the daughter of the Duke of Hamilton, the vast estate was known as "the Oaks," and Major-General John Burgoyne, Member of Parliament, budding playwright and a recognized wit, was made master of ceremonies for the occasion. He obliged by writing a drawing-room comedy which he called *The Maid of the Oaks*.

Producing and directing it himself at the wedding, with a cast made up largely of brothers, sisters, and cousins of the bride and groom, he saw his effort heartily applauded by the guests, who had already consumed considerable quantities of champagne. Gentleman Johnny was encouraged, nevertheless, and took the play to Garrick.

The great actor-producer-director read it, and sat down with the dramatist for what must have been a painful interview. On that occasion Gentleman Johnny became a professional, learning that successful plays are rewritten, not just written. Returning to the house in Belgravia and, for the first time, letting slide his attendance at the Commons, he struggled with a series of revisions.

Comedies of the period depended, in the main, on the wit and sparkle of their dialogue rather than on their plots, which were far-fetched, artificial, and more than a little absurd. The story of *The Maid of the Oaks* is no exception:

Sir Harry Groveby, as the play opens, is on the verge of marrying the lovely Maria, the ward of Mr. Oldworth. Sir Harry has an uncle, Old Groveby, described by the author as "an old crab," who is opposed to the match for reasons unexplained. The premarital festivities in the village are so moving that Mr. Oldworth breaks down and confesses that he is not Maria's guardian, but her father. His reasons for concealing the relationship are so complicated they strain credulity, but he now makes Maria the heiress to his entire fortune. She also charms Old Groveby, and he too makes her the heir to his estates, so the bride and groom marry, presumably living happily ever after.

The silly story is unimportant, and the play is saved by two high comedy characters who reveal that John Burgoyne had good reason to call himself a playwright. Mr. Dupely is a charming rogue, a rascal who devastates every women he meets. But he finds his match in Lady Bab Lardoon, a three-dimensional character whom Sheridan or Colley Cibber, the most successful playwrights of the day, would have been proud to invent. Lady Bab gambles and earns her living from her profits at the card table, making her a feminine version of a younger John Burgoyne. She is wise, shrewd, and witty, and she is unscrupulous in dealing with lechers like Mr. Dupely, thoroughly enjoying—with the audience—her ability to make a fool of him.

By the autumn of 1774 David Garrick decided *The Maid* was in sufficiently good shape for production, and keeping a promise he'd earlier made Burgoyne, directed the play himself. The success of the enterprise depended on the casting of Lady Bab, and Garrick hired an actress named Frances Abington for the role. Apparently she was perfect for the part, being somewhat like Lady Bab in her personal life, and Garrick, who was straight-laced, did not like her, considering her somewhat licentious. But he did not permit his personal tastes to stand in the way of business.

Gentleman Johnny attended the rehearsals, a new experience for him, and made further revisions in his script. The play opened on the night of November 14, 1774, at Drury Lane, and was acclaimed by an enthusiastic audience. The author and his wife were seated in a box, and Burgoyne was summoned to the stage for the curtain calls, winning an ovation when he gallantly kissed Miss Abington. *The Maid* was presented every night for a week, and thereafter became a standard production in the Drury Lane repertory, making it a rousing hit by every criterion of the period.

One curious feature of *The Maid* was that it contained a number of songs, thus placing it in a category with John Gay's *Beggars' Opera*, the first musical comedy, which had seen its initial production four decades earlier. Burgoyne demonstrated his versatility by writing both the music and the lyrics for these numbers.

His talents as a composer were meager, and he was a less accomplished lyricist, even though he liked to think of himself as a poet. But the music for one of the songs in *The Maid*, which was called "The World Turned Upside Down," was a sprightly air that gained immediate popularity and added to Burgoyne's renown. This additional fame pained him, however, because his lyrics were so insipid that his contemporaries promptly forgot them; the music was played everywhere, but the lyrics were happily ignored.

A footnote to the history of "The World Turned Upside Down" reveals an irony that could not have been lost on its composer. In 1781, after Lieutenant-General John Burgoyne's loss of the Battle of Saratoga had caused the eventual, almost inevitable collapse of the British cause in the struggle against the rebel Colonies, Lord Cornwallis surrendered his army to General George Washington at the conclusion of the Battle of Yorktown. When the Redcoats marched out onto the fields of Virginia on that momentous occasion, they kept time to a tune played by a regimental band. That lively air was Burgoyne's, "The World Turned Upside Down," and not even the composer could have imagined the ultimate significance of his title when he wrote it in 1774.

Certainly the success of *The Maid* made the playwright, Parliamentary slayer of the East India Company dragon, and major-general in the British Army, one of the towering, most eagerly sought men of his time, and his friendships were as varied as his talents were versatile. He and Fox, his distinguished young colleague in the Commons, were seen together frequently. He established a close relationship with Sheridan, who was so impressed by Frances Abington's portrayal of Lady Bab Lardoon in *The Maid of the Oaks* that he gave consideration to no other actress for the role of Lady Teazle when *The School for Scandal* was first produced in 1777.

In spite of his successes, however, Major-General John Burgoyne, M.P. and dramatist, was not a happy man. Lady Charlotte was ill, her physicians were unable to cure her ailments, and her health declined, even though she repaired frequently to Bath and took the healing waters there.

Another cloud was growing larger on Burgoyne's horizon. Great Britain's relations with her American colonies, which he admired, were deteriorating, and he was disturbed because he believed his country was in the wrong.

Six

Great Britain's dispute with her North American dependencies, which came to the surface in the years following the Seven Years' War, known on the far side of the Atlantic as the French and Indian War, was initially political and economic. The mother country imported the raw materials of her colonies, paying far less for them than other nations were willing to pay in the international markets, and the colonies were burdened with taxes which, although small, irritated them because they had no parliamentary voice in their imposition. Lord North knew little about the colonies and cared less about the attitudes of their inhabitants, a view shared by his monarch. King George and his Prime Minister believed that colonists were second-class citizens whose first duty was obedience to the orders of their masters.

Emotional factors crept in on both sides of the ocean, complicating the issues in the early 1770s, and the belligerence of an increasingly vocal minority in the colonies, combined with an intransigent inability to grapple with reality on the part of Lord North and the Tory majority in Parliament, made it more and more probable that force of arms would be required to settle the dispute.

The same group of political leaders who were responsible for the downfall of the East India Company took the part of the colonists in Parliament. Burke, Fox, and Burgoyne insisted in vain that the rights of the Americans be recognized and respected, and the Earl of Chatham was so exercised that, shortly before the outbreak of hostilities he directed his son and heir, William Pitt the younger, who would enjoy a career equal to his father's, to resign his position as aide-de-camp to Sir Guy Carleton, the Governor-General of Canada.

There were others in high places who shared the same sentiments. Major-General William Howe, running for a seat in the Commons from Nottingham in a 1774 by-election, announced that he would not take up arms against the Americans unless directly ordered to do so by the Crown. King George had a long memory, and when Howe was sent to take command of an expeditionary force in 1775, he received his command directly from the Crown.

Vice Admiral Augustus Keppel, who would become First Lord of the Admiralty and a viscount after the fall of Lord North's ministry in 1782, went even further. Under no circumstances would he draw his sword against the American colonists, he declared, and he went on the half-pay retired list rather than break his word.

Even more dramatic was the stand taken by General Lord Jeffrey Amherst, a hero in the Colonies as well as at home. King George personally offered him the post of commander-in-chief of all forces taking part in the war against the insurrectionists, but Amherst turned a deaf ear to the proposal, his attitude creating a permanent chill in his relations with the Crown.

Gentleman Johnny Burgoyne's position was somewhat more equivocal than that of his military colleagues. In 1774 he made several statements on the floor of the Commons that placed him squarely in the camp of those who took America's part in the growing dispute, on one occasion saying, "My heart grows heavy within me when I see a parent and child taking divergent paths. Let us show tolerance, patience and the love of a mother for her offspring before it is too late. The clock of destiny is already striking the fatal hour, and we can bind the American colonies to us only if we treat them with the honor and respect due a son who has grown to manhood and is capable of standing foursquare upon his own feet in the world."

At the same time, however, Burgoyne was a hot-blooded soldier who wanted action in the field. He had attained a rank that would give him major responsibilities in any campaign, and his vanity demanded that he achieve as much in his profession as a soldier as he had accomplished as a politician and as a playwright. His rigid concept of loyalty to the Army made it impossible for him to emulate General Howe and make a public statement to the effect that he would serve in the New World only if commanded by the King.

But he had an escape, and did not hesitate to utilize it. His wife's health was so precarious that only the gravest of emergencies could compel him to leave her side, and he took care to communicate this view to the future Colonial secretary, Lord George Germain.

Those of Burgoyne's foes who let it be known, delicately, that they thought he was taking a coward's way out of a dilemma in which his ambitions clashed with his principles were mistaken. A letter he wrote on his fifty-third birthday in January, 1775, to his brother-in-law and dearest friend, Lord Strange, indicates the depth of his sincerity:

> To separate for a length of time, perhaps forever, from the tenderest, the faithfullest, the most amiable companion and friend that ever a man was blessed with —a wife in whom during four and twenty years I never could find a momentary act of blame! The narrow circumstances, perhaps the distressed state in which

she might find herself at my death, add severely to my anxieties. To supply the requisites of her rank, to reward the virtues of her character, I could only bequeath her a legacy of my imprudence.

Men of the world in general are too callously composed to conceive what I endure. My intimates, even those of most sensibility, acquainted with the levities, the inattentions, and dissipations of my common course of life, might want faith in my sincerity; I therefore conceal my heart from all; and I even suffer my dearest Charlotte herself—not, I hope, to doubt what I feel—but rather to be ignorant how much I feel, than expiate on a subject that could be so afflicting to her in the tender and delicate state of her mind and health.

Relations with the Colonies grew worse, and the situations of individual generals became yet more sensitive. General Howe was asked whether he would accept the command of the British garrison in Boston, but he declined on the grounds that the post would embarrass him, since the city had erected a statue in honor of his late father, Brigadier Lord Howe, who had been killed at Ticonderoga during the French and Indian War.

Lord Dartmouth, the outgoing war secretary, decided to give a dinner party for the Army's senior officers in order to clear the air, and Burgoyne was one of nine general officers who attended. To his intense disappointment as well as that of his colleagues, no mention whatever was made of the Colonies. Several generals had prepared strategic plans to offer for discussion if the civilians wanted opinions and advice, but it appeared that no one wondered or cared what professional soldiers thought. The food was delicious and the claret and port were splendid, satisfying the palate of a gourmet as discriminating as Gentleman Johnny, but he was given no opportunity to talk about North America or his reluctance to accept a command there.

He left the dinner party quietly cursing the stupidity of senior civilians. But on due reflection he couldn't help wondering whether Lord Dartmouth had not outsmarted his top-ranking officers. Almost without exception the generals had no heart for fighting a war against rebellious American colonists, and the war secretary had been both wise and clever to give them no opportunity to air their opinions. When the time came—and the news from Boston, New York, and Philadelphia indicated it would come with a rush—the generals would be told rather than asked their future plans.

It became increasingly obvious to Lord North by the early spring of 1775 that something had to be done to bolster the Army garrisons in America, as it now seemed inevitable that hostilities would break out at any time. The two senior officers in North America were Major-General Thomas Gage, who had been sent to command the Boston garrison some months earlier, and General Sir Guy Carleton, the governor-general of Canada, who was directing all of his efforts to holding the king's Canadian subjects in line. Gage was the weak link in the military chain of command, and the War Office decided that Major-General John Burgoyne should be sent to Boston with several battalions of reinforcements, to act as Gage's deputy. The recommendation was sent to King George, who enthusiastically endorsed it, and the order was dispatched by special messenger to the house in Belgravia.

Gentleman Johnny's concept of honor made it impossible for him to refuse, so he obeyed the order. No details of his farewell to his wife are known, but his disturbed state of mind is indicated by an extraordinary letter he wrote at Portsmouth on April 18, 1775, leaving it with Charlotte's nephew, Lord Stanley, the future Earl of Derby, with instructions to deliver it only in the event of his death in the New World. It was addressed to King George III:

> Sire,
> Whenever this letter shall be delivered to Your Majesty, the writer of it will be no more. It may therefore be esteemed an address from beyond the grave, and under that idea I am persuaded Your Majesty will consider with indulgence both the matter and the expression.

My purpose, Sire, is to recommend to your royal protection Lady Charlotte Burgoyne, who at my death will have to combat the severest calamities of life—a weak frame of body, very narrow circumstances, and a heart replete with those agonies which follow the loss of an object it has long held most dear. What will be her consolation? Wretched state, when poverty is disregarded only because it is the least poignant of our sensations, and the pains of distemper are alleviated by the hopes that they send to our dissolution.

The first comfort upon which my mind rests in regard to that dear woman, in a crisis so trying, is a knowledge of her piety; the next a confidence in Your Majesty's compassion and generosity.

Your Majesty, acquainted with the value of female excellence, will hear without impatience a husband's praises. I protest, with the sincerity of a man who meditates death while he writes, and calls God to witness to his testimony, that in the great duties of life, I do not know that Lady Charlotte ever committed a fault, except that, if a fault it can be called, of love and generosity which directed her to me without consulting her family—even that is now cancelled in their eyes—upon a review of our happiness during a course of more than twenty-four years, no moment of which has been embittered, except by sickness or separation.

My heart tells me, Sire, that I am not presumptuous in this application. I received Your Majesty's commands for America with regret, the first sensation of that nature I ever experienced in a call for service, but I have not less a sense of duty; I have scorned to propose terms to my obedience, or to take advantage of the crisis of receiving your royal orders to prefer a petition for the provision of my family.

I rely on Your Majesty's heart to accept with indulgence this humble mark of my respect, and I take confidence to assure Your Majesty that, whatever may be my fate in my ensuing trials, I shall be found to my last moment

> Your Majesty's
> Zealous soldier
> And most faithful subject
> J. Burgoyne.

A friend named Hutchinson, who saw something of Gentleman Johnny in the period immediately prior to his departure reveals still more about his state of mind. Burgoyne's principal concern connected with his New World duties lay in his anxiety to determine how to conduct affairs in the event that martial law should be declared. He seemed unworried by the possibility that the Americans would resort to force, and that he would be compelled to fight them. He was free in his criticism of Lord North's government, saying the Prime Minister lacked direction and his councils were wanting in decisiveness. The entire administration, he said, was guilty of procrastination. In fact, even though he was scheduled to depart in eight days, he doubted whether any instructions had been prepared for him, and he was afraid he would be forced to go without a word from the War Office. In this he was correct.

Gentleman Johnny's sense of the dramatic made it impossible for him to leave without fanfare, and he made a brief address to his colleagues in the House of Commons, a speech so laden with false modesty that it sounded more like dialogue written by playwright Burgoyne for a pompous character in a comedy: "The utmost merit I shall be able to claim in this expedition will probably be that of an attentive, an assiduous, circumscribed obedience."

He sailed on a frigate of war, the *H.M.S. Cerberus*, in the company of two other major-generals, Sir Henry Clinton and William Howe, who would be knighted within a year. The trio spent most of their days together on the month's voyage across the Atlantic, and younger men watched in awe from a distance as they paced the decks together, engaging in earnest conversation while the tails of their scarlet and gold uniform coats flapped in the sea breeze.

They ate "tolerably well" on the voyage, Gentleman Johnny reported to his wife; she could not have been surprised, as he had fortified himself for the journey with boxes of foodstuffs and several cases of wine. Clinton and Howe having shown less foresight, common courtesy forced him to share his delicacies with them. Burgoyne was too much of a gentlemen to complain, even to his wife, but he must have been annoyed, often having denounced insufficient planning as the bane of a military man's life.

When the *Cerberus* reached Boston in May, General Gage gave a dinner for his colleagues to welcome them, and Burgoyne immediately assumed his duties as deputy commander of the Boston garrison. His first task was the writing of a proclamation in Gage's name, a pastime that kept him fairly busy thereafter, his superior being so verbose that he used that method of communication frequently, and so lazy that he wrote nothing himself.

Burgoyne's letters to his wife indicate that Boston offered him a number of pleasant surprises, even though he deplored the absence of theaters in the town. The unpopularity of Redcoats made it impossible for him to dine in any of the city's comfortable taverns or inns, but he was able to order the foods he wanted for his own mess, and consequently suffered no hardships. American ale and beer, somewhat stronger than that brewed in England, was superior in taste; good Spanish port was scarce, as was a palatable sack, but ample quantities of excellent claret could be purchased, and the far-seeing Gentleman Johnny laid in a supply. American oysters were better than those taken from the English Channel, the lobsters were magnificent, and the mussels were on a par with those served in London. He wrote frequently about another shellfish, found only on the western shores of the Atlantic, called the clam. It was he rather than Sir William Howe, to whom the observation has been attributed, who dubbed the clam "America's caviar."

Colonial beef was excellent, Burgoyne wrote, but was insufficiently aged, and American mutton was stringy. No one in all America, including his own British Army cook, he complained, knew how to make a trifle, but the tarts "are tasty, due to the fine quality of peaches and other fruits grown here, including several types of berries we do not see at home."

There were minor annoyances that made Burgoyne know he was not welcome in Boston. The heel on one of his boots came loose, but no local cobbler would repair it, and his orderly had to perform the task for him, ineptly. Boston's wealthiest citizen, ship-owner, and merchant, John Hancock, owned a magnificent house and set a handsome table, it was said, but Hancock was so active in the cause of those Americans who advocated independence that no invitation to dine was issued to the deputy commander of the garrison that was being made to feel it was an occupying force in a hostile, alien land.

General Gage, aided by General Burgoyne, had only one real responsibility, that of keeping order, and although the Redcoat leaders knew they were sitting on a keg of volatile gunpowder, there was little to keep them busy. Burgoyne loathed inactivity, and on June 14, 1775, he wrote a long letter to Prime Minister Lord North about an idea that had formed in his nimble mind. Other, more experienced generals, all of them senior to him in rank, could perform whatever military duties might await them in the Colonies. As for himself, he proposed that he don his other hat, that of a Member of Parliament, and that he travel through the Colonies, holding discussions with rebel leaders and trying to persuade them to work out their differences with His Majesty's Government on an amicable basis. His argument was concise:

> Not charged with any direct proposal from Government, nor authorized to treat with them in a publick character, I have not less zeal in my capacity as a Member of Parliament, a friend of human nature, and a sincere well-wisher to the united interests of the two countries, to forward as far as in me lies, the great work of reconciliation upon enlarged, solid honourable grounds. This sort of language would not commit Government in anything.

Regardless of the merits of Burgoyne's scheme—and in all

probability it would have come too late to be effective—his tactics were faulty. Had he written his plan to Burke, Fox, and some of America's other friends in the Commons, they might have been able to prepare the way for the sort of mission he proposed. Instead, by sending it direct to the unsympathetic Lord North, he sealed its fate.

The Prime Minister's reply, sent at the end of July, was equally long, even more flattering, and completely negative. If Burgoyne were captured during his travels through the colonies he would be too valuable a hostage; consequently "His Majesty fears your plan cannot be carried into execution."

Burgoyne's pen was busy in the early days of June, 1775. He wrote a long letter to his former subordinate, Charles Lee, who was now living in New Jersey, and proposed a reconciliation before it was too late. He also sent letters to several friends in the Army at home, stating frankly that the high command in Boston was incompetent, that the paymaster was keeping funds he should have distributed, including the sum of five hundred pounds due Gentleman Johnny for his travel expenses, and that the quartermaster-general was inept. Even Gage did not escape unscathed, Burgoyne calling him "unequal to his present station."

Then, on June 17, all hope for a peaceful solution vanished from Major-General John Burgoyne's mind, as did his petty criticism of his superior and subordinates. On that date was fought the Battle of Breed's Hill, known to posterity as the Battle of Bunker Hill.

Seven

History has concluded that the Battle of Bunker Hill or its equivalent was inevitable, American passions having soared to unbearable heights and General Gage having been too callous and clumsy to avoid a confrontation. Gage chose mid-June, when the Patriots were agitating for war, to fortify and expand his positions, to seize rebel stores in the town of Concord, and otherwise wave a red flag under the noses of men who were spoiling for a fight. His own Redcoats had been cooped up in the garrison for so long, enduring local insults on the few occasions they had been granted the freedom of the town, that they, too, were in an ugly mood.

Paul Revere and other American observers spread the word of Gage's maneuvers on the night of June 16, and on the following morning the British commander was awakened by a courier who brought him the astonishing news that American forces had established breastworks on Breed's Hill, and consequently commanded the heights above Boston. Had Gage been an expert tactician he would have moved a force to the American rear, and with the aid of the Royal Navy's heavy cannon it might have been a relatively simple matter to dislodge the inexperienced rebels. But Thomas Gage was a soldier of the very old school, and convinced that the Americans were mocking him, he decided to drive them from the field by launching a frontal assault on their position.

The advice of Major-General John Burgoyne was neither asked nor given, nor was the opinion of Major-General William Howe, who took part in the battle, solicited at any time. Burgoyne had literally nothing to do during the battle except stand at Gage's side, watch the action through his glass and shudder as his superior made error after error. Although meticulous in his restraint, as befitted a gentleman, Burgoyne was less circumspect in his subsequent, private correspondence. Gage, he declared, was "a stupid butcher, as our casualty figures show. Ninety-two of our officers were killed or wounded, a melancholy disproportion to the numbers killed and wounded of the private soldiers."

The Americans were forced to withdraw from the field when they exhausted their ammunition, but they hailed the Battle of Bunker Hill as a victory because men from all thirteen of the colonies had stood up to the heaviest fire of British infantry, cavalry, and artillery without breaking ranks or running away. The British also claimed a victory on the grounds that the enemy had evacuated the field.

There were men in Parliament who knew better, and those who did not soon received a liberal education. John Wilkes, an M.P. who was a strong American supporter, declared on the floor of the Commons: "What have we conquered? Bunker's Hill, with the loss of twelve hundred men! Are we to pay as dearly for the rest of America?"

The disgusted John Burgoyne gave vent to his feelings by writing a long letter to his friend, Lord Rochefort, who was also sympathetic to the American cause, perhaps hoping that his lordship would see to it that his critique was seen by the right people, men who could take appropriate action in the future. This communication is significant not only because it so aptly illustrates Burgoyne's keen powers of analysis, but because it marks a very sharp change in his attitude. The bloodshed had caused him to lose much of what he had felt for the colonists. They were the enemy now, and his grand scheme, his hope of acting as a conciliator, was forgotten. His contempt for the Americans was seen in his repeated use of the phrase, "a rabble in arms," and his tone indicated that he was taking a new, far more stern approach to the people he had called "our children."

Had he been in Gage's position, he said, he would have taken Samuel Adams, John Hancock, and other rebel leaders prisoners before they could commit mischief. He would have sent spies to scour the neighborhood for hidden arms and concentrations of men, he would have sent out detachments to seize caches of Patriot supplies, and, above all, he would have trained his own troops for combat instead of allowing them to "grow mold upon their uniforms" by sitting in their garrisons. He accurately described the so-called Battle of Lexington on April 19 as a "paltry skirmish," saying the Americans had made more of the incident than it had warranted in military significance, an opinion that posterity has confirmed. He also pointed out a number of errors made by the Americans in the Battle of Bunker Hill, stating flatly that commanders who were more experienced could have driven the British from Boston, "and from North America itself—without further conflict."

As for himself, Burgoyne declared, "the inferiority of my station as the youngest Major-General upon the staff left me almost a useless spectator. . . . In the general, regular course of business in this army, Major-Generals are absolute cyphers. My rank only serves to place me in a motionless, drowsy, irksome medium, or rather vacuum, too low for the honor of command, too high for that of execution."

His specific comments on Bunker Hill are worthy of note:

The enemy defence was well conceived and obstinately maintained; the retreat was no flight, no matter what our apologists may say; it was even covered with bravery and military skill, and proceeded no further than to the west hill, where a new post was taken and new intrenchments instantly begun.

Though my letter passes in security, I tremble while I write it; and let it not pass even in a whisper from your Lordship to more than one person: the zeal and intrepidity of the officers, which was without exception exemplary, was ill-seconded by the private men. Discipline, not to say courage, was wanting. In the critical moment of carrying the redoubt, the officers of some corps were almost alone.

Our present, general situation is melancholy, and offers little hope for the future. The country around Boston is all fortification; we are hemmed in here, and can enlarge our perimeter only by the slow step of a a siege; we are sadly lacking in wagons, hospital carriages and horses.

More than all else, Gage is not equal to his task; he might make an amiable governor, but is incapable of rising to military opportunity, although I must confess that even the great Caesar would be discouraged were he to take the command here. We have little money, so we have no cattle, no forage, and above all, no intelligence. We are ignorant not only of what passes in congresses, but want spies for the hill half a mile off.

In spite of the difficulties the British faced, Burgoyne was not pessimistic. He knew what he would do if he were given the command, and he outlined a sound strategy that, had it been adopted, might have been effective. He would occupy the heights that commanded Boston with the aid of the Royal Navy, and then, after leaving a garrison of three thousand men to maintain control of Massachusetts Bay Colony, he would embark on an ambitious program. He would create a number of diversions, the first of them the military chastisement of Rhode

Island Colony in order to draw American troops there. Withdrawing hastily before the enemy could force him into an engagement, he would occupy the whole of the Connecticut River, thus
giving him the control of the better part of New England. Meanwhile his agents would be active on Long Island, where the
residents were said to entertain strong Loyalist sympathies, and
he was certain New York Town, the third largest city in America, after Boston and Philadelphia, could be taken without the
firing of a single shot, provided the British high command
moved with dispatch.

But, alas! Gage was incapable of acting quickly. Burgoyne
wrote that he had interviewed many American prisoners of
war, and had found the majority "men of good understanding,
but of much prejudice and still more credulity." He had urged
Gage to send them off to their homes, telling them, "You have
been deluded; go to your homes in peace; it is your duty to
God and your country to undeceive your neighbors." But Gage,
he wrote, lacked the intelligence and wit to act on the suggestion.

Another of his ideas was adopted, however. He was responsible for the suggestion, accepted with alacrity by King
George and Lord North, that foreign mercenary troops be hired
to augment the British regiments, that native Indians be paid
to join forces with Britain, and that Canadians also be recruited
to serve in regiments of their own. "Our crying need is for men!"
he concluded, and not until much later, in his Saratoga campaign, would he realize the Indians were useless and that the
Canadians were reluctant to take an active part in engagements
beyond their own borders.

Few acts committed by the British throughout the entire
American Revolution created greater resentment in America
than the use of mercenary soldiers from Hesse and other German
principalities, and the policy solidified opposition to the mother
country on the part of many who had been unable to untangle
their loyalties. The extent to which Burgoyne can be credited—
or blamed—is difficult to determine.

There can be no doubt that the War Office and King George
saw his communication and were impressed by his arguments,

but it is likely that his recommendations merely bolstered a decision that had already been made in favor of hiring foreign troops. The use of mercenaries was widespread in the eighteenth century, and professional-troops-for-hire had been engaged by all of the major powers for the better part of one hundred years, most of them coming from the German states and Sweden. Certainly it can be argued that Burgoyne, in his capacity as a general officer, was thinking exclusively in military terms and did not consider the human repercussions to his proposal.

His personal reactions are far more evident in a letter he sent at the same time to Charlotte's nephew, Lord Stanley. Here his description of the Battle of Bunker Hill reflects the mind and emotions of Burgoyne, the author, as distinct from the critical observations made by Burgoyne, the soldier:

> As to the action of the 17th, you will see the general detail of it in the public print. To consider it as a statesman, it is truly important, because it establishes the ascendency of the King's troops, though opposed by more than treble numbers, assisted by every circumstance that nature and art could supply to make a situation strong. Were an accommodation, by any strange turn of events, to take place without any other action, this would remain a most useful testimony and record in America.

> To consider this action as a soldier, it comprised, though in a small compass, almost every branch of military duty and curiosity. Troops landed in the face of an enemy; a fine disposition; a march sustained by a powerful cannonade from moving field artillery, fixed batteries, floating batteries, and broadsides of ships at anchor, all operating separately and well-disposed; a deployment from the march to form for the attack of the entrenchments and redoubt; a vigorous defence; a storm with bayonets; a large and fine town set on fire by shells. Whole streets of houses, ships upon the stock, a number of churches, all sending up volumes

of smoke and flame, or falling together in ruin, were capital objects. A prospect of the neighboring hills, the steeples of Boston, and the masts of such ships as were unemployed in the harbour, all crowded with spectators, friends and foes, alike in anxious suspense, made a background to the piece; and the whole together composed a representation of war that I think the imagination of LeBrun [a seventeenth-century French artist commissioned by Louis XIV to paint scenes of the French army in combat] never reached. It was great, it was high spirited, and while the animated impression remains, let us quit it. I will not engage your sensibility and my own in contemplation of humanity upon the subject, but will close *en militaire* by lamenting that your brother Thomas was not arrived, because in a long life of service he may not, perhaps, have an opportunity of seeing any professional tragedy like it.

In the period prior to Bunker Hill and in the weeks following the engagement, Burgoyne also engaged in a heavy correspondence with Charles Lee, soon to be commissioned a major-general in the Continental Army. Inordinately ambitious and always too clever for his own good, Lee apparently hoped to win his former superior officer to his own cause. He did this in part by presenting philosophical and moral arguments he knew would appeal to Burgoyne, and he augmented this approach by clumsily denigrating the other senior British generals in America.

John Burgoyne's replies indicate he was more than Lee's match as a philosopher, and that he had the courage of his own convictions. After politely expressing astonishment that he and his former subordinate should find themselves on opposite sides in an armed conflict, he professed himself familiar with the works of John Locke, upon whose thinking the Americans based their arguments. He added, "I regard with reverence almost amounting to idolatry upon those immortal Whigs who adopted and applied such doctrine during part of the reign of Charles the First, and in that of James the Second."

Burgoyne proposed that he and Lee meet, and he even suggested a place for the conference, a house just inside the British sentry lines in occupied Boston, where he promised that his guest would be accorded every courtesy and protection. One paragraph in his letter created a sensation when Lee showed it to Silas Deane and other civilian Patriot leaders:

> Is it then from a relief of taxes or from the control of Parliament "in all cases whatsoever" we are at war? If for the former, the quarrel is at an end; there is not a man of sense and information in America who does not know it is in the power of the Colonies to put an end to the exercise of taxation immediately and for ever. I boldly assert it, because sense and information will also suggest to every man, that it can never be in the interest of Great Britain, after her late experience, to make another trial.

The letters were carried by uniformed messengers who were permitted to cross sentry lines and then were blindfolded while being transported to the places of delivery. They were seen by thousands of British and American troops, as well as by uncounted civilians, so it was literally impossible to keep the fact of the correspondence a secret. Then newspapers in New York and Philadelphia learned of the contents of the letter Burgoyne wrote in early July, 1775, and the flames of public speculation leaped higher.

Was Burgoyne, a Member of Parliament as well as a senior British officer, writing on behalf of Lord North's government? Or was he merely indicating his personal views? If he was acting in an official or semi-official capacity, it was possible that an accommodation could be reached. The Continental Congress, meeting in Philadelphia, talked about nothing else for days, and all but the radical element, led by John Hancock and Samuel Adams, that demanded separation from Britain at any cost, were eager to pursue the matter.

General Lee saw the chance to win immortality as the man

who ended the war, and submitted Burgoyne's letter to the Congress, which appointed its own representative, Elbridge Gerry, to attend the proposed meeting, form his own opinions, and report back to the civilian authority.

Burgoyne, the man of reason, was well aware of the stir he had created, and was delighted. Until now he had been acting solely in his private capacity, a fact he concealed from the Americans, but he saw himself in the role of an intermediary, and in mid-July, 1775, he wrote a long letter to Lord North. In it he presented arguments in favor of holding a dialogue with a former British military hero who, presumably, would understand the positions taken by His Majesty's Government.

Thoroughly familiar with the pressure tactics necessary to promote favorable action in Parliament, Burgoyne also wrote private letters to Charles James Fox, Lord Stanley, and Lord Rochefort. They were already sympathetic to the American cause, so he presented them with factual, military arguments in favor of a peaceful compromise settlement. The British Army at Boston was "bottled up like a cork," and could not advance overland to any destination. It was a besieged force, and would atrophy in hostile Boston, from which only escape by sea was available. The Royal Navy was hostile to the Army, and the senior officers of the fleet at Boston were incompetents who had no grasp of grand strategy, so the British cause in the Colonies was hopeless unless drastic action were taken in the immediate future.

The preferred course, Burgoyne declared, would be the opening of negotiations with a hard-headed man like General Lee, who could be trusted to carry unvarnished, unprejudiced accounts of the conversations to his own civilian government. The only alternative to such meetings, Burgoyne said, would be to adopt a whole new plan of military action. Should that course be followed, he recommended the evacuation of Boston and the taking of New York in order to make it the center of British operations. He recommended the former, since it would save bloodshed and civilian suffering; he also reminded his friends that the longer hostilities continued, the more Americans would resent the mother country and the more difficult it would become, consequently, to arrange a peace on any terms other than the granting of complete independence to the Colonies.

If the Parliament decided, however, that "national honor" made it necessary to prosecute the war, Burgoyne expressed his own willingness to do his duty, "no matter how painful that duty would be." But he stressed that the price would be higher than Lord North realized: it would be necessary to send "many corps of our troops" to the New World, to treble the size of the Royal Navy fleet operating in American waters, and to spend huge sums of money on provisions and armaments. Those who believed the British could live off the land had no concept of colonial life: there were no munitions plants in the New World, and even gunpowder would have to be imported from England. Aside from a few private tailors who made uniforms for senior American officers, there were no facilities in America for the making of uniforms, and no one to make them. As for food, local farmers would sell no supplies to the occupying forces, and actually hid grains, meats, and vegetables rather than permit them to fall into British hands.

Ships sailing across the Atlantic spent approximately one month traveling in either direction, so Burgoyne knew he had a long wait for a reply to his letters, and even longer before he could obtain a positive reaction to his proposals. In the meantime he had little to occupy his time. The Boston garrison maintained sentry lines, but did little else, and General Gage, consistently short-sighted in all military matters, rejected his deputy's suggestion that the regiments be trained for New World warfare, where vast distances, forests, and rugged terrain were responsible for battle conditions unlike those that even the most accomplished of veterans had known in Europe.

Reduced to making token inspections of the sentry outposts, soldier Burgoyne was bored by his existence, so playwright Burgoyne came to his rescue. Gentleman Johnny closed the door of his sitting room, put in supplies of ink, quill pens, and paper, and told his aides-de-camp that he was to be disturbed only in the event of an emergency.

Then, his Muse firmly perched on his shoulder, he wrote a

new play, a farce he called *The Siege of Boston*. It was presented by a cast of amateurs, all of them Army officers, civilian officials, or recruits from the ranks of the few British wives and daughters who had not yet been evacuated. The residents of occupied Boston snubbed the Redcoats, so only British audiences attended the play's three performances, but they were so enthusiastic in expressing their approval that the author sent a letter and a copy of the script to David Garrick, suggesting a possible London production.

Presumably Garrick replied, but no copy of his letter exists, so its contents are unknown. But the practical results speak for themselves: the play was not done in London, then or later, and aside from the three performances in Boston, was never done anywhere. David Garrick knew his business. *The Siege of Boston* is so crude, so sloppily conceived, and so badly written that it is difficult to believe the playwright was the same man who wrote *The Maid of the Oaks* and other plays vastly superior to it that were penned in the years after the American Revolution.

Had *The Siege* been Gentleman Johnny's only literary effort, it might be remembered as a curiosity, but as it was the work of a man who established a solid, deserved reputation as a dramatist, it can only be called unworthy of his talents. It is possible to excuse him on the grounds that he had other matters on his mind, and was so concerned with the issues of war and peace that it was difficult for him to concentrate.

One illustration of Burgoyne's writing in Boston is sufficient:

> Hold, let me be, you damned confounded dog,
> I am to rise and speak the Epilogue.

In a prologue Burgoyne urged the good citizens of Boston to attend the play, promising it would cheer them and help them forget the hardships to which they were being subjected. But the Bostonians, in their wisdom, elected not to compound their miseries, and absented themselves in large numbers.

The preparation and production of *The Siege of Boston* did

not occupy all of Burgoyne's time and energies, and at the end of July, 1775, he sent a long letter to Lord George Germain, in which he complained at length about London's procrastination in the prosecution of the war, which he termed fatal. His Majesty's Government, he declared, should decide whether it wanted peace or war, and if it chose the latter, it should act accordingly, sending enough armed, equipped men to perform the duty "that honor requires." Considerations of honor were ever-present in Gentleman Johnny's mind.

His estimates of American leaders are worthy of note. General Washington, he said, was very able, and were he an officer in the British Army, he would rise to the rank of lieutenant-general or even higher. Charles Lee, on the other hand, had no talent for strategic planning, and had he remained in the British Army would have been fortunate to rise as high as brigadier.

His opinion of Samuel Adams was unflattering, and in Burgoyne's opinion he was "a profligate hypocrite." At the same time, however, Burgoyne was one of the few contemporaries who recognized the value of Adams' contribution to the cause of American independence. He was "as great a conspirator as ever subverted a state, who has, by the exercise of his parts, availing himself of the temper and prejudice of the times, cajoled the opulent, drawn in the wary, deluded the vulgar, till all parties in America, and some in Great Britain, are puppets in his string."

His view of John Hancock, whom he called "Handcock," disagrees with that of posterity; Gentleman Johnny called him a "piddling genius." He dismissed the wealthy, shrewd Bostonian, President of the Continental Congress, as "one of Adams' tools, a mere vassal who is not capable of thinking or expressing his own thoughts."

Again Burgoyne stressed his theme that the British Army could not live up to its obligations in the Colonies unless it received appropriate support from the government. The Boston garrison, he said, had "neither bread-waggons, bat horses, sufficient artillery horses, nor other articles of *attirail* necessary for an army to move at a distance, nor numbers to keep up posts of communication and convoys, had we even magazines to be conveyed."

Burgoyne reserved his deepest scorn for the commander of the Royal Navy New World fleet, Admiral Samuel Graves, and history has confirmed his opinion of the man, who owed his rise to family connections. Even in his younger days Graves had been petty and incompetent, and age was rapidly increasing his deficiencies. Gentleman Johnny's handwriting grew perceptibly larger when he wrote:

> It may be asked in England, "What is the Admiral doing?" I wish I were able to answer that question satisfactorily, but I can only say what he is *not* doing.
>
> That he is *not* supplying us with sheep and oxen, the dinners of the best of us bear meager testimony; the state of our hospitals bears a more melancholy one.
>
> He is *not* defending his own flocks and herds, for the enemy have repeatedly plundered his own islands.
>
> He is *not* defending the other islands in the harbour, for the enemy in force landed from a great number of boats, and burned the lighthouse at noonday (having first killed and taken the party of marines which was posted there) almost under the guns of two or three men-of-war.
>
> He is *not* employing his ships to keep up communications and intelligence with the King's servants and friends at the different parts of the continent, for I do not believe General Gage has received a letter from any correspondent out of Boston these six weeks.
>
> He is intent upon greater objects, you will think, supporting in the great points the dignity of the British flag, and where a number of boats have been built for the enemy, privateers fitted out, prizes carried in, the King's armed vessels sunk, the crews made prisoners, the officers killed—he is doubtless enforcing instant restitution and reparation by the voice of his cannon and laying the towns in ashes that refuse his terms?

Alas! he is not. British thunder is diverted or controlled by pitiful attentions and mere Quaker-like scruples; and under such influences, insult and impunity, like righteousness and peace, have kissed each other.

Burgoyne also had cause for personal complaint. That "mere cypher, the youngest major-general in the British Army," as he continued to call himself, received no reply from Lord North. Summer gave way to autumn, winter approached, and still Burgoyne received no word from the government regarding his intended negotiations with the enemy.

Finally, in early December, 1775, only a short time after General Gage's recall for political reasons, the Army's youngest major-general received orders bringing him home on furlough. Since he had spent only seven months in America he jumped to the almost inevitable conclusion that he was being recalled to receive specific instructions for his talks. Other senior officers shared his view and regretted his departure, writing to their own families and friends that they were losing the most competent general officer in the Army, and regretting that his talents would be wasted in diplomacy.

General Lee heard of his impending departure, since nothing that happened in the British garrison escaped the attention of the superbly organized American espionage service. Lee conferred with various civilians, then hastily wrote another long, goading letter, in which he explained the American position in detail, then expressed the fervent hope that his former commander would return to America with the authority to enter into formal negotiations for a just and lasting peace.

On the eve of his departure Burgoyne wrote a courteous, brief and candid reply. He shared Lee's hopes, but had not been told what employment His Majesty's Government had in mind for him. Nothing would give him greater pleasure than "playing the role of an humble conciliator; I prefer success in such an endeavor to the command of armies that would make the Colonies secure to the Crown for ever."

Having purchased a number of trinkets, mementos, and

paintings of Indians, as well as several cases containing clothing, weapons, and other articles used by the Indians of North America, Gentleman Johnny Burgoyne sailed for London on December 9, 1775. His quarters on *H.M.S. Boyne,* a frigate-of-war, were spacious, which was fortunate, as he carried twenty-three travel boxes and a score of bottles of Spanish brandywine which he had obtained in mysterious dealings with unknown persons. The brandywine was first-rate, so he consumed only a small portion on his voyage, saving the rest for his wine cellar at home.

Eight

The *Boyne* cast anchor at Plymouth on January 4, 1776, her distinguished passenger having celebrated Christmas and the coming of the New Year with his aides-de-camp, one of them his wife's young nephew, Lieutenant the Honorable Thomas Stanley. The War Office had sent a carriage for the convenience of Major-General Burgoyne, but Gentleman Johnny had no need to use the official conveyance, Lord Stanley having traveled to Plymouth himself for the purpose of bringing his uncle-by-marriage back to London. Burgoyne immediately sensed the reason for his nephew's unexpected presence, but the news was even worse than he had imagined.

Lady Charlotte was seriously ill, having concealed her precarious state in her correspondence with her husband, and was not expected to live. Her brother, Lord Strange, had died while Burgoyne had been at sea, so there had been no way to inform him that his best friend had passed away. And Lord Derby was on his deathbed, surrounded by a corps of physicians who agreed there was no hope for him.

Burgoyne and Lord Stanley drove to London from Plymouth without stopping to rest, halting only long enough for changes of horses and the purchase of bread, meat, and cheese to eat on their journey. They arrived late on the night of January 5, and Gentleman Johnny, badly in need of a shave, his clothes rumpled and travel-stained, rushed to his wife's bedside. Lady Charlotte was lucid, but her health had deteriorated badly, and she had to be propped up with pillows before she could sit.

The next morning General Burgoyne called at the town house of his father-in-law, and was admitted without delay to the bedroom of the Earl of Derby, who died the next day. In the presence of several witnesses, including Lord Stanley, who would succeed to his title, the old man forgave Gentleman Johnny without reservation for his elopement a quarter of a century earlier with Lady Charlotte, and expressed the hope that all of the Stanley women would show as good choice in their selection of husbands.

Only after completing this visit did General Burgoyne report to the War Office, where he learned that King George awaited him at Whitehall. His Majesty's loyal servant repaired to the palace with due haste, and was received in audience by a monarch who refused to discuss specific aspects of the campaign in America, much less the prospect of peace negotiations. Burgoyne was offered a knighthood of the Bath, an order customarily reserved for distinguished Army and Navy officers, but surprised His Majesty by courteously rejecting it.

In all, over the course of several years, King George made such an offer on three occasions, and thrice was astonished to hear Gentleman Johnny decline. At first glance it appears to be out of character for an ambitious, vain man who would have become Sir John Burgoyne, K.B., to refuse such an honor. It has even been argued that on the first of these occasions Gentleman

Johnny was in a state of shock because of his wife's illness, the death of Lord Strange, and the impending demise of the Earl of Derby. According to this line of thought, he turned down the later offers, too, because he did not want to appear inconsistent.

These claims fail to take into account John Burgoyne's love of honor. As has already been seen, principle was all-important to him, and at no time would he knowingly compromise his standards. It is reasonable to suppose that he was as eager as any other Englishman to be made a knight, but he sincerely believed that his acceptance would have dishonored his own name and denigrated the Order of the Bath.

His argument was simple—and unanswerable. The knighthood of the Bath was conferred on officers who had distinguished themselves in service, but he had done nothing of note since his recall to active duty. He had spent seven months of almost complete inactivity in Boston, contributing nothing to the British cause and not even taking part actively in the Battle of Bunker Hill. So he would be guilty of bad taste if he accepted the honor, and the Order of the Bath itself would become something of a joke.

King George was forced to respect the sensible wishes of this reasonable subject, and the offer of the knighthood was temporarily withdrawn. But Burgoyne was given a brevet, or temporary, promotion to the rank of lieutenant-general, and was permanently confirmed in that grade the following year. His Majesty also hinted that a more active life was in store for the new lieutenant-general.

Burgoyne was granted a four-week furlough, and took Lady Charlotte to visit Bath in the hope that the waters there, combined with his own constant proximity, would restore her to good health. Few details of the stay of Lady Charlotte and Gentleman Johnny in Bath are known, but it must have become obvious to both, when her health failed to respond, that the end was in sight for her, and both thought it unlikely that they would be together when the time came.

Soon after Lieutenant General Burgoyne's arrival in Bath he received an even stronger hint regarding his future. He received a confidential communication from the War Office, signed by Lord George Germain, asking for his recommendations concerning the strengthening of Britain's military posture in Canada.

Burgoyne, like every other Englishman in a responsible position, already knew that the situation of General Sir Guy Carleton, the British governor-general in Canada, was precarious. The vast country was still a savage, underpopulated land, and even Quebec, the capital, was little more than a frontier outpost. General James Wolfe had captured the city in September, 1759, himself dying during the battle, and the rest of Canada, including the smaller town of Montreal, had fallen to the Redcoats the following year. Most of the inhabitants were still French-speaking, their loyalties lay with France rather than with Great Britain, and the English-speaking farmers, trappers, merchants, and fishermen loyal to King George were outnumbered at least four to one by the former French.

As a consequence, Carleton had to keep a tight rein on his domain, and found it necessary to hold several regiments of troops in reserve to put down possible local insurrections. There appeared to be little danger that Canadians would follow the example of their neighbors to the south, much less join forces with them. The former French subjects had little in common with the Americans, other than the problems of conquering, pacifying, and civilizing the wilderness. The Canadians were Roman Catholics, in the main, while the Americans, with the exception of Marylanders, were Protestant.

An American attempt to capture Canada that autumn and winter failed by a very narrow margin, and General Benedict Arnold, the Patriot leader, would have completed his mission had he commanded a larger force and been given more munitions and supplies. Now the principal fort between Canada and New York, Ticonderoga, had fallen to a band of American irregulars commanded by Colonel Ethan Allen, with the omnipresent Arnold also taking part in the fray. The Americans had transferred many of Ticonderoga's cannon to the heights overlooking the British perimeter in Boston, forcing General William Howe to evacuate that city, a course long advocated by Burgoyne.

Lady Charlotte spent at least a part of each day sleeping and resting, which gave her husband a chance to utilize his writing talents. He worked every day on a report he called *Reflections on the War in America,* which incorporated his thoughts on the role Canada might and should play in the conflict. It was destined to become the most important by far of the many political-military documents he wrote during his lifetime.

A few years later, after Burgoyne's permanent return from America, a vicious rumor was circulated in high places to the effect that Gentleman Johnny was unfaithful to the dying Lady Charlotte during the month they spent together at Bath. The reason for the story is easy enough to discern, since Susan Caulfield, a beautiful and talented young singer-actress, with whom Burgoyne became intimate after the completion of his American adventures, happened to be spending a sojourn of her own in Bath. Burgoyne, the playwright and theater buff, knew many prominent actors and even more actresses, so it would have been surprising had he not been acquainted with the lovely, blond Susan.

But there has been no evidence presented, down to the present, to indicate that anything other than the malice of Burgoyne's nameless enemies was responsible for the rumors. Common sense indicates that a man spending a few precious weeks with a dying wife to whom he had been faithful for twenty-five years would not have left her sickroom to enjoy an affair with a younger woman. The stories also fail to take into account the fact that Susan was escorted to Bath by her current protector, Lord Dunsmore, who was quite elderly but no fool, and who would not have appreciated her clandestine liaison with another, younger man.

Burgoyne's *Reflections* presented Prime Minister North, his Cabinet, and King George with their first comprehensive strategic plan for winning the war in North America. In a preface far longer than was really necessary to present his arguments, Burgoyne declared that a peaceful solution was preferred to armed conflict, and he repeated the Whig approach that had been contained in his letter to Lord North of the previous July, a series of claims already familiar to the ministers who were forced to listen to speeches in the Commons and Lords by Burke, Fox, Chatham, and their followers.

In the event that peace could not be obtained through negotiations, and Burgoyne pointed out that the American desire for total independence became greater with each passing month, he advocated a specific series of campaigns:

1. Boston, which was untenable, should be evacuated without delay. This much, at least, was done by the time the Cabinet began a serious consideration of his plan.

2. Diversionary attacks should be made on Rhode Island.

3. An Army corps, transported by the Navy in small ships, should capture the entire Connecticut River, which would cause the fall of Western Massachusetts and all of Connecticut.

4. Crown agents should flood Long Island in order to increase the "probability" that the residents would remain loyal to the king.

5. After these agents completed their task, a large force should be landed on Long Island to make it secure.

6. Simultaneously—and the timing was all-important—a surprise attack should be launched on New York Town. Blessed with the finest natural harbor "in all the world," New York should be an easy prey for a first-rate naval force, provided it was commanded by an officer more competent than Admiral Samuel Graves. The Patriots could be overwhelmed by ships that sailed at the same time up the Hudson and East Rivers, and Manhattan Island, "a fortress designed by Nature herself," would be "ripe for the plucking." Strong detachments of troops, preferably a force containing at least ten divisions, or twenty thousand men, would be necessary to guarantee the success of this operation.

7. In the meantime, Canada should be expanded as a base of operations. Strong reinforcements should be sent to Sir Guy Carleton, who was compelled to utilize his present garrisons exclusively for purposes of defense. Later in 1776, if possible, or in the spring and summer of 1777 if necessary, a strong expeditionary force should march south through Canada by way of

Lake George, recapture Fort Ticonderoga, and continue to march toward the south.

8. The dispatch of this expedition should be timed with the march of another, equally strong force that would march northward (presumably from New York Town) by way of the Hudson River.

9. These two forces should meet at a predetermined spot. It would be impossible to prevent American intelligence, which was excellent, from learning of these maneuvers, but the combined strength of the two expeditionary forces would prevent any American units, even the best, from winning a victory.

10. In order to further guarantee the triumph of His Majesty's New World armies, it would be wise to send a third corps, comprised of light cavalry and light infantry, from some area farther to the west, and it would meet the two larger forces at the predetermined place.

11. The success of the plan was predicated on the assumptions that (a) there would be enough fighting men available to win decisive victories by force of arms, and that (b) these forces would be supplied with ample quantities of provisions, weapons, and munitions of war.

The most significant section of Burgoyne's *Reflections* was devoted to a series of comments on the differences between Old World warfare and that in America. The formality of European wars and the rigid predictability of campaigns were a far cry from warfare in a land where distances were vast, the population small, and natural obstacles, such as broad, swift-flowing rivers, deep forests, and ranges of rugged mountains, made it necessary for armies to adapt to this new situation.

The Americans had proved themselves adept at warfare suited to their own terrain during their campaigns in the Seven Years' War. Burgoyne admitted that, during the heat of his emotional reaction to the Battle of Bunker Hill, he had called the Americans "rabble in arms," but he had done them an injustice. They were splendid fighting men because they believed in their cause, they served under such able leaders as generals George

Washington and Israel Putnam, and they were always told the reasons for fighting a specific battle at a specific place.

Their great weakness was their lack of military training, and "peasants, no matter how intelligent, are no match for equally intelligent troops who have enjoyed the benefits of discipline and training." Therefore the British Army should concentrate on the training of troops, with special emphasis to be laid on the conditions that combat units would face in America.

Since it would be impossible to retrain enough divisions and regiments in time to conduct a major campaign in the next two years, Burgoyne renewed his plea for the hiring of mercenaries. He did not yet know it, but such a program of recruitment had already been initiated in Hesse and Brunswick. He also urged the Cabinet to give further consideration to his suggestion that large numbers of Indians be recruited in America. He had met only a handful of them in Boston, he wrote, but he had been impressed by their "natural intelligence," and as they were already familiar with "every technique best suited to the conduct of warfare upon their Continent," it would only be necessary to teach them the use of firearms and supply them with muskets in order to transform them into effective allies.

Above all, Burgoyne pleaded for the dispatch of light infantry regiments to America. Sappers, or engineers, were indispensable for building bridges across rivers and similar tasks. Heavy infantry carried too much equipment for sustained marches through the North American wilderness. The function of artillery, although useful, was limited because it was so difficult to transport heavy cannon across countryside where there were no roads. Cavalry, his own first love, was always effective, but the problems of caring for horses in the wilderness made it difficult to utilize cavalry brigades on a large scale.

Burgoyne bolstered his request for light infantry by presenting a profile of the American soldier that was remarkably discerning:

> Accustomed to felling of timber and to grubbing
> up trees, they are very ready at earthworks and palisad-

ing, and they will cover and entrench themselves with surprising alacrity wherever they are for a short time left unmolested.

Composed as the American army is, together with the strength of the country, full of woods, swamps, stone walls, and other enclosures and hiding places, it may be said of it that every private man will in action be his own general, who will turn every tree and bush into a kind of temporary fortress, from whence, when he hath fired his shot with all the deliberation, coolness, and certainty which hidden safety inspires, he will skip as it were to the next, and so on for a long time till dislodged either by cannon or by a resolute attack by light infantry. In this view of the American militia, rebels as they are, they will be found to be respectable even in flight.

Light infantry, therefore, in greater numbers than one company per regiment, *must* be made an essential part of the general system of our army.

Returning to London in mid-February with the ailing Lady Charlotte, Burgoyne delivered his *Reflections* in person to Germain, and made sure King George would receive a copy by taking it to Whitehall and handing it in person to the monarch. It was at this time that the newly promoted lieutenant-general learned his new assignment, which was announced almost immediately thereafter.

Burgoyne was not surprised to hear he was being sent to Canada as second in command to General Sir Guy Carleton. Since he lacked experience and interest in the performance of administrative duties, he was given to understand that Sir Guy would remain in charge of these functions, while his deputy would be placed in over-all command of troops in the field. Nominally Burgoyne would be responsible to the governor-general in all that he did, but under a special arrangement it would be his duty merely to keep Sir Guy informed of his activities, which meant that for all practical purposes he would report direct to the War Office in London.

A day or two later Burgoyne was summoned to a conference with the Prime Minister, and was informed by Lord North that his peace plan was regarded as premature, and had been filed away for future reference. In other words, it had been shelved. The more radical of the Patriots in America were agitating in favor of making their break with the mother country complete and establishing an independent nation, so it was obvious to North and his Cabinet, as it was to the Crown, that the rebels had to be brought back into line.

Even the Earl of Chatham thought the Americans were going too far in their demands, and believed that if they persisted it would soon become impossible to deal with them. Burgoyne, who was essentially conservative in spite of his humanitarianism, shared this view. If the rebels would not deal with His Majesty's Government as reasonable men, the issues would have to be settled by force of arms. So the professional soldier put aside his plan to confer with General Charles Lee and concentrated on military matters.

He was delighted to learn that large numbers of veteran mercenary troops had already been hired in the German states, and that a full division of two thousand men from the state of Brunswick would accompany him to Canada, with several other divisions to follow as soon as the Royal Navy could arrange for troop transports and naval escort vessels. Burgoyne was also given funds for the recruitment of Indian warriors, but this appropriation was kept secret for fear that Charles James Fox would create a tempest in the Commons in the event that he learned of it. Fox was the most prominent member of a vocal group in both Houses of Parliament that believed Great Britain would be guilty of conduct unworthy of a civilized nation if she employed Indians to help subdue civilized insurrectionists. At no time had Burgoyne shared this opinion; like all professional fighting men, he was convinced that victory should be the only goal of a commanding general in the field, and he was irritated by the restrictions that well-meaning civilians tried to impose on armies.

Understanding the need for secrecy, he began to make his plans, and requested five thousand muskets for the Indian allies he hoped to enlist under the British banner. He felt certain he could recruit the warriors of two Canadian tribes, the Ottawa and Huron, and he held several private conversations with colonels who had served in the French and Indian War with regard to the possibility that he might be able to persuade the braves of the powerful Iroquois Confederation to join him.

His own personal problem continued to weigh heavily on his mind. Lady Charlotte showed no substantial improvement, and dreaded the thought that she might die while her husband was overseas. She was examined by two of King George's physicians, both of whom said they thought she would live for at least another year. The War Office appreciated Lieutenant-General Burgoyne's plight, and showing a rare compassion, agreed that he could come home on furlough whenever the cold of late autumn forced his divisions to go into winter quarters.

No details of Gentleman Johnny's parting from his wife are known, but it must have been painful for both of them. On this occasion he suffered his agony in private, committing none of his thoughts to paper.

Early in March, 1776, he went to Plymouth and boarded a frigate, *H.M.S. Blonde,* the command ship of a squadron that included transports for the division of troops from Brunswick. Immediately prior to sailing Burgoyne received a letter from Lord Germain, containing final instructions, and attached to the communication was a very human postscript. The commander of the *Blonde,* a Captain Pennel, would receive his distinguished passenger with great pleasure, the head of the War Office declared, adding, "It seems he is rich, so you need not fear putting him to expense."

Translated into less cryptic language, the postscript quickly becomes clear. Captain Pennel shared General Burgoyne's predilection for twenty-and-one, and could afford to lose at cards. It must be presumed that when the passenger was not reading various documents acquainting him with Canada, he found relief from the boredom of crossing the North Atlantic in a stormy season by playing cards with the frigate's commander. Having supplied himself with cases of food and wine for the voyage, he presumably suffered few hardships.

Lieutenant Stanley, who accompanied him as an aide-de-camp, wrote to his elder brother, "We enjoy most of the conveniences of civilization on board this frigate, and want only the company of ladies. Uncle John is zealous in his determination to pursue the enemy as soon as possible after we arrive at our destination."

Nine

History has failed to give Sir Guy Carleton his due, perhaps because he was one of the least flamboyant of the senior general officers on either side in the American Revolution. An exceptionally able administrator endowed with an unflagging devotion to duty, he was largely responsible for Canada's continuing loyalty to the Crown during and after the war. Having risen as high as he wished, he was not spurred by ambition, and was content to retire when relieved of his assignment in Canada. One of his talents was an ability to delegate responsibility to men he trusted, and when his new second in command reached Quebec in mid-April, 1776, the governor-general was pleased to discover they were kindred spirits. Both enjoyed fine foods and rare wines, both changed their linen daily, a habit which colleagues regarded as an eccentricity, and both were excellent whist players.

Carleton had seen and enjoyed a performance of *The Maid of the Oaks* in London, and cemented a friendship with his deputy by praising the play. The relationship became still closer when Carleton gave Burgoyne a free hand, allowing him to make his own military plans.

Gentleman Johnny wasted no time. The mercenaries from Brunswick were out of condition after their Atlantic crossing, but General Burgoyne gave them scant opportunity to become reaccustomed to life on land, leading them into the field only two weeks after their arrival at Quebec.

Carleton permitted him to use one thousand British regulars, and approximately five hundred Ottawa and Huron warriors also volunteered for his campaign. The firearms for the Indians had not yet arrived, so Burgoyne accepted them with their own weapons.

The campaign itself was minor, one of the least significant in the entire war, and has meaning only because it marked the first time Burgoyne went into the field as a general officer. The Americans held two small forts on Canadian soil, Fort St. John and Fort Chambly, and Burgoyne decided to flex his muscles by dislodging them.

The defending garrisons were small, and both retired in the face of an overwhelmingly superior force after desultory fighting, the capture of neither fort being a distinguished operation. But it is noteworthy that the general, in his victory proclamation, gave full credit to his troops for their twin victory, his love of the dramatic impelling him to add that the zeal and activity of his troops were "principles that cannot fail to produce the most glorious effects whenever the enemy shall acquire boldness enough to put them to the proof."

The most important result of the brief campaign was the rapport that General Burgoyne established with his subordinates. Abolishing physical punishment on the day he took command, he made it plain that any trouble-maker or insubordinate soldier would be transferred elsewhere without delay, and he would not hesitate to make life difficult for those who tried to take unfair advantage of him. He made several brief addresses to his regiments, explaining the goals of the campaign as well as possible problems that could be caused by the enemy, the terrain, and the weather. His door would be open at all times to junior officers, and any enlisted man who entertained a grievance could see him without delay by applying through the sergeant-major of the corps. The food supplied for the march was adequate, although not out of the ordinary, and he not only promised to do his best to obtain such delicacies as fresh bread and meat, but actually succeeded, advancing sums out of his own pocket for the purpose.

Officers and men alike responded to his gestures by pledging him their fealty, and from the outset he became the single most popular of all British senior officers in the New World. The men called him Gentleman Johnny, although not to his face, and were amused by his personal habits, boasting about them to other troops and writing about him at length in their correspondence. Certainly he gave them ample cause for talk. His own larder was extensive, containing no less than fourteen different kinds of fresh, smoked, and pickled meats and fish, numerous vegetables and fruits, as well as flour so his cook-orderly could bake bread. Two carts equipped with special springs that reduced their jolting motion carried his wines, and his tent of double, oiled layers of silk filled yet another cart. He even carried his own furniture on the campaign, including a bed, a desk, and a padded work chair with legs that could be collapsed. His clothing boxes contained several complete changes of uniforms, and a member of his personal party was a groom whose sole non-combat duty was that of caring for his horse. He traveled with two aides-de-camp, three orderlies, and the groom, and the aides were served by their own orderlies.

General Burgoyne rarely dined alone at the end of a day's march. His subordinate generals were frequent dinner guests, as were senior colonels, but he also made it a point to invite captains, lieutenants, and cornets who had distinguished themselves in one way or another to be his guests. These invitations were eagerly sought, and not merely because he set an extravagant table in the wilderness. The conversation was civilized, war was rarely mentioned, and the talk was reminiscent of that heard in gentlemen's clubs in London.

The medical aid provided for officers and enlisted men was extraordinary for the age. Burgoyne had seen sickness and death take heavy tolls of regiments because of a lack of proper facilities and of sufficient personnel, and had decided many years earlier that any corps he commanded would be adequately staffed with physicians and would carry enough supplies of medicines and bandages to afford good care. He was accompanied by a principal surgeon, who was aided by eight assistants, four of them physicians in their own right, and when the column halted at the end of a day's march, any man who felt ill was free to report to the surgeon as soon as the trumpeter sounded sick call. As a result of this basic consideration the incidence of serious sickness in Burgoyne's corps was far below that found in other armies. Most eighteenth-century generals, for all of the lip service they paid the cause of the Enlightenment, had much to learn from Gentleman Johnny, who was unique because he had acquired the odd habit of practicing what he preached.

Certainly the difference between Burgoyne and Carleton was partly responsible for the former's popularity. Sir Guy was remote in his relations with subordinates, his personal shyness combining with an inability to deal informally with inferiors to make him appear indifferent to their welfare. In the spring and summer of 1776 there were approximately eight thousand British regulars and five thousand mercenaries stationed in Canada, and most of them volunteered for duty in the corps commanded by Gentleman Johnny. Had Sir Guy Carleton been a jealous sort, his relations with his deputy would have become strained.

The Ottawa and Huron warriors contributed literally nothing to the success of Burgoyne's campaign in the spring of 1776. Refusing to respond to even rudimentary discipline, the braves came and went as they pleased, sometimes marching with the column, then vanishing into the wilderness to hunt and fish. When the paymaster made the mistake of giving them their wages at the end of a month they deserted in wholesale numbers, and complaints drifted back to the corps from farmers who found they had to contend with previously docile warriors made belligerent by the raw liquor sold at frontier trading posts.

John Burgoyne made his most serious error in judgment when he assessed the conduct of the Indians during the campaign. Unable to grasp the fact that their thinking, their very approach to life, in no way resembled that of professional troops from England and Brunswick, he found excuses for the misbehavior of the braves. They would learn discipline after they were associated with him for a longer time, he believed, and they would prove themselves more eager to fight after they were issued the muskets that had been promised them.

It did not occur to him that they found such firearms cumbersome and inaccurate, and had no use for the bayonets that were issued with muskets. They far preferred the long rifles favored by the frontiersmen of the rebel Colonies to the south and by Canadian wilderness dwellers, but these weapons were made in small numbers at local foundries, and were not available to the second in command of all Canada.

Sir Guy was concerned with the governing of His Majesty's diverse subjects, particularly the French-speaking waverers, and no one else was in a position to tell General Burgoyne that his estimate of the Indians was mistaken. Those who knew better, among them the guides, hunters, and trappers who were familiar with the ways of the Indians, had no easy access to a man of Gentleman Johnny's exalted rank. And those who did see him shared his ignorance, assumed he had other sources of information, and accepted his verdicts. He himself clung to his false notions for a long time, but in the autumn of 1777, a year and a half after his spring campaign of 1776, he paid dearly for his errors.

At the beginning of July, 1776, the Americans declared their independence, formally committing themselves to fight the war until it was won. Patriots rejoiced and Loyalists were glum, but no one on either side of the Atlantic was surprised by the turn of events. Gentleman Johnny, who had returned to Quebec to prepare for a more important campaign, had already assumed that the Americans would act as they did, and the news left him unruffled.

Of far greater importance to him than the word from Philadelphia was the arrival of his own deputy-commander, whom he had chosen himself for the post. Major-General William Phillips was an artilleryman who had served with Burgoyne in Spain, and they had become close friends, at least in part because they unfailingly reached the same conclusions when weighing a military question. Phillips, who held the honorary position of governor of Windsor Castle, was blunt where Burgoyne was diplomatic, forthright where his friend was suave. He paid little attention to what he ate or drank, limited himself to one aide-de-camp, and willingly slept on the ground during a campaign, rolling himself in a blanket and insisting he was as comfortable as he would have been in a featherbed.

The Army was Phillips' whole life, he expressed himself in a soldier's language, and he had no interest whatever in the theater that fascinated Burgoyne. But the two friends were far more alike than appeared on the surface. Honor was as important to Phillips as it was to Burgoyne, and like his superior, he always thought in long-range terms.

A few days after Phillips' arrival in Quebec he accompanied Gentleman Johnny to the headquarters of the governor-general, and he listened approvingly as Burgoyne outlined his newest plan. He intended to mount an expedition in the immediate future, he said, and hoped to capture Fort Ticonderoga, the gateway to New York and the other middle Colonies.

Sir Guy replied it was too late in the season for a major campaign, and vetoed the scheme. Gentleman Johnny was astonished to discover that the promises of independence he had been given by Lord Germain were worthless. Sir Guy was the Crown's representative in Canada, and his word was final.

But Gentleman Johnny, always thinking about the future, had spent enough time in the New World to have learned there was more than one way to skin a bear. He suggested that his deputy make a personal reconnaissance of the Ticonderoga area, and Phillips went off into the wilderness only six days after he had landed at Quebec.

The major-general spent six weeks traveling through the North American interior, and the report he submitted to Carleton and Burgoyne after his return to Quebec reflected his disgust. British sentry outposts were indifferently manned, and the troops holding them paid little attention to the enemy. The only scouts on hand were Indian warriors who were drunk and unreliable; the desertion rate was alarmingly high, and the officers neither maintained order nor disciplined their men.

Carleton believed the situation in the field validated the stand he had taken, but Burgoyne remained adamant and sent a firm letter to the War Office. Regardless of the difficulties that might have been encountered, he declared, an attempt should have been made earlier in the season to capture Ticonderoga before the coming of winter. At the worst, the British would have been forced to retire, and would have served warning on the Americans that they could not rest on their laurels after taking a British fort. Had the drive been successful, however, it would have given the British Army an important forward base in the wilderness, and this would have simplified the 1777 campaign. Now—assuming the Prime Minister approved of Burgoyne's over-all strategy—it would be necessary to do that much more in the coming year.

Early in October Burgoyne had to forget campaigning for a time, as he was bedded with an ailment variously described as the ague or as swamp fever. No matter what the diagnosis of his contemporaries may have been, he was suffering from what a later era would call influenza, and the attack left him shaken. He should have followed the instruction of his principal surgeon and remained in bed for several weeks, but the news from London regarding Lady Charlotte's health was alarming, and in late October, before the appearance of ice floes closed the St. Lawrence River to traffic, he sailed for home on board an aptly named frigate, the *H.M.S. New World*.

Burgoyne was so miserable on the crossing that he scarcely touched the food and wines he had brought with him. Lieutenant Stanley wrote that he suffered long bouts of fever that made him still weaker, and on several occasions, when he became delirious, he seemed convinced that his wife was dead.

The frigate landed him at Southampton in late November,

1776, and Burgoyne hurried to London, where his worst fears were confirmed: Lady Charlotte Stanley Burgoyne had died a few days after her husband had sailed from Quebec for England.

Gentleman Johnny had long been prepared for the tragedy, but its anticipation did not soften the blow. He visited his wife's grave in a driving rainstorm that severely aggravated his own condition, and for the only time in his adult life he was seen to weep in public.

That night he was confined to his bed, and had to remain there for a week. The War Office granted him an immediate furlough, and he went off to Bath to recuperate. Again the gossips were busy. He was a widower now, and Susan Caulfield, either by accident or design, also was a visitor to the spa, going there on this occasion without old Lord Dunsmore. On two or three occasions she and Gentleman Johnny were seen strolling together through the town, but no positive evidence exists to indicate their affair began at this time. Burgoyne was still in a state of shock over the death of his beloved wife, and wore a black band of mourning on the sleeve of his civilian coat. It would have been in the worst of taste—and Gentleman Johnny was rarely guilty of bad taste—for him to have slept with another woman at this time.

Besides, he was recuperating from a debilitating ailment of his own, and in addition he was very busy preparing another military document, which he called *Thoughts for Conducting the War from the Side of Canada*. He had, as yet, received no word to the effect that the over-all strategy he had recommended in his *Reflections* of the previous year had been approved by King George and his ministers. But he was going ahead on the blithe assumption that the affirmation would be forthcoming, and his *Thoughts* amplified the principles he had laid down in his earlier report.

He assumed that the Americans would keep a force of at least twelve thousand men at Ticonderoga, because they knew as well as did the British that possession of the fort was all-important to the control of vast American hinterlands to the south.

Based on this assumption of enemy strength, Burgoyne made a series of specific proposals:

1. He wanted the Royal Navy to provide him with a large number of small, manned boats on Lake George to assure his line of retreat, and he emphasized that he wanted these craft and their crews placed under his over-all command.

2. He felt certain that the Americans, if forced to retreat, would block the roads from Ticonderoga to Skenesborough to Albany by felling trees, smashing bridges, and building other obstacles. (It should be noted that this is precisely what Major General Philip Schuyler, the American commander, did do the following year.) These obstacles would make it necessary for the advancing British to alter their tactics somewhat, and in spite of the difficulties of transporting heavy cannon through the wilderness, he proposed that the British fortify themselves with the addition of a strong corps of artillery. General Phillips, he assured the Crown and the Ministry, would be equal to any task he might face.

3. He requested an exceptionally strong force, to consist of eight thousand regulars (both British troops and German mercenaries were included in this figure), an artillery corps of eight hundred to one thousand men, "a corps of watermen" (Navy personnel to be placed under his command, their numbers deliberately not mentioned), two thousand Canadians and one thousand Indians. The task of raising the corps of Canadians and of Indians was immediate, so he suggested that the responsibility be given to Sir Guy Carleton, a recommendation that, he must have realized, would annoy the governor-general.

4. Vast quantities of supplies, provisions and munitions of war should be gathered at the British fortress of Crown Point. This task was vital, and the success or failure of the entire campaign depended on it, Burgoyne declared, repeating that no army was stronger than the supply line it maintained and the merchandise that moved forward along that line.

5. At the beginning of the campaign a relatively small force should be sent on a diversionary expedition by way of Lake On-

tario and Oswego to the Mohawk River. Consisting principally of light infantry that could move rapidly, this force, after creating its diversion, should move eastward with all possible speed to effect a junction with the larger forces participating in the campaign.

6. As the force from Canada moved southward, Sir William Howe's army should march northward from New York Town, and the two main bodies should meet at Albany. This junction, when effected, would split the rebel Colonies irrevocably, and bring the war to a swift, successful conclusion.

After completing the document Gentleman Johnny did not linger in Bath, where he had already spent a full month. He allowed himself a single, additional day of rest, played whist with some friends for a few hours and then was seen dining, for the first and only time during his Bath sojourn, with Susan Caulfield. It was inevitable that posterity should engage in the useless pastime of speculating on the relationship of the couple at that time. The only known truth of the matter is that no information of any kind is available regarding the state of their friendship. If they corresponded after Burgoyne's return to London, their letters have been lost; Susan came back to London about a fortnight later, but General Burgoyne attended none of her performances at the theater, and at no time was seen with her in public. So common sense indicates that the grieving widower enjoyed only a casual relationship with the young actress-singer who had become one of the reigning stars of the stage.

General Burgoyne, attended by his aide and nephew by marriage, Thomas Stanley, who had just been promoted to the rank of captain, ate Christmas dinner at the home of the new Earl of Derby, formerly Lord Stanley. There had been so many deaths in the family during the preceding year that the affair must have been somber.

On the morning of December 27, 1776, Lieutenant-General Burgoyne, accompanied by Captain Stanley, paid the first official call of his sojourn in England at the War Office, where he left a copy of his *Thoughts*. To his astonishment he was so coldly received by Lord George Germain that he was forced to agree with the equally surprised Captain Stanley: he had been roundly snubbed.

Ten

Lord George Germain was one of the most complex men living in a complicated age, and the opponents of Lord North's ministry were even more correct than they knew when they claimed that his temporary appointment as head of the War Office was a disaster. Himself a former soldier who had been cashiered for cowardice during the Seven Years' War, Germain was temperamental, ultra-sensitive and secretive. Capable of rousing himself to almost frenzied pitches of energy, he habitually lapsed into periods of lethargy little better than a coma. Loving food, drink, and women, usually in that order, he was hypercritical of any subordinate who shared his tastes. Ambitious far beyond his talents, he dreamed of a dukedom, and he was ruthless in claiming full credits for the noteworthy achievements of his subordinates.

Germain had charm when he chose to exercise it, and at the

moment he had won the enthusiastic support of the plodding Lord North. He had also commended himself to King George, with the result that he had acquired a permanent portfolio, that of Secretary of State for the Colonies. As a consequence he, more than any other man, was responsible for the prosecution of the war in North America.

At one time or another Germain feuded with most of the able men who had the misfortune to serve under him, and at the moment he was barely on speaking terms with the efficient Sir Guy Carleton, having conceived the totally erroneous notion that the governor-general of Canada wanted to succeed him. According to the devious line of Germain's thinking, John Burgoyne shared Carleton's guilt because he was Carleton's deputy.

As a consequence he snubbed Gentleman Johnny. He was also convinced that Burgoyne's *Thoughts* were partly the product of Carleton's mind, and therefore he made it plain that he intended to do nothing with the laboriously produced document.

Gentleman Johnny was a veteran of London's personality wars, and decided to initiate his own campaign to secure the adoption of his master plan. The new Earl of Derby offered to help him, but for the moment he preferred to handle the matter alone, and went to Whitehall to pay his respects to King George. Only a few words were necessary to convince the monarch that he was growing heavy because he was neglecting the daily exercise his physicians had prescribed for him, and the following morning George III was seen cantering on the bridle paths in the company of Lieutenant-General Burgoyne.

They rode together daily for several weeks, so it was an easy matter for Gentleman Johnny to give his king a copy of the *Thoughts* and subsequently to persuade him to read the document. The result was predicted by a jubilant Captain Stanley, who won ten pounds on a wager to the effect that the monarch would endorse the Burgoyne plan. King George was so enthusiastic that he did not bother to discuss it with his ministers, and simply sent them instructions to adopt it.

Although the details of the plan were kept secret, London soon learned the story, and Germain was furious, but was forced to cooperate, his only alternative being his resignation from the Cabinet.

According to an unverified legend that has persisted down to the present day, a delighted Gentleman Johnny dined at Brooks's Club one day in January, 1777, and was joined at the fashionable men's establishment by his good friend, Member of Parliament Charles Fox.

They chatted over the oysters, soup, fish, game, and roast, and when the port was served they made a wager that was duly entered in the club's book, Burgoyne betting "one pony," or fifty guineas, that he would return victorious from America in time to celebrate Christmas, 1777, in London.

But Fox is said to have remarked, "Be not over-sanguine in your expectations. I believe when next you return to England you will be a prisoner on parole."

Judged by the hindsight of history, Lord George Germain appears to have done his best to make that uncomfortable prediction come true. Although King George approved of the Burgoyne plan in January, 1777, Germain procrastinated until March 26, when he finally sent a letter to Sir Guy Carleton, informing him of its formal adoption. Inasmuch as Carleton could not receive the communication until the end of April, it would be impossible for the governor-general to carry out all phases of the role he was expected to play.

The letter itself was ludicrous, and showed Germain at his muddle-headed worst. He opened by complaining that a letter he had sent to Carleton early the preceding August had been returned because the commander of the ship to which it had been entrusted, one Captain LeMaitre, had been forced to return home with the communication after failing in three attempts to find the entrance to the Gulf of St. Lawrence. It is difficult to refrain from drawing the conclusion that Germain employed men of his own caliber to act as his trusted messengers.

Outlining Burgoyne's plan, Germain charged Carleton with the task of raising the necessary Canadian and Indian forces, obviously an impossibility in a period of a few weeks, and also directed him to store enough provisions and arms at Crown Point to assure the success of the campaign. He neglected to tell the governor-general how this feat was to be accomplished, and it did not occur to him to obtain the necessary food, medicine, weapons, and gunpowder in England, then make arrangements to forward them to the New World.

After stressing the fact that the key to the entire plan was the junction of the armies of Burgoyne and Howe, Germain concluded his letter by stating: "I shall write to Sir William Howe by the first packet." In other words, Germain accepted full responsibility for notifying Howe, precisely as he should have done. In view of the sublime tragicomedy that would follow, this assertion is of primary significance.

It should be noted in passing that the British plan was not the great secret Whitehall supposed. General Washington, a superior strategist, had written as far back as July 4, 1776, "It seems beyond question that the enemy will attempt to unite their two armies, that under General Burgoyne and the one arrived here" (in New York, under Sir William Howe).

Only Sir Guy Carleton was kept in the dark as long as possible regarding the British plans, and, as will be seen, the campaign was kept so confidential that Sir William Howe was never informed of it.

Few errors in history place a greater strain on credulity. The entire British strategy was predicated on the union of the armies of Burgoyne and Howe, which was obvious to every thinking military man on both sides of the conflict. Even if Burgoyne had won the Battle of Saratoga, that victory would have been meaningless unless it were followed by a junction with the forces commanded by his colleague. That a man in a post of ultimate responsibility could have failed to perform the simple act of notifying one of the two commanders of the joint venture that he was expected to play a major part in the grand scheme indicts Germain on grounds of gross negligence.

There seems to be little doubt that a letter was written to Howe, and a copy of it is still stored in the archives of the British government. Precisely what happened to the original is a mystery that has never been solved.

After Sir William Howe's return to London from the war in America, he made an appearance before a special committee of the Commons making an investigation of the matter. Shown a copy of Germain's communication to Sir Guy Carleton, which stated flatly that Howe's instructions would be sent to him in the immediate future, Sir William made a flat statement. "The letter intended to have been written to me by the first packet," he said, "and which was probably to have contained some instructions, was never sent."

Germain, later Lord Sackville, refused to take a direct part in the controversy, and at no time could be persuaded to discuss the matter in public. But an anonymous book called *Letters to a Nobleman*, published in 1779 and probably written either by Germain himself or by someone close to him, made the flat charge that Howe had ignored his instructions. "By that neglect," the book said, "he sacrificed a British army and involved his country in a degree of disgrace it never before had experienced."

Sir William replied less than a year later with a broadside of his own. Replying to the *Letters to a Nobleman* in a short book entitled *Observations*, he not only repeated his denial that he had ever received the instructions, but challenged Germain to prove him wrong. Any official who received an important communication from a minister of the Crown was required to sign a receipt for it, and these receipts were returned to London and filed. Howe demanded that Germain either produce the receipt bearing his signature or admit he had erred. Lord George Germain did neither.

An undated memorandum written several years later by Lord Shelburne, another member of the Cabinet at the time of the incident, sheds further light on the question:

> Lord George having among other peculiarities a particular aversion to be put out of his way on any occasion, had arranged to call at his office on his way to the country in order to sign the dispatches; but as those addressed to Howe had not as yet been "fair copied" and he was not disposed to be balked of his projected

visit into Kent, they were not signed then and were forgotten on his return to town.

A more detailed version of the same story appears in the unpublished memoranda and correspondence of William Knox, who was Germain's under secretary in the Colonial Office. Discussing the occasion on which Germain refused to wait to attach his signature to a letter not yet prepared, Knox said that three persons were involved, the third being Deputy Secretary D'Oyly. He wrote:

> When all was prepared and I had them [*the letters*] to compare and make up, Lord Sackville [*Germain*] came down to the office on his way to Stoneland [*his country house*], when I observed to him that there was no letter to Howe to acquaint him with the plan or what was expected of him in consequence of it. His Lordship stared and D'Oyly started but said he would in a moment write a few lines. "So," says Lord Sackville, "my poor horses must stand in the street all the time, and I shan't be to my time anywhere." D'Oyly then said he had better go, and he would write from himself to Howe and enclose copies of Burgoyne's instructions which would tell him all that he would want to know. With this his Lordship was satisfied as it enabled him to keep his time, for he would never bear delay or disappointment.

If the Knox version is accurate, Germain depended on D'Oyly, and it was the latter who forgot to write Howe. Even if this was the case, Germain was in no way relieved of his own responsibility, as he should have made it his business, after his return to London, to inquire whether instructions had been posted to Sir William.

The incredibly slipshod manner of conducting affairs of state doomed Burgoyne's venture from the outset, but his plan was already encountering other troubles that made it highly unlikely he could succeed. Sir Guy Carleton received his own instructions from Germain at the beginning of May, 1777, and fired an angry verbal cannonade in reply.

The requests made by the secretary could not be fulfilled in sufficient time for Burgoyne to lead his expedition south that year, he declared, and emphasized that Quebec was not London. No man could recruit a corps of two thousand Canadians and one thousand Indians in the course of a few weeks, much less train them so their cooperation with regular troops would be meaningful. The only British weapons in Canada were the muskets, pistols, and swords carried by individuals, together with the few artillery guns that protected the Citadel at Quebec and the lesser forts of the realm. Ammunition for both muskets and cannon was scarce at all times, and there was not one foundry in all of Canada, so ammunition, other than that begged as alms from the Royal Navy squadrons that put into Quebec, did not exist.

As for gunpowder, there was none except the supplies sent out from the arsenals in England, and these stores were short. Much of the powder was coarse-grained, lumpy, and unfit for use in muskets, and Carleton doubted that any major expedition could fulfill its mission with what was on hand. Food supplies for an army of ten thousand men were equally difficult to obtain. Canada was producing only enough for her own needs, and the insurrectionist Colonies were hoarding their food supplies. Few farmers would be willing to sell grains, meat, and vegetables to an advancing column, so it would be almost impossible for Burgoyne to live off the land as he moved south.

Neither uniforms nor the materials to make them were available in Canada, and a shortage of tailors meant that all uniforms would have to be supplied by England. The situation with regard to boots was even more critical. There were only a handful of cobblers in Canada, largely because of a lack of raw materials. Cattle were precious, and could not be slaughtered for the production of cowhide; most settlers were happy to settle for native moccasins, which they fashioned themselves from buckskin. But troops who marched long distances would need footgear more substantial than moccasins, and a reserve supply of boots was urgently required.

By the time Carleton's letter reached London the unsuspecting Gentleman Johnny was already en route to Quebec, dreaming of the great victory he would win. He assumed, based on assurances he received from Lord George Germain, that all of his requirements were being met, and he had no idea that critical shortages of almost all of the sinews of war awaited him in Canada.

Had Germain been efficient it might have been possible for him to meet Burgoyne's needs. Arsenals in England were filled with cannon, muskets, ammunition, and gunpowder. Barrels by the thousands, filled with salted meats and fish, dried beans, rice, and other foodstuffs, were piled high in warehouses for the use of the Army and Navy. Germain received Carleton's letter around the beginning of July, 1777, and had he responded promptly, an armada of merchant vessels, escorted by a few of the many Royal Navy ships at anchor in British ports, could have sailed for Canada with the necessary supplies and provisions.

But Germain, as usual, did almost nothing. He made a few half-hearted inquiries, learned that thousands of uniforms and pairs of boots were stored in the vicinity of London, and then took no action whatever to have them moved to Quebec, where they were so badly needed. Critics of Lord North's ministry charged, prior to its fall in 1782, that the American victory was due as much to the total incompetence of Lord George Germain as to the intrepidity of American fighting men, and it is difficult to disagree with them.

Knowing nothing of the ineptitudes that would guarantee his failure, Gentleman Johnny spent the month of March, 1777, relaxing in London. He had already been ordered to sail for Quebec early in April, and although he indicated that the sooner he reached the New World the sooner he could prepare for his operations, Germain informed him, in a waspish note, that no ship suitable for the transportation of an officer who held the exalted rank of lieutenant-general would be available for another month.

Part of Gentleman Johnny's reputation as a woman-chaser stems from the active life he led in London during the weeks prior to his departure on his great adventure. He had recovered from the initial shock of Lady Charlotte's death, his own health had been restored, and he was a vigorous fifty-five years of age, free to give greater expression to his appreciation of feminine beauty than his principles and concept of honor had permitted during the quarter of a century he had been married.

Undoubtedly spurred by the thought that he might be killed during his forthcoming campaign, he made up for lost time with a vengeance that made him the talk of London's clubs. He was seen nightly in the green rooms of various theaters, invariably departing with one or another of the young actresses who were not averse to the granting of favors to prominent men of influence and means. On other occasions he was seen with aristocratic young women whose reputations were somewhat tarnished.

One of these girls was Lady Sarah Hedley, who was considered so lacking in morality that no man who valued his reputation would be seen in her company. But Gentleman Johnny rode in carriages with her through the heart of town, escorted her on a number of shopping expeditions, and even took her to the homes of friends for visits. He was careful not to offend the sensibilities of more virtuous ladies, however, and Lady Sarah did not go with him to the home of the Earl of Derby or to any of the other great houses of London.

This romantic idyll was short-lived, however. An initial flurry of gossip indicated that Lieutenant General Burgoyne was contemplating marriage to the blonde Lady Sarah, who was approximately thirty years his junior. But before these stories gained force a disagreement of some sort caused a parting, and the couple stopped seeing each other.

Specific information on Burgoyne's romances during this hectic period were difficult for his contemporaries to glean, and have proved equally elusive for posterity to piece together. He took his sobriquet seriously, and neither talked nor wrote about his various affairs; they were strictly his own business.

It seems fairly certain that one young woman who did not go to bed with him during this month was Susan Caulfield. In later years Burgoyne freely admitted that he had been attracted to her from the time of their first meeting, but in the month before sailing to Quebec it appears he did not make love to her. Whether this was due to his own abstinence or to Susan's refusal to become intimate with him has never been determined. What is certain, however, is that they were destined to enjoy a far different experience, one unique in Gentleman Johnny's long life.

Eleven

In the spring and summer of 1777 only the most optimistic of American Patriots dared to believe that the War of Independence could be won. General George Washington's little army of approximately eleven thousand men was gradually being forged into a military force of veteran soldiers, but the process was long and the obstacles appeared insurmountable. The Continentals, or regulars, were already formed in cohesive units, but the ragged militia, who volunteered for periods as brief as eight weeks, were almost useless, and the commander-in-chief never knew when he awakened each morning how many men had deserted during the night. Supplies and munitions were painfully short, only a few wealthy officers wore real uniforms, and Burgoyne's observation that the foe was a rabble in arms was shrewdly accurate.

Washington was retreating steadily through New Jersey and

Pennsylvania, hounded by the army of Sir William Howe, who lacked the strength and mobility to destroy him. The Americans were incapable of making a real stand; the British, already occupying New York, would take possession of Philadelphia, the Patriots' capital, in September. Thereafter Washington would spend the winter in the "natural fortress" of Valley Forge, where almost unbearable hardships would form the cement that would enable him to unify his forces.

Under the circumstances it appears strange, at first glance, that Burgoyne was not sent direct to New York, or, at the very least, that he did not use Quebec as a staging area and then move south with his army to reinforce Howe in New Jersey and Pennsylvania. The overwhelming strength of the combined forces would have made it possible for the British to have achieved the decisive victory they sought, and the war would have come to an end.

Burgoyne envisaged the possibility of such a campaign and included a discussion of it in his *Thoughts* as an alternate plan. The whole concept was rejected on the personal authority of King George himself. Writing in his own hand, the Monarch prepared a three-page paper he called *Remarks on the Conduct of the War from Canada,* and his final paragraph left no opening for further discussion:

> The idea of carrying the army by sea to Sir. Wm Howe, would certainly require the leaving a much larger part of it in Canada, as in that case the rebel army would divide that province from the immense one under Sir W. Howe. I GREATLY DISLIKE THIS LAST IDEA.

So the British were committed to Burgoyne's first plan, that of sending an army overland from Canada to make a junction with Howe at Albany. And, at least on the surface, Burgoyne's corps appeared invincible. In spite of Carleton's complaints, large quantities of artillery had been amassed by the competent General Phillips, who would act as second in command of the expedition. Far larger quantities of food and ammunition than the

Americans would see at any one time in the war had been gathered by Carleton, even though only relatively small amounts had been forwarded to the depot at Crown Point.

The corps was already formed for the campaign, and the officers were among the best professionals on earth. The British infantry commander, also chosen by Burgoyne, was Brigadier Simon Fraser, a combat-hardened Scotsman who instinctively knew where to find trouble spots during a battle, and just as quickly understood how to solve his problems. Only thirty-six years old, he was the youngest brigadier on active service in the British Army.

The commander of the German mercenary contingent, which included regiments from Hesse as well as units from Brunswick, was one of the most distinguished soldiers in Europe. Only thirty-nine years of age, Major-General Baron Friedrich Adolph von Riedesel had been a professional fighting man since his mid-teens. He knew his business so well that he had already ordered his troops to put aside their cumbersome, high-crowned brass helmets, which would impede their progress on a wilderness march, and to substitute either the stocking caps worn by the Canadians or the square-crowned fur hats, complete with raccoon tails, that were a favorite of hunters, trappers, and guides.

Two of Riedesel's immediate subordinates were also men of the highest caliber. Lieutenant-Colonel Friedrich Baume, the commander of the horseless German dragoons, may have been the most professional soldier in Burgoyne's entire corps. Unlike virtually all German officers, he was not of aristocratic stock, but had performed the feat, extraordinary in the eighteenth century, of rising through the ranks to his present place. Equally tough was Lieutenant-Colonel Wilhelm von Breymann, the German infantry commander, who had served under Riedesel in a number of campaigns. What none of the British, including Burgoyne himself, knew at the outset was that Breymann had an almost pathological hatred of Baume whom he considered an upstart, and that his intense dislike was reciprocated.

Lieutenant-General John Burgoyne, master planner and commander of the expeditionary force, landed at Quebec on May

6, 1777, and found his entire army lined up on the parade ground at the Citadel to greet him with the pomp and respect that his high rank deserved. He watched his force of approximately eight thousand men pass in review: there were four thousand British regulars, including the 9th, 20th, 21st, 24th, 47th, 53rd and 62nd regiments; the German contingent numbered about three thousand men; there were one hundred and fifty Canadians, all of them such individualists that they were suited exclusively for duty as scouts; and bringing up the rear were approximately five hundred Indian warriors, most of them Ottawa and Huron, who made no attempt to maintain even the semblance of a military formation. General Phillips' artillery was massed at one end of the field, and was so large it spread far beyond the confines of the actual parade ground. In fact, a dozen or more of the larger guns were too heavy to be rolled into such cramped quarters, and had been left in the open country beyond the city of Quebec, where they were guarded by several batteries of bored artillerymen.

Although the command was the largest that had ever been assembled at any one time or place in the New World by any single army, Gentleman Johnny was disappointed, having asked for far more. He was a good soldier, however, allowing no one but Sir Guy Carleton to know his real feelings, and determined to do what he could with the men available to him.

Within twenty-four hours of his arrival Burgoyne became aware of a number of grave problems, the most serious of them being the unhappiness of the German officers. Under a rule promulgated by the War Office, British officers were permitted to command German troops, but under no circumstances, even during combat emergencies, were German officers allowed to give orders to British soldiers. This situation caused the Germans to feel they were being treated like second-class military citizens, and they asked Baron von Riedesel to obtain a correction of the unfair situation.

Burgoyne and Riedesel had met in London on a number of occasions, and had formed a friendship based on mutual trust and respect. They were so close, in fact, that Burgoyne made no protest when he learned that the handsome Baroness von Riede-

sel and her three daughters, the youngest of them an infant-in-
arms, would accompany the expedition, as would a number of
other German officers' wives.

Riedesel approached Burgoyne to voice the complaints of his
subordinates, making it plain that he shared the views of his officers. In the blunt soldiers' talk that followed, Burgoyne emphasized that he could do nothing to overrule or ignore the War
Office's policy. He disagreed with it, and he sent off a letter to
London asking for a change in the status of mercenary officers,
but until he learned that the policy had been changed, he was
compelled to obey it.

Since he sympathized with the German officers, however,
he was willing to establish some rules of his own that would al-
low them to keep their pride intact. The mercenary regiments
would fight as a unit, with Riedesel reporting direct to the commander-in-chief, and no one but Burgoyne or Phillips, his deputy,
would be permitted to give orders to the major-general commanding the troops from Brunswick and Hesse. Riedesel understood that Burgoyne was making a considerable concession, and
was grateful.

Other problems required equally prompt solution. It was a
long-established custom in the British Army for only cavalry
or infantry officers of high rank to assume command of large
units that included men of services other than their own. Officers
of the artillery and sappers, much less the quartermaster corps
and others that performed housekeeping duties, were regarded
as distinctly inferior to the dashing horsemen and the sturdy
foot soldiers. Yet none other than an artilleryman had been
named second in command of the entire expedition.

Burgoyne wasted no time straightening out the situation.
As Will Phillips wrote to his wife in a letter filled with admira-
tion and tinged with awe, Burgoyne summoned his entire corps of
officers to a meeting in the assembly hall at the Citadel. Minc-
ing no words, he told them he had learned they were disgruntled, and he proposed to rectify the situation: General Phillips
would continue to serve as his deputy, and the commander-in-
chief would accept the resignation, on the spot, of any officer who

was dissatisfied with the arrangement. Those who elected to accept it would be expected to obey General Phillips as readily as they would the commander-in-chief himself. And any who failed at any time to accord General Phillips the respect and obedience due his position and rank would be subjected to a field court-martial within twenty-four hours of his insurrection.

General Phillips wrote to his wife that he felt confident he would encounter no difficulties with subordinate commanders.

Yet another problem proved to be a blessing in disguise. The new uniforms for the British contingent of four thousand men had been "lost," the fine, efficient hand of Lord George Germain again being evident, and it seemed unlikely they would be located in time for the march. This necessitated the trimming of long coattails to use as patches, and the removal of broad, bent brims from hats, so that the soldiers' headgear now resembled high-crowned skullcaps. Burgoyne was privately pleased, as he had long believed the cumbersome British field uniform unsuited for wear in the wilderness.

The most startling of the problems awaiting the commander-in-chief of the expedition was insoluble. His march route was his most closely guarded secret, as was the plan to link forces with Sir William Howe, and presumably was known only to Carleton and Phillips. Less than forty-eight hours after his arrival in town, however, he was astonished to hear from Captain Stanley, still his aide, that every merchant, tavern-keeper, and harlot in Quebec was familiar with all of the details.

A personal survey conducted that same day proved Stanley was correct. Neither the route of march nor the planned junction with Howe was even a loosely kept secret. Although Burgoyne did not realize it until much later, the only man kept completely in the dark was Lieutenant-General Sir William Howe.

Carleton and Phillips were totally trustworthy, professional soldiers, so it was obvious that neither had spoken out of turn. The furious Burgoyne launched an investigation of his own, in which Governor-General Carleton cooperated fully, and together the two senior officers learned what they might have guessed from the outset: the culprit was none other than Lord George

Germain. The bumbling Minister of State owned several large tracts of property in Canada, and hoping to offer good cheer to the men who managed them for him, he had written them detailed accounts of Burgoyne's projected movements. Germain's stupidity becomes all the more amazing when it is remembered that he had been unwilling to keep his horses waiting for a few minutes so he could sign a letter to Howe.

One of the few cheering factors in Burgoyne's situation was the assistance rendered him by Sir Guy Carleton, who faced the prospect of being overshadowed by an officer far junior to him. Burgoyne paid a glowing tribute to the governor-general, concluding a letter to the War Office with the remark: "I should think myself deficient in justice and honour were I to close my letter without mentioning the sense I entertain of General Carleton's conduct; his zeal is manifest, exemplary and satisfactory."

But Sir Guy was neither a miracle-worker nor a magician. Heavy inducements had been offered to Canadians and to Tory refugees from the rebel Colonies, but only a handful had enlisted. The Indians had proved equally reluctant to join the expedition, although Carleton, who knew them well and considered them untrustworthy, believed their absence would be no loss.

There was a severe shortage of horses and wagons, too, Canadian farmers having been unwilling to sell their precious animals and conveyances for any price. The requisition for gun carriages had arrived only a few weeks before Burgoyne himself had reached Quebec, Germain's tardiness again being responsible, but they were now being constructed of green wood and would be ready in time for the march—provided they did not warp. At Burgoyne's urgent request an immediate order was given to build an additional five hundred two-wheeled carriages, and the offers to farmers for horses were doubled, making the price irresistible, and ruining the budgets for the operation that had been carefully devised by the War and Colonial offices.

Immediately prior to Burgoyne's arrival in Quebec good news had been received from the commander of the force that was to create a diversion in the west, Colonel Barry St. Leger. His light infantry was on the move, and he wrote that he would do what was expected of him.

The same could not be said of Sir William Howe. Carleton had heard, indirectly, that Howe was skirmishing with Washington in Pennsylvania, and had no intention of moving elsewhere unless Washington moved there, too. This news was so bewildering that Gentleman Johnny found it difficult to give the story credence, but found an explanation in his own mind, and wrote accordingly to the young Earl of Derby. It had been Howe's intention to devour Washington's army, he said, but Sir William, his former fellow-passenger on a trans-Atlantic voyage, was a reliable officer—and a complete gentleman. Therefore he would respond with all due alacrity when he received his orders from Lord George Germain. It was a trifle strange, perhaps, that he had not already received those orders and acted accordingly. On the other hand, Howe was a wily lad and a competent officer, so he undoubtedly knew how long it would take him to march north from Pennsylvania to Albany. So, in all probability, he was hoping to confuse the enemy by waiting until the last possible moment before severing contact with Washington's forces, wheeling toward the north and then making a rapid march to the rendezvous at Albany.

Comforting himself with his rationalizations, Gentleman Johnny turned to other problems. His commissary-general, a colonel, was seriously ill with the ague, and no other commissioned officer experienced in the art of transporting large quantities of supplies, munitions, and all of the gear necessary for a large corps on the move was available. Consequently it would be necessary to hire a civilian, preferably someone who knew the wilderness and was familiar with the problems of moving bulky goods through it.

The very man happened to be living in Quebec, and was willing to accept the task. Felix Loescher was an exceptionally able man who had been the proprietor of the general store at Ticonderoga when the British garrison had been stationed there, and had become wealthy selling various merchandise to the officers and their families. When the Americans had captured the fort he fled to Quebec with his fortune stuffed in sacks, which he had carried in a small cart. Now he was a respected, still prosperous Quebec merchant, but he hated the Americans who had caused him to become a refugee, and he leaped at the opportunity Burgoyne offered him.

Loescher accepted the position of commissary-general on one condition. His wife, who was less than half his age and was said to be part Indian, was a flighty girl, and he was afraid she would get into trouble if he left her behind. Therefore he would accompany the expedition only if he could bring her with him.

Burgoyne was in no position to refuse, and actually had no reason to deny Loescher's wife the questionable privilege of making the long march. Ever since it had become known that the Baroness Riedesel and other German ladies would accompany their husbands, a number of English officers' wives had also applied for the privilege, and they, too, had been accepted. Warfare was still conducted in a civilized manner in the eighteenth century, and it was not uncommon for ladies of rank and standing to go into the field when their husbands were campaigning. They were circumspect, they traveled with the rear guard, and they understood they could join their husbands in the evening only when the military situation of the moment permitted. General officers usually welcomed their presence, believing that officers were more inclined to remember they were gentlemen, less likely to associate with the camp followers who associated with ordinary soldiers when they dined with the wives of colleagues.

The situation was complicated, to be sure, because some officers utilized the opportunity to bring their mistresses on campaigns with them. But these women usually could not be distinguished from the wives of other officers.

Gentleman Johnny Burgoyne's initial reaction to Fanny Loescher was not recorded, but a man with his eye for beauty must have recognized certain qualities in her. He soon explored them.

Twelve

It was typical of the England of Gentleman Johnny Burgoyne's era that, proud of her heritage as the most civilized of Western nations, she forgave the commander of the losing army at the Battle of Saratoga for his sins of commission, as well as those of omission that were not his fault, but expressed horror when it was learned he had employed Indian warriors. No less a statesman than the Earl of Chatham thundered in the House of Lords, "We have sullied and tarnished the arms of Britain for ever by employing savages in our service, by drawing them up in a British line, and mixing the scalping-knife and tomahawk with the sword and firelock." It might be noted, more or less parenthetically, that his Lordship had a convenient memory, having forgotten that, as William Pitt, he had been delighted with the part played by the Indians in the capture of Quebec during the French and Indian War.

For his own part, even before leaving Quebec, Burgoyne had cause to regret his decision to utilize the services of Indian warriors. Following his usual friendly, open-handed policy of dealing with his troops, he had not observed the old custom of closing all taverns of the town to his men. This meant the Huron and Ottawa braves could buy liquor, a prospect that filled anyone familiar with the New World with horror. As everyone who had lived for any length of time in Canada or the new United States believed, Indians were congenitally incapable of coping with alcoholic beverages.

Captain Thomas Stanley, himself enjoying a night on the town, was instrumental in preventing a riot involving townspeople, off-duty troops, and a band of drunken warriors. He suffered a broken arm and several broken ribs for his pains, forcing him to remain behind when the expedition marched and making it necessary for the commander-in-chief to find a replacement as aide-de-camp.

Burgoyne was angry, and with justice, but quickly learned there was nothing he could do about the situation. If he tried to punish the Indians who had become intoxicated, he was told by no less an authority than Sir Guy Carleton, his entire regiment of braves would vanish into the wilderness, taking with them the muskets they had been given, as well as any other supplies, provisions, or arms they could steal on their way out of town.

Gentleman Johnny discussed the situation with several of his officers experienced in New World living, Brigadier Hamilton, the adjutant-general, Colonel Kingston, and the quartermaster-general, Colonel Money. All agreed with Carleton, so Burgoyne felt obliged to accept the advice.

A new contingent of officers arrived in Quebec on May 13, and Burgoyne immediately appointed several of them to posts of trust. Major the Earl of Balcarres was made commander of the light infantry, and the exceptionally competent Major John Acland, who was married to the daughter of an earl, was given the command of the grenadiers, or heavy infantry. Two new aides were appointed to take the place of the disabled Stanley. Lord Petersham, who wanted to be a diplomat, had an opportunity to practice for that profession when he was made senior aide and given the responsibility of acting as liaison officer with the commanders of subordinate units. The junior aide was the young and impetuous Sir Francis Clark, who was destined to lose his life at Saratoga.

The presence of the dynamic Burgoyne in Quebec caused a stir, and in the days following his arrival Canadians continued to volunteer for the expedition. The need for increased manpower made it almost impossible to reject any man who appeared before the recruiting officer, but Burgoyne had lost faith in what he had previously envisaged as a corps of Canadian fighting men, and on May 14 he sent an unhappy letter to Germain:

> I cannot speak with much confidence of the military assistance I am to look for from the Canadians. The only corps yet instituted, or that I am informed can at present be instituted, are three independent companies of 100 men each, officered by Seigneurs of the country who are well-chosen; but they have not been able to engage many volunteers. The men are chiefly drafted from the militia, according to a late regulation of the Legislative Council. Those I have yet seen afford no promise of arms—awkward, ignorant, disinclined to the service; and spiritless. Various reasons are assigned for this change in the natives since the time of the French government. It may partly be owing to a disuse of arms, but I believe principally to the unpopularity of their Seigneurs, and to the poison which the emissaries of the rebels have thrown into their mind.

Having delivered himself of his complaint, the commander of the Army of the North, as the corps was now designated, took his leave of Governor-General Carleton. Burgoyne expressed a reluctance to advertise his departure, but it is unlikely that anyone in Quebec, resident or visitor, was unaware of what he was doing. His personal baggage train consisted of no less than forty-three two-wheeled carts, all of them piled high with furniture, food, racks of wine, uniforms, two spare swords and three braces of pistols, a half-dozen flags, and more than two hundred books, including a number of plays he wanted to read.

Burgoyne's immediate destination was Montreal, the assembly point for his entire force, most units having preceded him there. He was accompanied only by the members of his "private party," which included his two aides, his and their orderlies, six in all, two Canadian guides, and a double company of grenadiers, who formed his honor guard. Although he could have traveled by boat on the St. Lawrence River he made the journey of approximately one hundred and seventy miles overland, following the frequently used trail that ran more or less parallel to the river.

This was Gentleman Johnny's introduction to the North American wilderness, and it delighted him. The Canadian forests were lovely in May, the trees were in full leaf and wildflowers were everywhere. The monotony of travel through the woods was broken by the occasional appearance of spacious farmhouses, owned by some of Canada's most prosperous "planters," and they gave the distinguished lieutenant-general a royal welcome, serving him their finest smoked ham and choice cuts of beef. Although Burgoyne did not yet realize it, the trail from Quebec to Montreal no longer qualified as a genuine wilderness road. Traffic between the two growing communities was increasingly heavy, and the hardships of real frontier travel had become a thing of the past. As Gentleman Johnny would discover, the difference between this journey and the longer march that lay ahead of him was vast.

He arrived at Montreal on May 22, and immediately plunged into the task of organizing the Army of the North for the coming campaign. In later years he was criticized for his preponderance of artillery, and some of his own officers, principally men who were new to North America, let it be known at a council of officers that they were concerned about the problems of moving heavy guns across country where no roads existed. But Lieutenant-General Burgoyne, the veteran observer of the Battle of Bunker Hill, made short work of their arguments. He had seen American fighting men in action, and knew they could be dislodged only by artillery and light infantry. Cavalry and heavy infantry were useless unless the enemy could be compelled to fight after the fashion of European armies, and he knew of no way to accomplish that end.

"We must adapt ourselves to the American methods if we hope to give the rebels a drubbing," he told his officers, and they agreed with his wisdom.

Gentleman Johnny was not one to forget the amenities, and on the evening of May 24 he gave a dinner party in the log fort he was using as his Montreal headquarters. All of the ladies who would accompany the expedition were present, with Baroness von Riedesel seated on the host's right and the wife of Major Acland on his left. Not even the pressures of a military campaign could cause Gentleman Johnny to forget that the latter was the daughter of an English earl. No record of the menu was kept, but it is known that eight separate courses were served and that quantities of champagne, among other beverages, were consumed.

Only one of the ladies failed to powder her hair. Fanny Loescher was proud of her blue-black tresses, which were piled high on her head, and some of the women subsequently wrote that Burgoyne's attention was called to her because of her unfashionable individualism. Perhaps they were right, but it is more likely that the experienced ladies' man was drawn to her because of a subtle expression that he alone noted in her dark eyes. Whatever his reason, he spent more than a half-hour chatting with her at the end of the dinner, and Frederica von Riedesel, a shrewd observer and compulsive letter-writer, informed one of her many correspondents, "The Army has suffered its first casualty, General Burgoyne having fallen victim to the charms of Mme. Loescher. She is animated and has a certain charm, but she lacks the poise and grace of many of our ladies, so several of us were surprised that the General spent so long a time in her company." It later became evident that Fanny Loescher was endowed with a

quality that set her apart; she was amenable, which the other ladies were not.

For the moment more important matters were paramount in
Burgoyne's mind. The Canadians who had enlisted were already
deserting. He was annoyed, but addressed himself to the problem, and conceived a new idea, which he mentioned in a letter to
Carleton on May 26:

> When the plan of my expedition was framed, the
> ideas of Government respecting armed Canadians
> went to six times the number. . . . Without that depend-
> ence I have reason to believe the proportion of Regu-
> lars would have been larger. To remedy in some meas-
> ure this deficiency I have to propose to your Excellency
> a Corvee of one thousand men to attend the expedition
> for a limited time for the purposes of labour and trans-
> port.

Carleton, who better understood the New World, realized it
would not be feasible to form a Canadian labor corps, and in his
reply he could not resist the opportunity to take another slap at
the man responsible for so many of the expedition's problems,
Lord George Germain:

> The Desertion you give me Notice of in your Let-
> ter does not surprise me; it has been the same here,
> and was no more than I expected. If Government laid
> any great stress upon assistance from the Canadians,
> for carrying on the present war, it surely was not upon
> Information proceeding from me. Experience might
> have taught them, and it did not require that to con-
> vince me, these People had been governed with too
> loose a Rein for many years, and had imbibed too
> much of the American spirit of Licentiousness and In-
> dependence, administered by a numerous and turbulent
> Faction here, to be suddenly restored to a proper and
> desirable Subordination.

That ended Burgoyne's hope of establishing a labor corps. Meanwhile the Indian warriors were creating a new problem: denied the use of alcoholic beverages by order of the commander-in-chief, they obtained what they wanted in the way of liquor by stealing rum from the stores carried to provide the daily ration that British and mercenary soldiers considered a necessity. The increasingly irritated Burgoyne took care of that unfortunate situation by doubling the guard detail posted to maintain sentry duty in the vicinity of the liquor supplies, and ordered the troops to shoot any intruders.

Only temporarily foiled, the braves began to steal into the quarters of the officers in search of liquor, cash, and any other valuables they might find. Sir Francis Clark caught two warriors of the Huron who were trying to sneak into Burgoyne's own bedchamber in the fort, and the general, ignoring the advice of subordinates experienced in the ways of the New World, promptly dismissed the pair and ordered them to leave his camp.

They departed without delay, but were followed by forty of their comrades, most of them either relatives or close friends. At this rate, Burgoyne complained, his corps of five hundred Indians would soon be depleted, and for the first time he began to wonder whether it was worth his Army's while to retain the services of the warriors who remained. His need for manpower was so great that, after weighing the matter, he decided not to disband the corps, much to his subsequent regret.

In the main, however, he was in high spirits regarding his great enterprise, as a letter he wrote from Montreal to a colleague in the War Office, General Harvey, clearly indicates. The troops were in good health and eager for the campaign to begin, Sir Guy Carleton had given him every possible assistance, in spite of his "natural resentment" over the treatment accorded him by an unnamed Minister of State. The letter continues:

> My intention is, during my advance to Ticonderoga, and siege of that post, for a siege I apprehend it must be, to give all possible jealousy on the side of Connecticut. If I can by maneuver make them suspect

that after the reduction of Ticonderoga my views are pointed that way, it may make the Connecticut forces very cautious of leaving their own frontiers, and much facilitate my progress to Albany.

I mention this intention only to Lord George and yourself, and I do it lest from any intelligence of my motions that may reach England indirectly, it should be supposed I have suffered myself to be diverted from the main object of my orders. The King and His Majesty's Ministers may rest assured that whatever demonstrations I may endeavor to impose upon the enemy, I shall really make no movement that can procrastinate my progress to Albany.

One thing more occurs. I had the surprise and mortification to find a paper handed about at Montreal, publishing the whole design of the campaign, almost as accurately as if it had been copied from the Secretary of State's letter. My own caution has been such that not a man on my own staff has been let into the secret. Sir Guy Carleton's, I am confident, has been equal; I am therefore led to doubt whether imprudence has not been committed from private letters from England, and wish you would ask my friend D'Oyley, to whom my very affectionate compliments, whether there is any person within the line of ministerial communication that he can suspect to be so unguarded? It is not of great consequence here, except as far as regards St. Leger's expedition; but such a trick may be of most prejudicial consequence in other cases, and should be guarded against.

Since it was impossible to accuse a Minister of State of being indiscreet without positive proof, Burgoyne chose the next best approach to the problem. Apparently he felt confident that the deputy secretary for the Colonies would read between the lines and, hopefully, would find some way to muzzle the ever-talkative Germain, who was as incapable of keeping a vitally important official secret as he was of communicating that information to the man who most needed to know it.

Before departing from Montreal, Burgoyne also sent a crisp communication to Germain himself. The personal tone that had been present in previous letters to the minister was absent, and he was coldly official:

> The only delay is occasioned by the impracticability of the roads, owing to late extraordinary heavy rains, and this difficulty will be speedily removed, by exerting the services of the parishes as soon as the weather clears. In the mean time I am employing every means that water carriage will admit for drawing the troops and their stores to the point. I trust, I shall have vessels sufficient to move the army and stores together, and in that case, will take post at once, within sight of Ticonderoga, and only make use of Crown Point for my hospital and magazine.
>
> A continuation of intelligence from different spies and deserters, confirms the design of the enemy to dispute Ticonderoga vigorously. They are also building bow-galleys at Fort George, for the defence of that lake, etc., fortifying on the road to Skenesborough. It is consigned to the New England colonies to furnish supplies of men and provision to oppose the progress of my army, and they have undertaken the task, upon condition of being exempt from supplying Mr. Washington's main army."

Burgoyne closed on a hopeful note. He wrote that Colonel St. Leger was not already at Lake Ontario, as he had supposed, but came to Montreal for a conference with the commander-in-chief before setting out on his own diversionary expedition. The general and the colonel coordinated their plans, and Burgoyne reported that all was in readiness for the great adventure that would make military history and bring the rebellion of the Americans to a swift end.

Thirteen

Colonel Barry St. Leger consciously modeled himself on Gentleman Johnny Burgoyne, so it was small wonder the two men established an immediate rapport in their personal relations. A cavalryman like Burgoyne, the younger St. Leger was handsome, personable, and dashing. He wore his uniforms with an air, he had been reckless in combat as a junior officer, and he even traveled through the North American wilderness with his private larder and portable wine cellar. But there the similarities ended.

Selected for his position of trust by Lord George Germain, in spite of Burgoyne's protests that the place should be given to a major-general, or at the very least to a brigadier, St. Leger had never held an independent command, had only a vague grasp of the principles of strategy, and knew literally nothing about the sharp differences between Old World fighting and the battle techniques used in the vast, uncivilized interior of North America. Learning nothing from his mistakes, which he invariably blamed on others, he lost encounters he should have won and had an extraordinary talent for converting ordinary blunders into monumental disasters. Had a competent officer held his command, Burgoyne might have won the Battle of Saratoga, in spite of Sir William Howe's absence from the area, but the fine hand of Lord George Germain was everywhere, and St. Leger proved himself incapable of performing the task given him.

It is possible to dispose of him and his expedition with the dispatch his enemies showed. St. Leger's mobile corps consisted of about seventeen hundred men, the majority veteran British light infantry who, like their commander, knew nothing about American methods of fighting a war. He was also accompanied by several regiments of Hessian mercenaries, who were even more ignorant of the New World, and by three battalions of Tories. These men, American born, had received no training, and many were city dwellers who had never before used firearms. A regiment of Indians rounded out the corps, and like Burgoyne's warriors, they were independent, and volatile.

Setting out through the wilderness beyond Montreal in June, St. Leger stumbled into Oswego, New York, a month later after making several unnecessary detours, and on August 3, tardy but triumphant, he finally arrived before the post that was the strong-point of the entire Mohawk Valley, Fort Schuyler, named by the Americans after Major-General Philip Schuyler, the Albany war-horse, but known to the British as Fort Stanwix.

The garrison of Americans, most of them militia, consisted of approximately seven hundred and fifty men, less than half the size of the attacking force, and was commanded by a tough old colonel of Dutch colonial stock, Peter Gansevoort, who had spent his entire adult life on the Mohawk Valley frontier and could not be bluffed by Indians, Redcoats, or anyone else. He had long been acquainted with the leader of St. Leger's Indians, the legendary Joseph Brant, and the two men had detested each other ever since they had quarrelled at a pre-war conference of settlers and Indians at Albany.

Mistakenly thinking he was conducting a siege in France or the Low Countries, St. Leger drew up his troops in parade formation, marched them around the square, log fort and then, personally, read aloud a proclamation written for the occasion by none other than the noted playwright, Gentleman Johnny Burgoyne. The reading lasted for more than twenty minutes, accompanied by gestures, and was one of Burgoyne's more pompous, less inspired efforts.

If the Americans within Fort Schuyler refused to surrender, St. Leger intoned in a voice that offered no threat to the primacy of David Garrick on the London stage, "the messengers of justice and of wrath await them in the field; and devastation, famine, and every concomitant horror that a reluctant but indispensable prosecution of military duty can devise will bar the way to their return."

A lack of an audience marred St. Leger's performance. No American defenders could be seen on the catwalks around the fort, but long rifles that protruded from gunports indicated that the good St. Leger was not giving an audition for the benefit of his own troops. As a matter of fact, Colonel Gansevoort's position was precarious. His supplies of gunpowder were low, most of his salt beef had been improperly cured and was rotting, and his men had to melt their bullets, then fashion them again because they did not fit the frontier long rifles. In spite of these difficulties, however, the thought of surrender did not cross Peter Gansevoort's mind, and at the end of St. Leger's peroration he politely but firmly ran up his flag.

That night neither side slept, thanks to the shrieks of Brant's Indians, who danced and cavorted around the palisades from sundown until sunrise. Apparently they exhausted themselves in the process, for they felt in need of rest and recuperation, and telling no one their intentions, they vanished. Some returned to their homes, while about half of the original contingent returned to demand more money from the increasingly annoyed and bewildered St. Leger. When he refused to pay them for a job not yet completed, the temperamental braves took umbrage, and many of those who remained melted away into the forests. By the time the siege and its aftermath ended a few days later, only a handful of Indians remained with St. Leger's corps.

The fighting began in earnest on August 4, and the British commander, who had assumed he was confronting farmers who knew as little about warfare as the peasants of Portugal, Spain, and France, was astonished to discover that the marksmanship of the American sharpshooters was remarkably good. He hastily withdrew his forces beyond the range of the long frontier rifles, but maintained his siege.

Meanwhile Gansevoort's plight was called to the attention of the American commander for the Mohawk Valley, pipe-smoking, Bible-reading Brigadier-General Nicholas Herkimer, like so many of his neighbors a land-owning descendant of the early Dutch settlers. Hastily assembling a force of about nine hundred men, most of them militia, he hurried to the assistance of Fort Schuyler. The resulting action, fought on August 6, is known as the Battle of Oriskany.

Herkimer and his men, who presumably knew better, made the error—fatal in the wilderness—of not sending out enough scouting parties, so the Americans walked into an ambush. But the British and Hessians had been trained to fight in formation on open fields, and the incompetent St. Leger was unable to take advantage of a situation that might have enabled him to win a decisive victory had he acted with greater dispatch and intelligence.

The Americans in the fort heard the sounds of musket and rifle fire, and came out to assist their comrades. St. Leger found the enemy behind him as well as in front of him, but the area immediately surrounding Ft. Schuyler had been cleared, and he knew how to fight in the open. His regiments held firm, and could not be dislodged.

General Herkimer, who was wounded early in the battle, directed operations while leaning against the trunk of an oak tree, and remained calm, in complete possession of his faculties, even though he died of his wounds a few days later. The two forces were evenly matched, and neither side was able to utilize leverage by fighting in its own style. When the Americans retreated into the forest the British pursued them, and were bewildered by frontier tactics; when the Americans emerged again into the open, they were incapable of advancing against British and mercenary regiments drawn up in hollow squares, a formation made invincible in Bavaria, the Low Countries, and France three-quarters of a century earlier by the Duke of Marlborough and Prince Eugene of Savoy.

Eventually Herkimer was forced to withdraw, and Gansevoort's men were compelled to return to their fort, but the latter did not fall, and the Battle of Oriskany ended in a draw. St. Leger failed to realize that the engagement had accomplished literally nothing, and sent an ecstatic report of the flight of Herkimer's men to the commander-in-chief of the Army of the North.

He also sent a messenger, under a flag of truce, to inform Colonel Gansevoort that his cause was hopeless because General Burgoyne had captured Albany. The hard-headed Gansevoort refused to believe the story without positive proof, and continued to hold out.

The discouraged St. Leger was learning that warfare in the New World was not conducted according to any rules he knew. Virtually all of his Indians had deserted, his supplies and munitions were running low, and he could obtain neither food nor gunpowder in the hostile Mohawk Valley. While he debated his next course, his enemy taught him yet another lesson.

He had hired several local inhabitants as spies, believing they were Loyalists, but they were actually imaginative Patriots, and they concocted a story strictly for his benefit. A force consisting of "many thousands" of Continentals under the command of Major-General Horatio Gates was on the march, they told him, and the corps of Redcoats and Hessians soon would be overwhelmed by an army four or five times its size.

Barry St. Leger was no coward, but he saw nothing to be gained by making a futile stand against superior numbers, so he retreated to Oswego, thus automatically lifting the siege of Fort Schuyler, and then returned to Canada, his mission unfulfilled. All he had really accomplished had been to further alert the Americans with his gratuitous announcement that Burgoyne had captured Albany. If the Patriot high command had entertained any doubts regarding Gentleman Johnny's ultimate destination, they were dissipated.

Not until many months later did St. Leger learn he had been fooled by a false rumor, and even then he would not believe that the so-called American army sent to destroy him had been the figment of clever double espionage agents' imagination. It was too humiliating to accept the truth, so St. Leger rejected it, and after his return to England he continued to maintain that only the approach of a large rebel army had made it necessary for him to retreat.

As a matter of fact, the Americans were hard-pressed to put an army into the field for the purpose of halting Burgoyne. Washington, as has been noted, had known since the summer of 1776 that an attempt would be made to cut off New York and New England from the other states by two large British corps. This conviction was confirmed by the time Burgoyne left Quebec, and even the squabbling politicians of the Continental Congress realized that Gentleman Johnny would try to capture Fort Ticonderoga and then march south to Albany.

Attempts were made, within the limits of manpower and resources, to strengthen the American position. Perhaps the single greatest contribution was made by Thaddeus Kosciusko, the Polish patriot who had volunteered to help the former colonists win their independence, and who vastly strengthened Ticonderoga's defense bastions.

A great deal more was needed, but the almost frantic Washington had no troops to spare, thanks to Sir William Howe's attempt to win the war single-handed. Commanding an army of approximately twelve thousand British and mercenary regulars, with another four thousand under his deputy, Sir Henry Clinton, holding the garrison in occupied New York Town, Howe believed that the capture of Philadelphia, the Patriot capital, would end the war.

Washington believed otherwise, and necessity forced him to adopt a strategy that posterity would regard as brilliant, but that the panicky members of the Continental Congress failed to appreciate. The American commander fought a series of delaying actions on the approaches to Philadelphia, his irregulars attacking Howe's long supply lines through New Jersey, but he was determined to sacrifice Philadelphia, if that should prove necessary, while he reorganized and obtained more men to continue the fight.

The over-all command of the Army of New York was vested in the patrician Major-General Philip Schuyler, the oldest and probably the wealthiest general officer in Patriot service. Bluff and hearty in his dealings with frontiersmen, suave and diplomatic in the company of his peers, Schuyler owned a large town house in Albany, as well as vast estates and several country houses in the sparsely settled countryside to the west. He was also forced to bear several handicaps that made it difficult for him to retain his command.

No man was more devoted to the American cause than Schuyler, but his wealth and grand style of personal living aroused the hostility of troops from Connecticut, Massachusetts, and New Hampshire, most of them farmers, who were placed under his command. Their complaints reached the ever-open ears of their representatives in the Congress, who decided he needed to be replaced because he was middle-aged.

Their real reason was their desire to find a suitable command for the man whom many politicians were considering as a replacement for Washington, whose wealth also made him the target of the envious. It is possible that Major-General Horatio Gates was the most overrated man in the entire American field force.

British-born, Gates had served in Portugal under Brigadier John Burgoyne, then had seen duty in the New World, where he had observed and absorbed the principles of wilderness fighting. Retiring from the British Army with the rank of major, he had migrated to the colonies in 1772, and had been among the first to volunteer for duty with the Continentals, or regulars. His experience had been responsible for his swift rise, and being ambitious, he wanted to climb still higher, so he became the natural magnet for those who opposed Washington.

If George Washington was upset by the machinations of those who wanted him removed as commander-in-chief he kept his feelings to himself. Certainly he disliked the idea of replacing Schuyler with Gates, but he was too busy warding off Sir William Howe's blows to defend himself from the politicians who connived behind his back, and so he was forced to accept, with as much grace as he could muster, the decision of the Congress to give Gates the command in the north.

Washington's faith in Gates was limited, and so was that of the general officers and colonels who would fight under the banner of the Army of New York. Horatio Gates was a petty-minded martinet who failed to understand the temperament of his new fellow-countrymen. Americans had to be led, under no circumstances could they be driven, and they would not tolerate, much less do their best for a man who patronized them.

The appointment of Gates in the late summer of 1777 made it necessary for Washington to find someone who would neutralize the personality of the commander and make up for his deficiencies as a soldier. One man came to mind, and Washington rammed the appointment of the meteoric, controversial Brigadier-General Benedict Arnold through a reluctant Continental Congress.

No American was endowed with greater military talents than the Connecticut-born Arnold, and few enjoyed his infinite ability to make personal enemies. He had come within an eyelash of taking Quebec, he had played a major role in the capture of Ticonderoga, but had seen Ethan Allen given all the credit, and he had been so vain, quarrelsome, and disagreeable that the Congress had repeatedly passed him over for promotion until Washington intervened—after the Battle of Saratoga—to obtain for him the rank of major-general to which his exploits and accomplishments entitled him.

Under Washington's plan, Gates was the supreme commander in the north, but would confine his principal activities to administrative duties, at which he excelled. What was more, it was convenient to have Gates in charge, as his friends in the Congress would see to it that the Army of New York received a fair share of the food and arms, uniforms, lead, and gunpowder that were in such short supply.

But the troops would be led in battle by Arnold. Those who had served previously under his command worshiped him—he had the knack for winning the affection and loyalty of subordinates, no matter how difficult it was for him to get along with his peers, and he was also endowed with another quality that Washington recognized and appreciated. A self-taught soldier, like so many of the Americans' general officers and colonels, Arnold had an instinctive grasp of battlefield tactics. When engaging in combat he knew from moment to moment what needed to be done and he did not hesitate to give commands accordingly. Equally important, he taught by example, and actually relished the exhilaration of leading his men into a fight.

It was Washington's hope that Gates and Arnold would complement each other. Assuming they would behave like grown men, it did not occur to him that Gates' jealousy and Arnold's lack of tact would set them clawing at each other's throats—and thereby place the whole future of the new United States of America in jeopardy.

Fourteen

A book published without fanfare in Berlin, in 1800, has earned the Baron and Baroness von Riedesel the eternal gratitude of posterity. Called *The Letters and Reports*, it contains their separate and joint accounts of the years they spent in the service of the British in the New World, beginning with General von Riedesel's employment in 1776 and lasting until the end of the American War of Independence in 1783. The Baroness was remarkable, thinking nothing of accompanying her husband on a campaign through the wilderness of North America and taking with her their three small daughters, Frederica, Gustava, and Caroline, the last an infant less than one year old.

The Baron was a trencherman who conceived a strong dislike for English cooking from the day he reached England on his way to Quebec; he drank only wine, and he would not permit the troops under his command to be given rations of rum, claiming that strong drink befuddled the mind and weakened the body of a fighting man. The food rations of the British Army were inferior, he said, because they consisted principally of salt meat, salt fish, and rice. There were no fruits, and the British were uncivilized because even the officers ate no vegetables. In fact, when local produce was available, Redcoat officers and soldiers alike refused to touch it. Britain, he wrote, was at least one hundred years behind the Continent of Europe in its food preparation and tastes, a view repeatedly confirmed down to the present day by the gourmets of many nations, who have found the fare unpalatable when they have strayed from cosmopolitan London.

The Baroness was a tiny woman with a waist so small that her husband could span it with his hands. She was also exceptionally pretty, with dark hair and enormous eyes, and she was devoted to the Baron and her children. As the wife of a soldier who had no income other than what he earned with his sword she was always money-conscious, and complained bitterly about the prices she found in London. Even clothing was so expensive there that she hated to buy new, warm attire for her children, but she believed she had no choice, having been told that only raw flax was available in the New World. She had also been informed that the only food in plentiful supply on the far side of the Atlantic was oats, which people boiled, but even this erroneous information did not deter her from going with her husband and taking her daughters on what was one of the stranger military odysseys of the eighteenth century.

Frederica von Riedesel allowed nothing to compromise her personal standards. The ladies she met in Quebec were beneath her contempt because their clothes and hair were dirty. She did not object to the fact that their gowns were ill-fitting, she wrote, but there was no excuse for their grime.

From the time of the Baroness' first meeting with General Burgoyne, in London, she disliked him:

He bends too low and too often over one's hand;

he finds paltry reasons for offering one his arm; he is too quick to laugh and smile, even when one does not jest. It is true that he exercises care not to show overly much attention to a lady whom he knows to be happily wedded, but there is at all times an expression in his eyes that causes one to feel discomfort. He is known as gallant, but one does not expect the gallantry of the Continent in an Englishman.

In other words, Burgoyne was too much of a gentleman for the taste of the sober and somewhat puritanical Baroness. It was a strange complaint, even though she took pains to emphasize that he tried to take no liberties. King George offended her in somewhat the same way, although she was careful not to chastise him. She was taken to Whitehall to be presented to His Britannic Majesty, and in the course of their interview he found her so charming that he kissed her on the cheek. Her only comment was to the effect that the royal gesture was so sudden and unexpected that it caused her to redden.

Gentleman Johnny and Fanny Loescher began their affair soon after the Army of the North left Montreal, and thereafter the diary-commentary of Baroness Riedesel became sternly disapproving. On a number of occasions, she noted, the commander-in-chief was "very merry, and spent the whole night singing and drinking and amusing himself with the wife of the Commissary, who was his mistress, and who, like him, was very fond of champagne."

She criticized Burgoyne's food tastes, too. She herself had discovered that bear steak was delicious, provided it was well done, and she enjoyed the aroma when it was cooking, but it shocked her that Gentleman Johnny liked his bear served rare. She also was horrified when one of her husband's aides informed her that the commander-in-chief enjoyed a local delicacy, rattlesnake soup.

At the same time she was grateful for Burgoyne's advice in making wilderness living easier. Burning cedar-branches kept flies and mosquitoes at a distance, and cedar sap rubbed on the arms, legs, and faces of her children prevented them from being bitten. The inner boughs of white pines, she learned from Gentleman Johnny, made first-rate mattresses when the luggage train bogged down in autumn mud and her own mattress was not available. No New World berries should be eaten when green, he informed her, and one Sunday afternoon on the march, when he had ordered a longer than usual rest, he amused her by taking her and Lady Acland into the nearby forest, where he entertained them by pulling up edible roots for them.

General Burgoyne, the Baroness observed, was as dapper in the deep woods as he was in the drawing room, and she was disconcerted by his every-present poise. It bothered her, too, that her husband held his superior in high regard. Burgoyne was one of the great soldiers of the age, Baron von Riedesel declared, and his military standing was in no way lessened by the fact that he slept with Fanny Loescher. In fact, his private life was no one's business but his own, the Baron said, and evidently Gentleman Johnny had reached some sort of understanding with Commissary General Felix Loescher, who seemed blind and deaf for the duration of the campaign.

The Army of the North left Montreal behind schedule, undermanned and ill-equipped, on June 1, 1777, marching southward through rolling country in the direction of lakes Champlain and George. The weather was pleasant, the roads and trails were dry enough after torrential spring rains to support even the weight of the heaviest artillery pieces, and Fanny Loescher's company after a bachelor dinner every evening was delightful.

The muse stirred in the breast of author Burgoyne, and knowing it would have been improper for him to begin writing a new play, he penned a proclamation for the edification of his troops. On June 20 he had it read for his regiments. The reading was essential since most of the English soldiers were illiterate and the mercenaries knew too little English. The less than immortal work showed Burgoyne in one of his more sonorous moods:

By John Burgoyne, Esq.
Lieutenant-General of His Majesties Armies in

America, Colonel of the Queen's Regiment of Light Dragoons, Governor of Fort William in North Britain, one of the Representatives of the Commons of Great Britain in Parliament, and Commanding an Army and Fleet employed in an expedition from Canada.

The forces intrusted to my command are designed to act in concert and upon a common principle with the numerous armies and fleets which already display in every quarter of America the Power, the Justice (and when properly sought) the Mercy of the King. The cause in which the British armies are exerted, applies to the most affecting interest of the human heart, and the military servants of the Crown, at first called forth for the sole purpose of Restoring the rights of the Constitution, now combine with the love of their country, and duty to their Sovereign, the other extensive incitements which spring from a true sense of the general privileges of mankind.

To the eyes and ears of the temperate part of the public, and to the breasts of the suffering thousands in the Provinces, be the melancholy appeal, whether the present unnatural Rebellion has not been made a foundation for the completest system of tyranny that ever God in His displeasure suffered for a time to be exercised over a froward and stubborn generation. Arbitrary Imprisonment, confiscation of property, Persecution and torture unprecedented in the Inquisition of the Romish church, are amongst the palpable enormities that verify the affirmative. These are afflicted by Assemblys and Committees, who dare to profess themselves friends to Liberty, upon the most quiet subjects, without distinction of age or sex, for the sole crime, often for the sole suspicion, of having adhered in principle to the Government under which they were born, and to which, by every tie, Divine and human, they owe allegiance.

To consummate these shocking proceedings, the

profanation of religion is added to the most profligate prostitution of common reason; the consciences of men are set at naught, and multitudes are compelled, not only to bear arms, but also to swear subjection to an usurpation they abhor.

Animated by these considerations, at the head of troops in the full power of health, discipline and valour, determined to strike when necessary and anxious to spare when possible, I, by these presents, invite and exhort all persons, in all places where the progress of this army may point, (and by the blessing of God I will extend it), to maintain such a conduct as may justify in protecting their Lands, Habitations and Families. The intention of this address is to hold forth security, not degradation, to the country. To those whom spirit and principle may induce to partake in the glorious task of redeeming their countrymen from dungeons, and re-establishing the blessings of Legal Government, I offer encouragement and employment, and upon the first intelligence of their associating, I will find means to assist their undertakings.

The domestic, the industrious, the infirm and even the timid inhabitants I am desirous to protect, provided they remain quietly in their houses, that they do not suffer their cattle to be removed, nor their corn or forage to be secreted or destroyed; that they do not break up their bridges or roads, nor by any other acts, directly or indirectly, endeavor to obstruct the operations of the King's troops, or supply or subsist those of the enemy: every species of provision brought to my camp will be paid for at an equitable rate and in solid coin.

The consciousness of Christianity, My Royal Master's Clemency, and the honour of soldiership, I have dwelt upon in this invitation, and wished for more persuasive terms to give it impression; and let not people be led to disregard it by considering their distance from the immediate situation of my camp. I have but to give stretch to the Indian forces under my direction (and they amount to thousands) to overtake the hardened enemies of Great Britain and America. I consider them the same wherever they may lurk. If notwithstanding these endeavors, and sincere inclinations to effect them, the phrensy of hostility should remain, I trust I shall stand acquitted in the eyes of God and men in denouncing and executing the vengeance of the State against the wilful outcasts. The messengers of Justice and wrath await them in the field: and Devastation, famine and every concomitant horror that a reluctant but indispensable prosecution of military duty must occasion, will bar the way to their return.

Presumably the Redcoats and German mercenaries were duly enlightened and inspired by these pompous words. Properly speaking, the address should have been heard by the residents of the American colonies who had turned against the Crown, but there were none in the immediate vicinity. Gentleman Johnny nevertheless felt he had done his duty.

He had left a permanent record of his attitude toward the rebels and of his appeal to them. If they chose to ignore his outstretched hand, woe betide them, even though they might be ignorant of the fact that he had extended it to them. Besides, he kept copies to read or post when he took possession of towns and villages along the way. The document would be particularly effective when he captured Albany, he informed Sir Francis Clark.

He had exercised dramatic license, to be sure, when he had indicated that Crown justice, as personified by Lieutenant-General John Burgoyne, stretched everywhere in the United States. He showed poor taste and a rare lack of understanding of the American temperament when he threatened to use his Indians as instruments of justice, and he exaggerated in the worst way when he claimed that thousands of them were enrolled under his banner.

The Patriots, to be sure, were unaware of his threat and would have been indifferent had they learned of it. The American settlers had succeeded in driving the Indians westward, a process that was continuing throughout the war, and they could not be intimidated by the threat that the braves would be sent on the warpath against them. The brandishing of Indians in a club-like fashion over the heads of the Patriots could have no effect other than that of stiffening their resistance to the King and his Lieutenant-General for the armies in North America.

Few Americans ever learned of Burgoyne's proclamation, but the document became well-known in England when the author thoughtfully sent copies to Charles James Fox and other friends in Parliament. Had Burgoyne won the Battle of Saratoga and ended the American Revolution, it is possible that nothing further would have been made of his threat. But his defeat left him vulnerable, and he was subjected to such a barrage of criticism by enemies like Horace Walpole that his nickname was used ironically to taunt him. The very phrase, Gentleman Johnny, was understood to refer to an advocate of shockingly uncivilized conduct.

Burgoyne knew that fellow Englishmen, including such friends as Fox and Burke, would be dismayed by his use of Indians, so he tried to forestall or circumvent their opposition by delivering a brief address to his warriors. The scene itself invited parody, although Burgoyne was too immersed in the complexities of his mission to realize it. He wore full dress for the occasion, and one of his aides helped him to climb onto the top of his collapsible table, then held it steady while he delivered his speech to the warriors. The braves stood impassively, their naked torsos gleaming with grease, their hair matted with fish oil and dust, and listened as interpreters translated the words of the resplendent figure in scarlet and gold.

There were certain laws, Burgoyne declared, that all Indians serving under his banner had to obey, and there were customs of civilized warfare to which they had to conform:

"I positively forbid bloodshed when you are not actively opposed in arms.

"Aged men, women, children, and prisoners must be held sacred from the knife and hatchet, even in the time of actual conflict. I will punish any man who breaks this rule, no matter the excuse for conduct otherwise that he may offer.

"You shall receive compensation for the prisoners you take, but you shall be called to account for scalps.

"In conformity and indulgence to your customs, which have affixed an idea of honour to such badges of victory, you shall be allowed to take the scalps of the dead, when killed by your fire, and in fair opposition; but on no account, or pretence, or subtlety, or prevarication, are they to be taken from the wounded, or even dying; and still less pardonable, if possible, will it be held to kill men in that condition, on purpose, and upon a supposition that this protection to the wounded would be thereby evaded."

Burgoyne was trying so hard to persuade his Indians to behave in a manner alien to them that he failed to realize how ludicrous he could be made to look by his peers. London was far more upset by the mere fact that he employed "savages" in the first place than by his loss of the Battle of Saratoga, and even men he regarded as close friends could not resist charring him on the coals of ridicule. A satiric comment made by Edmund Burke in the House of Commons set the tone. Burke imagined that a great riot took place on Tower Hill in London, and that the keeper of the royal zoo in the old Tower of London delivered an address to the wild animals the Crown intended to set free for the purpose of restoring order. The keeper, Burke said, donned his finest clothes and climbed onto the top of the beasts' cages, then addressed them: "My gentle lions, my humane bears, my sentimental wolves, my tender-hearted hyenas, go forth: but I exhort ye as ye are Christians and members of a civilized society, to take care not to hurt man, woman or child."

Fortunately for Gentleman Johnny's vanity, he did not learn of the snickers at his expense for a long time, and by then far more urgent matters filled his mind. His friends and enemies were wrong, of course, to single him out for criticism. Indians were used as scouts and volunteer riflemen by the top-ranking generals of both armies throughout the War of Independence, and it is irrelevant that they served with equal unreliability, regardless of whether they served with the Redcoats or the Patriots.

In most instances throughout his career Burgoyne enjoyed good fortune in his dealings with the public, but his luck ran out when he employed Indians, exhorted them in an absurd manner, and used them as a threat in his dealings with the rebels. Other generals kept quiet about Indians, but Burgoyne's concept of honor made it impossible to maintain a false front while engaging in a sly activity behind the back of the public.

It might be argued that a man who had time to write long proclamations and deliver addresses on civilized warfare to Indian braves had little else to occupy him. This was true during the first days of Burgoyne's march, but thereafter he was far too busy to write anything except relatively curt field orders.

Fifteen

Ticonderoga, known as "the Gibraltar of the American Revolution," was an extensive wooden fort located on the west bank of the narrow waterway that connected Lake Champlain to its north with Lake George to its south. Directly above it, about ten miles away, stood a smaller fort, Crown Point, that was still in British hands and was used as a supply base. Off to the east lay the thinly populated Vermont District of New Hampshire, already agitating for separate statehood, and about eighty miles to the south stood Gentleman Johnny Burgoyne's destination, Albany.

In the autumn of 1776 Fort Ticonderoga reached its peak strength, but by the following spring and summer it had declined appreciably in spite of Kosciusko's engineering feats and the exertions of the Patriot commander there, Major-General

Arthur St. Clair. Generals Washington and Schuyler were aware of the fort's deterioration, which was reported to them in detail in May, 1777, but they lacked the reinforcements, supplies, and sinews of war to be of any appreciable help.

Out of a total of approximately two thousand men in the garrison, as many as five hundred, or one-fourth of the total, were incapacitated by swamp fever, which later generations would call influenza. Blankets were in short supply, stores of boots and stockings had been exhausted the previous winter, and food was running low. There was so little to eat, as a matter of fact, that St. Clair coupled his requests for reinforcements with equally shrill demands that newcomers bring their own provisions with them. His own garrison, he wrote, lacked enough food for the summer. Game was scarce in the surrounding wilderness, and only the abundance of fish in Lake George, combined with shrinking barrels of flour in the garrison's pantry, kept the troops fed.

The fort itself leaked so badly that the men had to live in tents, but they had been patched so often they were worn threadbare, and were useless when it rained. The powder supply was rotten, and in spite of St. Clair's attempts to protect it, at least fifty pounds were rendered useless by rain each week. The garrison had no paper to make cartridges for rifles, and lacked the tar to seal the boats they made for use on the lakes and connecting waterways.

St. Clair rightly saw his situation as desperate. He needed a force of ten thousand men to render Ticonderoga invincible, and he wrote to General Schuyler that with a garrison of that size he would prevent any British army, regardless of its strength, from passing. At the very least he needed bayonets, a count revealing that there were only two hundred in the fort.

On the other hand, there seemed to be no cause for alarm. St. Clair knew from his own scouts and a few friendly Indians that a Redcoat corps had left Montreal and was headed in his direction, but he was informed by the War Board of the Continental Congress in early June that the move was only a feint by a weak column. The main British Army of the North was being transferred by troop transports to aid Sir William Howe on his drive toward Philadelphia, the report said, so it would be a simple matter for St. Clair to repel the few invaders who approached his palisades.

St. Clair relaxed a trifle, but remained suspicious of the report, and queried General Schuyler about it. The blunt Philip Schuyler was already inundated by troubles of his own. His troops from Connecticut and Massachusetts, along with several small but shrill battalions from Rhode Island, were agitating for his removal from command, and he had good reason to suspect they were being spurred by the ambitous General Gates, who wanted to succeed him. New Englanders in the Congress were blocking Schuyler's own requests for more men, provisions, and munitions, and he wrote to his wife that he was "bound hand and foot by forces of ineptitude."

He could only reply to St. Clair in all honesty that he had received a copy of the Congress' report on British intentions in the area, but that, lacking any specific information, he was unable to verify or deny its authenticity. Not until June 15 did St. Clair finally learn from a captured British espionage agent that Lieutenant-General John Burgoyne and his entire Army of the North were marching south toward Ticonderoga, intending to capture it and make it their own headquarters for a drive that would extend much farther south.

St. Clair raised the alarm, but it was too late to send him the men and supplies he needed. The question was theoretical, to be sure, since food, gunpowder, and boots were unavailable, the Continentals receiving only a trickle and the militia of the various states doing without. It was obvious that the Patriot defenders of Ticonderoga faced a bleak and uncertain future.

The commander of the British Army of the North had better cause to be in high spirits than even he realized. His march south from Canada into upper New York was progressing smoothly, the weather was fair, and the forest was pleasant beyond his imagination. The artillery and the carts of his long baggage train passed over hard ground, and only rarely did one of the big guns become mired in mud. The few Canadian members of the expedition proved their worth by ranging far afield on hunting expeditions, and returned with deer, elk, bear, and other delicacies, General Burgoyne always being given his choice of cuts. Berries and wild fruits were abundant, and Gentleman Johnny discovered, somewhat to his own surprise, that he quickly developed a taste for the edible roots of the wilderness.

His large tent of double-layered silk was raised for him every night, and he shared his featherbed with the amenable Fanny Loescher, whose husband was earning such a large sum as commissary general for the corps that he chose to look in another direction. There were problems, of course, but they were minor.

Most of the difficulties were caused by the ladies, principally Baroness von Riedesel and Lady Acland, who were outraged by the wanton behavior of Fanny Loescher and wanted nothing to do with her. On several occasions they made excuses rather than dine with her, and Gentleman Johnny quickly realized he was being snubbed, so he put his wilderness house in order.

Thereafter he dined only with invited officers on most occasions, joining the willing Fanny later in the evening. On one or two evenings a week he entertained the ladies of the expedition at his table, but Fanny always found an excuse to absent herself, so direct confrontations were avoided. Burgoyne was enjoying the best of all worlds, and his supplies of wine seemed inexhaustible. His personal orderly had to boil a large quantity of water every evening in order to keep the general's linen spotless, but Gentleman Johnny took such services for granted and did not concern himself with them.

On July 1, with a cloudless sky overhead, the Army of the North embarked on its waiting fleet to cross Lake Champlain. Sir Guy Carleton had provided all of the ships that the far-seeing Burgoyne had requested, and the flotilla that awaited the expedition was impressive. Two frigates, the *Royal George* and the *Inflexible*, acted as escort vessels; the troops were loaded aboard barges, canoes awaited the Indians, and there were pinnaces for each of the senior generals, Burgoyne, Riedesel, and Phillips.

Regimental bands played lively airs, and the ladies raised parasols to protect their fair complexions from the early summer sun.

It was said that Major-General Arthur St. Clair could hear the martial music from the redoubts of Fort Ticonderoga, but that was an exaggeration. His scouts did report to him that a force of seven thousand to eight thousand men, accompanied by the largest artillery train ever seen in North America, was rapidly approaching, and the outnumbered Americans made frantic preparations for the battle they had been told would never take place, a battle that even the most optimistic knew they could not win.

Late in the afternoon the refreshing cruise came to an end, and the Army of the North moved ashore at a spot a few miles above Ticonderoga, where Lake Champlain narrowed to the width of a river. Burgoyne and Phillips made a personal reconnaissance of the area, and the latter became excited over the possibilities presented by Sugar Loaf Hill, an exceptionally steep eminence that rose to a height of six hundred feet. The two defense bastions, Forts Ticonderoga and Independence, located directly opposite the hill on the far side of the lake, were within reach of any cannon of the caliber of twelve pounders and more.

It was astonishing that the hill had not been fortified by the defenders. As a matter of fact, a young American artillery officer, John Trumbull, had demonstrated some months earlier that guns firing from Ticonderoga could reach Sugar Loaf Hill, so it was obvious that the reverse also would be true. But General Horatio Gates, who had witnessed the experiment, had decided that the hill was too steep to fortify, so the defenders had done nothing.

Will Phillips felt otherwise, and his comment became a motto for British artillery: "Where a goat can go a man can go, and where a man can go he can haul up a gun."

Immediate orders were given to fortify the hill, and Burgoyne promptly changed its name to Fort Defiance. The sappers, under the command of a Lieutenant Twiss, began to hack out a road up the side of the hill, and General Phillips personally supervised the entire operation. Work began at dawn each day and continued until long after sundown, with Phillips driving the sappers and artillerymen until they were too exhausted to stand. A crude road was built, and the cannon were hauled up to a point just behind the crest by slinging ropes around stands of oak and hoisting the guns from tree to tree. The task was completed on the evening of July 5.

That night General St. Clair and his senior officers held a council of war inside Fort Ticonderoga in an atmosphere of unrelieved gloom. The garrison had been augmented by the arrival of approximately nine hundred militiamen, but they had brought no food with them, which meant the garrison would be unable to withstand a prolonged siege. Even worse, the enlistments of the militiamen were due to expire within a few days, and these part-time soldiers made it clear they intended to go home the moment they reverted to a civilian status.

British guns could pound the log forts into kindling, and General St. Clair decided it would be the better part of wisdom to withdraw, saving his wilderness-toughened garrison of two thousand to fight again on a later date. His officers agreed, and Ticonderoga was evacuated early on the morning of July 6 without the firing of a single shot by either side.

Burgoyne entered the Gibraltar of North America in triumph, and as soon as the Union Jack was raised he sent off a hastily written note to inform London of his spectacular victory.

Both sides were aware of the significance of the victory. The British had been brooding over the loss of the fort, and its recapture was a moral as well as a military triumph. It was said that when the news reached London on August 22, George III ran into the Queen's sitting room shouting, "I have beat them! I have beat all the Americans!"

Lord Derby was summoned to Whitehall and was informed that His Majesty was pleased to offer the Order of the Bath to General Burgoyne. But Gentleman Johnny, who had previously indicated a reluctance to accept the honor, had anticipated the offer, and Lord Derby made it plain to the bewildered monarch that his uncle by marriage had no intention of accepting. The story quickly made the rounds of aristocratic London, and it was rumored that Burgoyne was waiting until he ended the war with an even greater victory, at which time it would be impossible for the Crown to offer him anything less than a viscountcy.

Lord North announced the capture of Ticonderoga to a cheering joint session of both Houses of Parliament, and Gentleman Johnny was the hero of the day. Bonfires were lighted throughout Great Britain, and Ethan Allen, who was being held as a prisoner of war in England, broke down and wept.

Alarm and dismay swept the United States when it was learned that Ticonderoga had fallen. There were demands for the court-martial of both St. Clair and Schuyler, but neither was actually brought to trial. General Schuyler, who was blameless, shared the bewilderment of his fellow citizens, writing to the New York Council of Safety, "What could induce General St. Clair and the general officers with him to evacuate Ticonderoga, God only knows."

Even General Washington, who had grown accustomed to taking bad news in his stride, was badly shaken by the loss, and said in a letter to Schuyler, "It is an event of chagrin and surprise, not apprehended nor within the compass of my reasoning: this stroke is severe indeed, and has distressed us much."

St. Clair's only defense was brief. Refusing to discuss the details of his reasons for evacuating Ticonderoga for fear the American public would become too discouraged, he merely said, "We have lost a post but saved a province."

Events were to prove him right, but military historians have continued to debate the matter for the better part of two hundred years. Arthur St. Clair's detractors have argued that had he endured a siege of any duration the Americans might have been able to rally a force sufficiently large to send the British Army of the North reeling back to Canada in disarray.

It appears that Burgoyne himself was inclined to share this opinion. He had enjoyed a rare stroke of good fortune, he knew, and his assessment of the military situation was shrewd. He was becoming familiar with the wilderness, and the deeper he penetrated into the interior of the rebel domain the more complex his task became. He neither anticipated an easy, ultimate victory nor placed undue emphasis on what he had already accomplished.

In a letter to Lord Derby, a portion of which was later reprinted in London's *Gentleman's Magazine*, Burgoyne was candid in his analysis of the wilderness as a theater of war:

The American woods have in some places a great deal of underwood, in other parts none at all. The difficulties of making roads in such situations may be reduced to three. First, the trees in general, in their natural state, are very close to each other. In the second place, fallen trees lying in all directions, some sound, blown down by winds, others in a rotting state, are as plenty as lamp posts upon a highway about London, and frequently as thick as the lamps upon Westminster Bridge; these being irremoveable, and almost innumerable, the road is continually upon the turn to one side or the other, to get clear of them. In the third place, about every two or three miles, probably, there is a bridge to be made, twenty, thirty or forty feet high, and twice or three times as long, over a creek, or rather a great gutter, between two hills, and the avenues, when the ground is very high, want levelling. The sum of the perplexities must be charged to the account of the swamps.

The ensuing difficulties in keeping open a direct lane for the bringing forward of supplies, provisions and munitions of war tax the ingenuity of even those long accustomed to warfare in these woods. The enemy move about with greater freedom, it being their custom for every man to carry his own supplies of food, gunpowder and the like. But a civilized army, long and habitually acclimated to a far different method of waging war, cannot enjoy a similar freedom of movement, being encumbered with gear of all kinds and the necessities of sustaining life that a more salubriously civilized life has impressed upon them.

Had I known, before setting out on this enterprise, the many difficulties I would encounter in freely moving forward my artillery and munitions, I would have been reluctant to engage so great a train of artillery. But, it being impossible to dislodge the rebels from the woods without these pieces, the commander of any British army which maneuvers in this wooded area faces this same dilemma. It can be resolved only by pressing forward with the greatest of diligence, circumventing and overcoming the perplexities caused by the woods, and, by giving the enemy no opportunity to gather his opposing forces in strength equal to that of the attacking corps, to achieve the eventual victory which honour and the justice of one's cause demand.

It appears that although Gentleman Johnny was suffering doubts caused by second thoughts, his resolution did not waver, and he remained convinced that he would triumph.

Sixteen

The immediate aftermath of the American loss of Ticonderoga offered no cause for rejoicing in the British camp, and General Burgoyne began to realize that his problems were even more complex than he had anticipated. He sent Brigadier Simon Fraser, commanding the light infantry, and Major-General Baron von Riedesel, in command of his mercenaries, in pursuit of the retreating Americans, a standard procedure which any competent army chieftain would have ordered. His directions were simple: pursue and destroy the enemy, he declared, and showing a preference for the bayonet in close combat, he added, "The onset of Bayonets in the hands of the Valiant is irresistible."

Fraser wasted no time, and caught up with the American rear guard near the village of Hubbardton, where the retreating

Patriots turned and gave as good as they received. The British were outnumbered, but in spite of their unfamiliarity with wilderness fighting techniques they held their own. Lord Balcarres led a charmed life throughout the engagement, and more than thirty Patriot bullets passed through his uniform, but he suffered no injury worse than a slight graze on one hip.

The absence of the mercenaries made it impossible for the British to achieve a decisive victory. Baron von Riedesel had moved forward with Brigadier Fraser's vanguard, but he and his personal aides-de-camp were the only Germans on the scene. Von Riedesel rode back and forth, cursing in a fluent, unending stream, but his Brunswickers and Hessians did not appear until more than two hours after the start of the engagement.

They could be heard long before they were seen. Not only did they make a "great noise," as Fraser said in his report, crashing through the forest in their cumbersome uniforms, but they were singing Lutheran hymns at the top of their voices.

St. Clair's corps was duly warned that British reinforcements were coming, and broke off the fighting. The Americans resumed their retreat, and Fraser, by now realizing that the mercenaries were useless in this type of warfare, gave up the pursuit. Neither side actually won the battle, but the Americans managed to escape after suffering only light losses, so General Burgoyne interpreted the affair as an enemy victory. Baron von Riedesel was mortified, but knew it was impossible to find lighter uniforms, footgear, and back-packs for his men.

During this engagement Burgoyne himself won another bloodless victory at a place called Skenesborough by its sole resident. A former major in the British Army, one Philip Skene, appeared at Ticonderoga and offered the commanding general his "help." The proprietor of a vast tract of land on lakes Champlain and George, Skene had built himself a handsome fieldstone house, the only dwelling in what he liked to call Skenesborough. He had been forced to evacuate it because of his Loyalist sympathies when the Americans had captured Ticonderoga, and it had been occupied since that time by a small American garrison. Now was his chance to regain possession of his property, and the innocent Gentleman Johnny was happy to oblige.

The general crossed the lake himself at the head of a double brigade, and the Americans, who saw the Redcoats coming, promptly left the place. Skene accomplished his end with such ease that he sought the help of the British in a far more ambitious project. His property was cut off from Albany by the wilderness, but a road that cut through the deep woods would enhance its value, and he pursuaded Burgoyne to build such a road from Skenesborough to Fort Edward, which lay twenty miles to the east.

General Burgoyne's agreement to construct such a road on his own route to Albany has been called his single greatest error in the entire campaign. Even by the most charitable standards he was inexplicably foolish. The Americans had already built a good road on the western side of Lake George, and the fleet of small boats and transports that had carried the Army of the North down Lake Champlain could have been used again for simple, expeditious transport. But Gentleman Johnny trusted Skene; after all, the man was an obvious gentleman, having risen to the rank of major in His Majesty's service. So it did not occur to Gentleman Johnny that he was being duped by a clever operator, and he ordered the road built.

A relatively minor incident should have set off alarm bells in the mind of the commanding general. The skirmish at Hubbardton was still fresh in his mind, and was followed by another incident of the same sort. The Americans still held a tiny frontier outpost called Fort Anne, off to the east, and the 9th Regiment of British regulars was sent to capture it and destroy the garrison. The Redcoats fought gallantly, but the outnumbered Americans were not only courageous but wise in the ways of the forest. When it became apparent that they were outnumbered they set fire to Fort Anne, then slipped away to join their comrades at Fort Edward, and the British captured only the ashes of the burned log fort.

Burgoyne had not yet realized that speed was essential to victory in the wilderness. Having achieved one victory at virtually no cost, he should have pursued the Americans to Fort Edward, then struck again, incapacitating them before they had the opportunity to regroup, find reinforcements, and gain new strength. Not until much later did it occur to him that Arthur St. Clair had been right, and that victory, in the European sense, was meaningless in the vast reaches of a semi-explored continent. Although the Americans themselves did not know it, they were experts in the art of what would come to be known two centuries later as guerrilla warfare.

The building of the new road was an almost impossible task, and the light infantry, the grenadiers, and the artillerymen joined the sappers in cutting down trees, constructing bridges, and clearing the wilderness. General Schuyler added to the discomfort of the invaders by sending a force of about one thousand men experienced in forest lore to fell trees across the rough trail that already existed and to destroy bridges.

The sweating Redcoats battled through the forests, made their way through mosquito-infested swamps and struggled across swift-flowing rivers. Every step was a nightmare, and soldiers who knew what to do in close-order drill and in combat proved useless when wielding an ax. The previously maligned Canadians again came to the rescue, and Burgoyne was astonished when he saw that one Canadian could cut down more trees in a single day's work than eight British soldiers. No one counted the score of the Brunswickers and Hessians, and the Indians, obviously thinking the white men insane, went off into the forest and quietly drank themselves into insensibility.

The unseen Americans who were creating new problems ahead may have been responsible for an ailment that sent mercenaries by the score to the hospital, from which less than fifty per cent emerged alive. It was dawning on the Germans that they would not be able to win battlefield victories in the style to which they had been accustomed for centuries. They could hear Americans chopping down trees in the distance, creating new obstacles, but no advance patrols ever caught sight of the elusive Patriots. The omnipresence of the forest itself was oppressing, and Baron von Riedesel's troops became the victims of what their perplexed commander called "the homesickness fever."

The symptoms were always the same. For two or three days a man became increasingly morose, unable to eat or sleep, and eventually he collapsed. Removed by stretcher to the hospital at Ticonderoga, he was placed in the care of physicians and surgeons who could find nothing wrong with him. Yet, in a majority of cases, the victim died within a week, never showing any physical signs of distress, never running a temperature, never making a specific complaint. The alarmed Baron von Riedesel would have taken his men home had he not signed a contract with George III —and had there been transportation available for his ailing men. He estimated that he lost almost fifteen per cent of his fighting strength in less than a month, and the end was not yet in sight.

General Burgoyne was becoming perturbed, and his Indians were contributing nothing to his peace of mind. His officers were bringing him rumors that the Indians were ignoring his instructions and were killing and scalping settlers who lived in isolated farmhouses. He remonstrated in vain with their leaders, having previously convinced himself that Americans by the hundreds, perhaps thousands, would flock to his liberating banner. That they failed to respond to his presence in the neighborhood could be the fault of no one but the braves, who continued to steal liquor from the regimental supplies, no matter how large the sentry parties that guarded the rum.

On July 11 the commander of the Army of the North discussed the matter frankly in a report to Lord George Germain:

> Your Lordship will have observed I have made no mention of the Indians in the pursuit from Ticonderoga. It is not possible to draw them in many respects from the plunder of that place, and I confidentially acknowledge this is not the only instance in which I have found them little more than a name. If, under the management of their conductors, they are indulged, for interested reasons, in all the caprices and humours of spoiled children, like them they grow more

unreasonable and importunate upon every new favour;
were they left to themselves, enormities too horrid to
think of would ensue; guilty and innocent, women and
infants, would be a common prey.

Burgoyne could not resist the opportunity, in the same
communication, to throw a barb at Germain, whose orders had
tied him and held him to a single permissible course of action:

> Your Lordship will pardon me if I a little lament
> that my orders do not give the latitude I ventured to
> propose in my original project for the campaign, to
> make a real effort instead of a feint upon New England.
> As things have turned out, were I at liberty to march
> in force immediately by my left, instead of to my right,
> I should have little doubt of subduing before winter
> the province where the rebellion originated.

July 11 appears to have been a day when Gentleman Johnny
busied himself with letter-writing, perhaps finding it fatiguing
to watch his troops laboriously chop down trees. On that date
he sent a communication to Sir Guy Carleton, asking the governor-general to send one thousand Canadians to supply a garrison force at Ticonderoga. Apparently this question had not
been settled before Burgoyne's departure from Quebec.

But Carleton discovered he was in no position to honor the
request, as he could not find any volunteers for the purpose. This
forced Burgoyne to leave more than nine hundred of his own
effectives behind, and he admitted that this reduction of his own
combat wing made his situation "a little difficult."

It was at this time that the tragic scandal of Miss Jane or
Jenny McCrae shook the Army of the North, causing violent
repercussions throughout the United States and England. Miss
McCrae was engaged to marry a Loyalist officer serving under
Burgoyne, a Lieutenant David Jones, and as she lived only a
short distance from Skenesborough, Jones planned to bring
her to headquarters so he could present her to the commanding
general.

Before he could go off to fetch her, however, two intoxicated warriors went to the McCrae home, and one of them returned to camp waving the scalp and long, blonde hair of the girl he had murdered. Young Jones had to be restrained by his superiors, who, regardless of the justice of the officer's reprisals, did not want to start a war with the Indians. The brave escaped into the forest, still carrying the girl's scalp-lock, and it was impossible for Burgoyne to catch him.

A thrill of horror spread through the United States, and Major-General Horatio Gates took it upon himself to chastise the British commander-in-chief. Writing in a hand larger and bolder than usual and thoughtfully making copies for the American press, Gates was unsparing in his heavy-handed sarcasm:

> That the savages of America should in their warfare mangle and scalp the unhappy prisoners who fall into their hands is neither new nor extraordinary; but that the famous Lieutenant-General Burgoyne, in whom the fine gentleman is united with the soldier and the scholar, should hire the savages of America to scalp Europeans and the descendants of Europeans, nay more, that he should pay a price for each scalp so barbarously taken, is more than will be believed in England until authenticated facts shall in every gazette convince mankind of the truth of this horrid tale.
>
> Miss McCrae, a young lady lovely to the sight, of virtuous character and amiable disposition, engaged to be married to an officer of your army, was with the other women and children taken out of a house near Fort Edward, carried into the woods, and there scalped and mangled in the most shocking manner. . . . The miserable fate of Miss McCrae was partly aggravated by her being dressed to receive her promised husband; but met her murderers employed by you.

Burgoyne was already deeply distressed by the tragedy, and his anger was exacerbated by his realization that he could do nothing to right a grievous wrong. The receipt of Gates' letter, which was delivered to him under a flag of truce, aroused him to even greater heights of fury, and he replied to the American commander, his former subordinate, in one of the most pompous and scornful communications he ever wrote:

> I condescend to inform you that I would not be conscious of the acts you presume to impute to me for the whole continent of America, though the wealth of the worlds were in its bowels and a paradise on its surface.
>
> Respecting Miss McCrae, her fall wanted not the tragic display you have laboured to give it, to make it as sincerely abhorred and lamented by me, as it can possibly be by the tenderest of her friends. The fact was no premeditated barbarity, on the contrary two chiefs who had brought her off for the purpose of security, not of violence to her person, disputed who should be her guard, and in a fit of savage passion in the one from whose hands she was snatched, the unhappy woman became the victim.
>
> Upon the first intelligence of the events, I obliged the Indians to deliver the murderer into my hands, in absentia, he having fled, and though to have punished him by our laws and principles of justice would have been perhaps unprecedented, he certainly would have suffered an ignominious death, had I not been convinced by circumstances and observation beyond the possibility of a doubt, that a pardon under the terms I prescribed and they accepted, would be more efficacious than an execution to prevent similar mischiefs.

The fate of Jane McCrae created as great a furor in England as it did in America, and in 1779 a special committee of the House of Commons investigated the tragedy. Burgoyne was exonerated without qualification, thanks to the testimony given by the young Earl of Harrington, who had served with the Army of the North as a Captain in the 29th Foot. He said that when the news of the murder was received at headquarters, General Burgoyne had gone at once to the Indian camp, threatened the killer with death and insisted that he be delivered without delay to the British. When informed he had escaped, Burgoyne had remained adamant and had demanded that his fellow warriors find, capture, and return him.

There were many officers, Harrington declared, "and I own I was one of the number, who feared he would put that threat into execution. Motives of policy, I believe, alone prevented him from it. And if he had not pardoned the man, which he did, I believe the total defection of the Indians would have ensued, and the consequences, on their return through Canada, might have been dreadful, not to speak of the weight they would have thrown into the opposite scale, had they gone over to the enemy, which I rather imagine would have been the case."

If the Jane McCrae affair blackened Gentleman Johnny's good name for a time, the Battle of Bennington virtually destroyed it, and there were many Americans who, for the next quarter of a century, spoke of him only in harsh terms. There were two villains, the ubiquitous Skene and Lieutenant-Colonel Friedrich Baume of von Riedesel's command. The disaster they concocted followed close on the heels of other grave troubles.

The building of "Burgoyne's nightmare," as the troops called the new road, seemed to last an eternity. The actual construction task took twenty days, the corps progressing at a snail's pace of one mile per day. When they finally reached Fort Edward they discovered that the nimble General Schuyler had a new surprise in store for them: the Americans had vanished again.

Although Gentleman Johnny did not yet know it, the Patriots were buying precious time through their employment of tactics that a man trained in European warfare could not visualize. While Burgoyne plowed deeper into American territory the enemy not only refused to come to grips with him, but General Washington had the opportunity to scour the new United States for troops to meet the threat, and already men were marching in small numbers, by platoons, companies, and occasionally battalions to join generals Gates and Arnold, who were still supported by the loyal General Schuyler, even though he had been supplanted.

On the morning of August 3, while General Burgoyne and his men were resting for a few days at newly captured Fort Edward, a messenger who had spent many days on the road avoiding rebel patrols arrived with a letter for the commander-in-chief from his friend and colleague, Sir William Howe. After extending his warm felicitations for the capture of Ticonderoga, Howe revealed his own plans:

> My intention is for Pennsylvania, where I expect to meet Washington, but if he goes to the northward and you can keep him at bay, be assured I shall soon be after him to relieve you. After your arrival at Albany, the movements of the enemy will guide yours.
>
> Success be ever with you.

The brief letter turned Lieutenant-General John Burgoyne's whole world upside down, and he could scarcely believe the contents. *"My intention is for Pennsylvania."* Had the letter not been written in Howe's tiny, easily identifiable hand, Gentleman Johnny would have suspected that he was the intended victim of a gigantic hoax perpetrated by the enemy.

It was inconceivable to him that Howe was deliberately ignoring Lord Germain's instructions and placing the entire campaign-to-end-the-war in jeopardy. It was equally beyond credence that the entire master plan of operations could have been changed so drastically without his knowledge.

Burgoyne sent off letters to Germain and Sir Guy Carleton, urgently demanding an explanation. But he was in no position to sit for three months in the middle of the North American wilderness awaiting word from London. Unless he called off his march and returned to Canada without delay, a course of action so dishonorable that he could not even consider it, something had to be done.

He was in dire need of gunpowder, food, and transport. The artillerymen were weary, bone-tired after hauling his one hundred and thirty-eight cannon so far. Von Riedesel's dragoons were disgruntled because they had no mounts and were reduced to the status of mere light infantry.

And the Army of the North desperately required reinforcements. In addition to the nine hundred men who had been left behind at Ticonderoga, it would be essential to staff a garrison at Fort Edward. The main body was dwindling, and Burgoyne needed no one to tell him that he weakened himself each time he left some of his men behind.

He not only had to act, but the preservation of the Army of the North made it mandatory that he act without delay.

Seventeen

In spite of the blow that destroyed John Burgoyne's plan to end the American Revolution with a devastating victory, it did not cross his mind to deviate from his orders. He was a professional soldier, and for all he knew the War Office and Colonial Ministry had evolved a new scheme, perhaps a refinement of his own strategy, and would inform him of it in due course. He had been directed by Lord George Germain to march to Albany and capture the city, so march to Albany he would.

Spies and scouts informed him that the rebels were gathering near a village called Stillwater, twenty miles away from Fort Edward, on the west bank of the Hudson's headwaters. So Burgoyne made up his mind to smash them there, then go on in triumph to Albany itself. After all, Colonel Barry St. Leger would be joining him at any time now with his wilderness-hardened corps, so it should not prove too difficult to take Albany—provided horses, food, and gunpowder could be found somewhere in this Godforsaken land of endless forests.

Burgoyne's "good friend," Philip Skene, whom Gentleman Johnny eventually would call his "evil genius," was as helpful as ever. Dining with the commander-in-chief on venison soaked in burgundy, Skene had all the answeres at his facile fingertips. To his positive knowledge, he said, the rebels had been accumulating vast quantities of food and military stores at two small towns in the Vermont District of New Hampshire, Bennington, and Manchester. The farmers of the area, all Loyalists at heart, had many horses they would gladly sell to His Majesty's lieutenant-general commanding the Army of the North. And best of all, the people of the District were confirmed monarchists, ready to participate in the march to victory, so it was possible, even probable, that hundreds of volunteers who knew the wilderness well would gladly join the colors.

Too little is known about Philip Skene to speculate on his possible motives in weaving his fanciful tale. Posterity must assume, for want of other evidence, that he was somewhat simple-minded, as well as crafty when it came to looking after his own interests, and that he hoped to ingratiate himself with Burgoyne by telling Gentleman Johnny what he wanted to hear. There is no evidence available even hinting at the possibility that Skene was a secret agent in the employ of the Patriots, even though the services he inadvertantly performed for their cause were worth several divisions of troops.

There was literally no truth whatever in Skene's assertions. No food supplies or gunpowder had been stored at either Bennington or Manchester; the hard-working farmers who were trying to coax a living out of unfriendly soil owned few horses and certainly had none to spare. Above all, it was unlikely that more than an inconspicuous handful of Loyalists could be found living in Vermont, the home of Ethan Allen and his fiercely independent Green Mountain Boys. Few Americans had shown greater unanimity in supporting the cause of American liberty than the residents of the Vermont District, whose favorite toast as they drank their home-made ale was, "Damn King George and may he hang."

But Colonel Baume knew none of this, and neither did Skene, who was endowed with an unlimited ability to delude himself. Baume was the least imaginative of the German officers, a stolid, humorless martinet who demanded unquestioning obedience from his subordinates. Among his other less attractive traits was his difficulty in distinguishing between the Anglo-Saxon and German methods of dealing with civilians caught in the backwash of war. The Americans and British believed in the principle that noncombatants should be treated with consideration and never abused; there were violations of the theory on both sides throughout the American Revolution, to be sure, hot-headed young men sometimes forgetting what they had been taught all their lives.

But no such niceties cluttered the limited mind of Friedrich Baume. Helpless peasants in Poland, Bavaria, and Latvia had known the terror wrought by his rampaging mercenaries, and Baume agreed with the members of his command. Friendly civilians were robbed and abused, but rarely beaten, while those whose sympathies lay with the enemy could expect murder, looting, rape, and the torch. The obstacles would have been difficult for any competent officer, and Baume was less than competent.

Immediately prior to Baume's departure with about five hundred men, most of them Germans, Skene suggested to the commanding general that these military ambassadors-of-good-will concentrate their efforts on Bennington and its environs, as they might waste too much time if they went to Manchester, too. Burgoyne approved of the idea, and in the hearing of a dozen or more British officers verbally altered Baume's orders. When the intrepid colonel indicated that he understood, Burgoyne took pains to remind him that the operation was being conducted in America, not the far reaches of Silesia, and that the column would do far more harm than good if civilians were mistreated. Baume's assent indicated, falsely, that the words of the commanding general had penetrated his consciousness, and off he went, escorted by Skene, who had a few scores of his own to settle with the Americans who had occupied his home and caused him untold inconveniences.

A snail might have marched more rapidly than Baume, but no snail was hampered as were the mercenaries. Each man carried a heavy musket, sixty rounds of ammunition, a hatchet, a cumberstome water canteen, a knapsack, and a haversack, this equipment weighing approximately seventy-five pounds. He also carried a broadsword weighing twelve pounds and an eight-pound container of flour, so he could make his own bread. His metal helmet, from which decorative feathers protruded, was said to weigh an incredible forty-eight pounds, and beneath it he wore a wig, which cushioned his head. His boots were enormous and came above his knees, his breeches were fashioned of stiff leather, and he was also required to wear awkward gauntlet gloves. It is surprising that he could march anywhere in the wilderness during the heat of summer, and it need only be added that the Americans fought in their buckskin shirtsleeves.

The Patriots also had another advantage: every frontier settler was faithful to the cause, and warning after warning was sent to the rear, notifying General Schuyler, who was still in charge of the area's defenses, that the enemy was moving forward. Baume made certain he advertised his slow advance by stupidly disobeying orders. His men stole provisions from every farmhouse, killed the settlers who protested, and raped the women. A tidal wave of outrage and horror rolled across New York and Vermont as Baume crept toward Bennington.

The Patriots were organizing to meet Burgoyne's advance, and the troops nearest to Baume's dismounted grenadiers were several regiments of militia, about two thousand men in all, commanded by Brigadier-General John Stark. As it happened, these were no ordinary militiamen, and John Stark was no run-of-the-mill commander. Previously passed over for promotion, Stark had very stubbornly gone home and remained there until the Continental Congress had seen the light and made him a general officer. His men, virtually all of them from New Hampshire, the Vermont District, and western Massachusetts, were farmers with previous military experience in the conflict. Baume's raids were being conducted against their friends, neighbors, and relatives, so they had a personal stake in the matter of teaching the mercenaries a lesson.

Stark had been ordered by General Schuyler to take up a position on the east bank of the Hudson, so it was an easy matter for him to double back across the New York-Vermont border and go in search of the marauders.

Friedrich Baume and his dragoons were not difficult to find. The column had been accompanied by a party of about fifty Indian warriors, and the braves, having found the supplies of rum being carried to offer solace to professional soldiers in the wilderness, had gone completely out of control. Not only were they slaughtering farmers' cattle so they could steal cowbells, but they were even making off with the horses of the mercenary officers.

Wearily plodding forward, his heavily encumbered men dragging four-pounder cannon behind them, Colonel Baume caught sight of a large number of farmers at the far end of a clearing directly ahead. These were friends who had come to offer their services, the foolish Philip Skene declared, so Baume stood in his saddle and waved in his most cordial manner.

The farmers astonished him by firing a salvo at his vanguard with their long frontier rifles, and their marksmanship was so good that the truth dawned on Baume. These were not Loyalists but enemies who knew their business. Halting without further ado and saving a few choice words for Skene, to be delivered when he had the opportunity, Baume immediately dug in, establishing his command post at the crest of a high hill, and sent a mounted messenger to General Burgoyne, asking for immediate reinforcements.

Baume was so rattled by the rude reception he had received that his message to headquarters was woefully incomplete, and he forgot to mention what was happening to him, who was opposing him, or why he needed aid. Burgoyne obliged by sending forward the German light infantry, commanded by Colonel Breymann. Perhaps Breymann was in no hurry because of the reputed bad blood between him and his colleague, a situation which Burgoyne may or may not have known, or it may be that the delay was caused by the fact that Breymann kept halting to straighten his lines of marching men, no mean feat in the forest. Whatever the reason, the relief column advanced at a pace even slower than Baume's, progressing at a rate of one mile every two hours.

It took Breymann a day and a half, marching without rest, to reach the dismounted dragoons, and the confusion was so great that, as he approached, Baume's four-pounders opened fire on him. This mistake did nothing to heal the breach between the two German lieutenant-colonels.

John Stark, whose force still outnumbered the enemy by about two to one, saw his chance to win a significant victory. According to legend he sent his men into battle with the stirring cry, "There are the Redcoats and Tories! Conquer them, or tonight Molly Stark will be a widow!" Someone erred in repeating the story, as Mrs. Stark's name was Bessie, not Molly, but the tale deserves mention.

Regardless of Mrs. Stark's Christian name, her husband's militiamen responded to the challenge. Rain had fallen for more than twenty-four hours, hampering both sides as well as contributing to Breymann's delay, but the sky cleared early on the morning of August 16, and the militiamen enjoyed what they called a fandango, a word adapted from the Spanish to mean an all-day picnic. A lack of coordination between the two German commanders enabled the Americans to attack Baume simultaneously from the front and rear, decimating his forces. Then Breymann was subjected to the same treatment, and he was himself wounded when he made a gallant but ineffective attempt to rally his troops.

Scores of Germans were wounded, and more than two hundred out of the total force of aproximately one thousand were taken prisoner. The mercenaries, assuming that their frontier foes had adopted the customs of the Indians, fell on their knees when approached by their captors and begged for mercy.

Baume and Breymann were forced to retreat separately,

staggering through the lines of American sharpshooters, and the orderly march quickly gave way to a disorganized rout. So precipitate was the flight of the professionals from Brunswick and Hesse that they left their artillery behind, allowing it to fall into American hands. This abandonment was regarded as a cardinal sin when perpetrated by professionals, and officers who were that inept were usually subjected to courts-martial.

The Indians and Canadians who accompanied the Germans knew better than to fight for a lost cause, and hastily took themselves elsewhere. Baume courageously rallied the remnants of his force, and made a stand until his ammunition was exhausted. He refused to surrender even then, and an American marksman put a bullet into his heart, ending his mortification and allowing him to be remembered as something of a hero.

The entire action lasted two hours, and the laconic Stark, who had seen action with Wolfe at Quebec in the French and Indian War and had participated in the Battle of Bunker Hill, called it the hottest he had ever known. Waxing lyrical with atypical fervor, he said, "Our people behaved with the greatest spirit and bravery imaginable. Had they been Alexanders or Charleses of Sweden they could not have behaved better."

According to John Burgoyne's definition of a gentleman, one who remained gallant in the face of disaster deserved the title, and on those grounds alone he earned the name of Gentleman Johnny. When the remnants of the expedition limped into Fort Edward, with Breymann bringing up the rear on a stretcher, the commander of the Army of the North shook the hand of every survivor and "encouraged him with warm words."

Whether he showed the same cordiality to Philip Skene, who arrived unscathed and full of excuses, is unknown. Burgoyne made no mention of Skene by name in his official report, but left no doubt regarding the identity of the man he regarded as the culprit:

> It appears that Lieutenant-Colonel Baume, not having been able to complete his march undiscovered, was joined at a place called Sancoix Mills, about four miles short of Bennington, by many people professing

themselves to be Loyalists. A provincial gentleman of confidence who had been sent with the detachment, as knowing the country and the character of the inhabitants, was so incautious as to leave at liberty such as took the oath of allegiance.

His credulity and their profligacy caused the first misfortune. Colonel Baume was induced to proceed without sufficient knowledge of the ground. His design was betrayed; the men who had taken the oaths were the first to fire upon him; he was attacked on all sides. He showed great personal courage, but was overpowered by numbers.

Even in defeat Philip Skene was unable to control his unbridled imagination, and Friedrich Baume was no longer alive to correct his tall story. No Americans had pretended to swear allegiance to the Crown and then turn on the mercenaries; the truth was that Skene had assumed the men he saw ahead were friendly farmers, and had been as astonished as Colonel Baume when they had turned out to be Patriot militiamen spoiling for a fight.

General Burgoyne was faced with a number of immediate problems, the most urgent being that of restoring morale, so he issued a general order that was read to every member of the Army of the North. The catastrophe, he said, was in no way due to any want of gallantry or courage on the part of either the officers or men who participated, but to "the credulity of those who managed the department of intelligence and who suffered great numbers of the rebel soldiers to pass and repass and perhaps count the numbers of the detachment, and upon an ill-founded confidence which induced Lieutenant-Colonel Baume to advance too far to have a secure retreat." A secondary cause was Breymann's tardiness in reaching the scene with his reinforcements, but Gentleman Johnny took care to absolve Breymann of any personal blame. The delay was occasioned, he declared, by exceptionally foul weather, impassable roads, and the exhaustion of both men and horses.

In the presence of his men Gentleman Johnny continued

to exude good cheer and confidence in the future, and not even his personal aides saw him show any sign of concern. But he conferred privately for a long time with General Phillips behind the closed flap of his tent, and although there is no record of their conversation, Burgoyne sat down immediately thereafter and sent a confidential letter to Lord George Germain. Dated August 20, it reflects his growing uneasiness.

Fort Stanwix was still holding out, he declared, and he had received no word of Colonel St. Leger's progress; it was obvious he had not yet heard that Barry St. Leger was hurrying back to Canada, chased there by a nonexistent corps of Patriots. The Loyalists, Burgoyne wrote, were not rising in arms and coming to join him, in spite of the predictions freely made by all of the so-called authorities who believed they knew the temper of the American people. A total of no more than four hundred Loyalists had flocked to his banner, many of them unarmed, and of these only about half were reliable; the rest, he was afraid, would vanish if he suffered reverses.

As for the enemy, their tactics were causing him increasing concern:

> Wherever the King's forces point, militia to the amount of three or four thousand assemble in twenty-four hours. They bring with them their subsistence, etc., hence are able to move about with all great speed; the alarm over, they return to their farms. The Hampshire Grants (the Vermont District) in particular, a country unpeopled and almost unknown in the last war, now abounds in the most rebellious and active race of the continent, and hangs like a gathering storm upon my left.

Finally, after discussing all of his other woes, Burgoyne came to the crux of his worry: he had received only one communication from Sir William Howe, who had written the astonishing, numbing news that his "intention is for Pennsylvania." Gentleman Johnny could not get the phrase out of his mind. He added that Sir Henry Clinton remained in New York Town with his garrison of four thousand, and presumably would act as developing circumstances would direct.

No longer able to conceal the news from his own command that the Army of the North would not be meeting Howe, Burgoyne indicated to Germain that he was compelled to reveal the truth to his men. Fully aware that his situation was grave and that he had to modify the high hopes he had entertained for so long, he closed the letter on a somber note:

> No operation, my Lord, has yet been undertaken in my favour: the highlands have not even been threatened. The consequence is that Putnam has detached two brigades to Mr. Gates, who is now strongly posted near the mouth of the Mohawk River, with an army superior to mine in troops of the Congress, and as many militia as he pleases. Had I a latitude in my orders, I should think it my duty to wait, perhaps as far back as Fort Edward, where my communication with Lake George would be perfectly secure, till some events happened to assist my movement forward, but my orders being positive to *"force a junction with Sir William Howe,"* I apprehend that I am not at liberty to remain inactive longer than shall be necessary to collect twenty-five days of provisions and to receive the reinforcements of the additional companies, the German drafts and recruits now (and unfortunately only now) on Lake Champlain.

> The confusions that abound in head quarters other than my own add to the precariousness of the military situation in which I find myself placed, and which daily becomes more severe. Certainly I had not foreseen that, due to no fault in perseverance or honour on my part or that of the diligent officers and men under my command, I would be left to pursue my way through such a vast tract of country and hosts of foes, without any co-operation from New York. Lack-

ing that assistance essential if His Majesty's arms are to triumph in America, I must confess to your Lordship that I do not believe such an overwhelming victory to be within my present grasp."

Fanciful in his playwriting, Burgoyne was a hard-headed realist in his analysis of military affairs. He was short of provisions, and his supply lines were growing longer as he moved south and east; the reinforcements being sent to him from Canada by way of Ticonderoga were few in number as well as inexperienced, and his spies daily brought him word that Horatio Gates' army was growing rapidly. Worst of all, his grand plan for the conquest of America was in a shambles because, for reasons he could not fathom, Sir William Howe had no intention of meeting him at Albany. The Army of the North was isolated in a hostile, alien land, and only a miracle wrought by a prodigious feat of arms could save it from destruction.

Eighteen

Lord George Germain may have been myopic as well as lazy, but he could see well enough to read handwriting written in large, clear graffiti on a wall when his own reputation and interests were at stake. Burgoyne's letter indicated that a major catastrophe might be in the offing. Unable to admit that his own negligence was responsible for the presence of Howe's army in Pennsylvania rather than on the Hudson River approach to Albany, the Minister of State sent a memorandum to his deputy in an attempt to clear himself before the storm broke:

> I am sorry to find that Burgoyne's campaign is so totally ruined. The best wish I can form is that he may have returned to Ticonderoga without much loss. His private letter to me, 20th of August, contains nothing material about the affair near Bennington, but what

alarms me most is that he thinks his orders to go to Albany to force a junction with Sir William Howe arè so positive that he must attempt at all events the obeying [of] them.

If a flood of public indignation swept the land following a major defeat of Burgoyne's army, Germain intended to prevent any mud from clinging to his own boots. His evasion was not foolproof, of course, but he was building the dike of his defenses.

Others, in both England and the New World, were equally stunned by the turn of events. William Knox, the number-three man in the Colonial Office, declared, "I am sorry the Canada army will be disappointed in the junction they expect with Sir William Howe, but the more honour for Burgoyne if he does the business without any assistance from New York."

Sir Henry Clinton, Howe's deputy, who remained behind in New York while his superior chased General Washington's ragged army through the thickets of Pennsylvania, was horrified by the turn of events long before he learned that Burgoyne's grand plan had been aborted. A far better soldier than Howe, Clinton wrote to him on several occasions suggesting that he return north to meet Burgoyne. When Howe indolently brushed aside the idea, Clinton sent a messenger north, offering Gentleman Johnny the assistance of his own garrison, saying he would send two thousand of his men to the Hudson rendezvous if Burgoyne wished. By that time, unfortunately for the British cause, it was too late for Clinton's corps to do any good.

No one knew better than Burgoyne himself that his back was pressed against a high, prickly wall. He continued his dogged advance in the last days of August and the first part of September, 1777, in spite of repeated disappointments. The new troops from Canada, only a few hundred in number, proved to be raw recruits who would be useless in combat. The stores at Ticonderoga were inexplicably depleted, and not until much later did Gentleman Johnny learn that light-fingered officers whom he had trusted too much had diverted food and equipment into private channels. So the Army of the North was short of rations, and both ammunition and gunpowder were running low because the corps was harassed by invisible American irregulars as it moved forward. Redcoats and mercenaries fired blindly at adversaries they never saw, and precious munitions trickled away.

Meanwhile General Washington's genius for strategy remained intact. Sensing a possible victory of the first magnitude in the north, the American commander-in-chief depleted his own already weak forces by sending some of his best units to Gates. Among them were such regiments as Dan Morgan's Virginia riflemen, perhaps the best light infantry to take the field on either side in the entire conflict.

On September 13 the Army of the North, a noose tightening around its throat, reached the west bank of the Hudson River. Before daybreak the sappers built a bridge of boats, and Gentleman Johnny crossed to the east side of the river with his vanguard, then established his camp on the heights near the village of Saratoga.

That evening he issued a five-word general order. "The army must not retreat," he said. With those words he crossed the Rubicon as well as the Hudson, committing his forces to a forward advance to Albany, no matter what the cost. The odds against him were high, and Burgoyne has been criticized for being a gambler who hoped to accomplish alone what could not be done in concert with Sir William Howe. Gentleman Johnny knew he was taking a gamble, to be sure, but he was convinced he had no alternative, no matter how great the odds. His orders to proceed to Albany had remained unchanged, and he could be court-martialed, dismissed from the British Army in disgrace if he failed to obey them. What was more, his flaming, ever-present sense of honor made it impossible for him to contemplate changing his course unless and until he received new, specific instructions from London.

Certain elements were still in his favor, and he weighed them with care, discussing them at length with General Phillips, Brigadier Fraser and Baron von Riedesel. According to what

Phillips later wrote to his wife, Burgoyne saw several advantages. Sooner or later, and he thought the day would come soon, he would fight a pitched battle against the main body of the enemy. When that time came the experience of his own regulars and of the mercenaries would stand him in good stead, since even the best of the Americans were relative newcomers to the art and science of making war.

And the artillery that had been hauled all the way from Canada was still intact. Some guns had been emplaced at Ticonderoga, to be sure. Burgoyne had a precious one hundred and twenty-six field pieces, only a few having been lost on the long journey, and as not one of them had as yet been fired, his supplies of ammunition for them were ample. A difficult fight against superior numbers awaited him, but he was sure he could give a good account of himself, and if luck favored him he could win.

Perhaps his greatest single advantage, Gentleman Johnny believed, was the caliber of his principal opponent, Major-General Horatio Gates. Burgoyne knew him well, and held an opinion in which posterity has concurred. Gates, said Gentleman Johnny, "is a fool wise enough to persuade others he is no fool, but that talent does not make him any less a fool."

It was a relief and the best of good fortune to learn that Major-General Philip Schuyler, whom the British had come to respect, had given up the command to Gates, and was now only in charge of the defenses of upper New York State. The one man Burgoyne overlooked in his calculations was Benedict Arnold, but his mistake was natural enough. Inasmuch as Arnold was Gates' deputy, it was assumed that he would follow his superior's orders, and no one could have known that a man of Arnold's talents, ambitions, and temperament could not be held in check by a milksop like Horatio Gates.

The Army of the North was drawing near its ultimate destination, so the ladies accompanying the expedition, who had remained behind at Ticonderoga in July, were brought forward under a strong escort. Burgoyne remembered Jane McCrae, and wanted no repetition of that tragic affair. The column was led by the doughty Baroness Riedesel, her youngest daughter in her arms, the other two clutching her skirts. Lady Acland was in the advanced stages of pregnancy, but showed a remarkably cheerful disposition, as did the thirty to forty other women. Riding apart from the rest was Mrs. Fanny Loescher, who was given quarters of her own and who did not go to the tent of the commanding general until that evening.

She was soon to discover that a significant change had taken place in Gentleman Johnny. He was engaged in a serious business now, and although he would not think of sitting down to a dinner without wine, he had no time for a dalliance enlivened by champagne. Fanny remained for only two days and then took her departure, traveling all the way back to Quebec, by way of Ticonderoga, in the company of armed messengers carrying dispatches and mail. Gentleman Johnny was too preoccupied to see her off, although he gave her a gift of a small diamond brooch the night before she left, and she vanished from his life. Thereafter she took up housekeeping again with Felix Loescher in Quebec, her reputation permanently tarnished by her liaison with Burgoyne, and for the rest of her days she was snubbed by ladies of high station and virtue.

The Battle of Saratoga was actually a series of engagements, two of them major confrontations, the first taking place on September 19, 1777, and variously known as the Battle of Freeman's Farm, the Battle of Bemus' Heights and the Battle of Bemis' (sic) Bluff. The Americans held a strong position, which had been selected by Arnold, who had been joined by other general officers in overcoming the objections posed by Gates, and the camp had then been fortified by Kosciusko. Captain James Wilkinson, who was destined to become, after the turn of the century, almost as notorious a traitor to his country as Benedict Arnold, wrote at length that the Battle of Freeman's Farm was an accident, and that neither of the commanding generals planned to fight when and where they did. Wilkinson was mistaken, and merely should have said that Horatio Gates had not planned to engage in battle.

John Burgoyne knew the time had come to destroy the enemy and push south to Albany, while Benedict Arnold, spoiling for a fight, realized he could win lasting glory if he annihilated the British Army of the North.

The American camp was located four miles from that of the British, and Burgoyne laid out his plan to his principal subordinates at a council of war held the night before the battle. The Army of the North would march at daybreak, with the commanding general himself leading the center. Fraser would be on his left, Riedesel on his right, and Phillips, who would move the artillery forward with all possible speed behind the main body, would join Burgoyne as soon as his duties permitted.

Early the following morning the advance began, and American scouts quickly carried the word to Gates. The American commander wanted to wait behind the earthworks he had erected, and apparently was so sure he would be beaten that he had his baggage wagons packed for a hasty retreat. General Arnold wanted to advance into the open to meet the British, and quarreled so bitterly with Gates that the pair parted on nonspeaking terms. But Gates had his way, and the Americans waited.

Burgoyne fully intended to force the Americans to fight his kind of battle, but it was easier said than done. The British had to advance through woods, and American snipers were busy, but the Redcoats and mercenaries advanced stubbornly, holding their fire, and the main bodies clashed at about two o'clock in the afternoon.

The battle raged for about four hours, and was the single biggest confrontation that had taken place in the entire war, with about sixteen thousand men, in all, taking part. Trying to describe the fight, Lord Digby later wrote, "Such an explosion of fire I never had any idea of before, and the heavy artillery joining in concert like great peals of thunder, assisted by the echoes of the woods, deafened us with their noise."

Horatio Gates followed the British custom of remaining in the rear and giving his orders from a safe place, but John Burgoyne adopted the American system, and recklessly exposing himself to enemy fire, personally led the 20th, 21st and 62nd regiments in charge after charge against the American breastworks. He was taking chances even greater than he knew because Dan Morgan's riflemen, who distinguished themselves throughout the entire action, were on the move constantly, sounding their shrill "turkey calls" and directing their deadliest fire against British officers.

According to a report later made by a British soldier, the conduct of his commanding general on the field was exemplary: "General Burgoyne during this conflict behaved with great personal bravery. He shunned no danger; his presence and conduct animated the troops, for they greatly loved the General. He delivered his orders with precision and coolness and in the heat, danger and fury of the fight maintained the true characteristics of the soldier, a serenity, fortitude and undaunted intrepidity."

Burgoyne was a thinker as well as a fighting man, and the Patriots gave him cause to ponder long and hard, even during the heat of the battle. In almost every direct confrontation of consequence that had been fought in the two years since the war had begun, Americans had retreated, usually in confusion, when they had faced the massed power of British infantry and artillery. But the Patriots at Freeman's Farm were not yielding an inch. John Stark and his tough brigade demonstrated why the Germans had encountered such difficulties at Bennington. Morgan's Virginians were little short of superb, Henry Dearborn and his two regiments proved to be unmoving rocks, and Ebenezer Learned's brigade showed the British that Americans could display stubborn courage under fire, too.

Gentleman Johnny was everywhere, enjoying himself thoroughly, and Colonel Dan Morgan later paid him the highest of compliments, saying, "Burgoyne is either mad or the bravest man I ever saw." Seventeen bullets slashed through Burgoyne's uniform, but failed to draw blood, and he repeatedly showed the cuts and rents to any Redcoats who happened to be nearby, convincing them, as he himself was convinced, that he led a charmed life.

Then, as the commanding general declared in his report of the battle to Lord George Germain, ignoring his own losses of more than five hundred men:

Just as the light closed, the enemy gave ground on all sides, and left us completely masters of the field of battle, with the loss of about five hundred men on their side, and, as supposed, thrice that number wounded.

Totally exhausted Redcoats, Brunswickers, and Hessians dropped to the ground and remained there, unable to move. But the coming of night caused them to rise to their feet without further delay and return to their own lines. Indians, regardless of whether they were nominally serving with the British or the Americans, appeared on the field, and with striking impartiality began to murder and scalp the wounded of both sides who had not yet been removed to safety.

The British believed they had won, but they knew they had merely bought time and that their victory had been expensive. The American army was still intact, in spite of its losses, and the Army of the North had suffered severely, too.

Burgoyne changed into a clean uniform and fresh linen, then sat down to a dinner of beef cutlets and claret with his senior officers. He himself wanted to renew the fight the following morning, but Phillips later declared that Fraser protested, saying the grenadiers and light infantry badly needed a rest.

Gentleman Johnny agreed, probably for reasons other than Brigadier Fraser's persuasiveness. A messenger awaited him when he returned to his headquarters from the field of battle, and handed him a letter, dated September 12, signed by Sir Henry Clinton. Too wise a strategist and too sharp a tactician to lose the opportunity that Sir William Howe continued to ignore, Clinton declared his intention of marching north, capturing the small enemy garrisons that stood between him and Albany, and joining forces with Burgoyne. "I will continue my march northward until we meet, wherever you may be."

Clinton was demonstrating rare courage, too, as he was forced to leave half of his garrison in occupied New York Town, which meant he could march with only two thousand men.

But Gentleman Johnny was overjoyed. He would not only be reinforced by two full divisions of veteran British troops whose presence might give him the added strength he so desperately nedeed, but Clinton would provide a diversion that would drain away some of the Americans still facing him. Experience had taught Gentleman Johnny that the Patriots would rally from their defeat at Freeman's Farm, and that fresh units of Continentals and militia would materialize out of nowhere to compensate, perhaps doubly or trebly, for the losses the Patriots had suffered.

Not only would the Army of the North be given a chance to rest, but Gentleman Johnny's master plan for the conquest of the rebels was being revived, albeit in miniature. Since some hope was better than none, he decided to wait for Clinton.

Nineteen

Sir Henry Clinton, unfairly criticized by a number of military historians for his failure to keep his word to John Burgoyne, did his best with limited manpower and under trying circumstances. He marched north along the Hudson from New York Town, as he had promised, and captured two small Patriot forts, Montgomery and Clinton (named after Governor George Clinton of New York). But he suffered such severe losses in these engagements that it was impossible for him to continue unless he received help from his own superior, Sir William Howe. So he sent off a letter to Howe, requesting immediate aid, and realizing that he himself was vulnerable to an attack by a larger enemy force in the field, he returned to New York to await Howe's answer. Billy Howe was not only a poor correspondent, but was so busily engaged in his campaign against Washington that he did not reply in time to change the surge of history, and even when he finally found the time to scribble a few lines he merely said that he could spare no men.

Meanwhile the situation of the Army of the North was deteriorating. The Indians sensed the direction of the wind and began to take themselves elsewhere in ever-increasing numbers, and the Canadians were discovering that urgent affairs at home required their immediate attention. Daily skirmishes between British and American patrols took their toll, too, and the lists of the wounded grew longer.

As Burgoyne had anticipated, the Patriot strength was increasing. By the beginning of October he estimated that he could rely on no more than five thousand men in combat, while the Americans had almost twice that number. His official dispatch of October 3 reveals the depth of his predicament:

> I have continued to fortify my camp and watch the enemy, whose numbers increase every day. I thought it advisable, this day, to diminish the soldiers' ration in order to lengthen out the provisions, to which measure the army has submitted with the utmost cheerfulness. The difficulties of a retreat to Canada have been clearly forseen, as has the dilemma, should the retreat be effected, of leaving at liberty such an army as General Gates's to operate against Sir William Howe.
>
> This consideration has operated forcibly to determine me to abide events as long as possible, and I have reasoned thus. The expedition I command was evidently meant at first to be *hazarded*. Circumstances might require that it should be *devoted*. A critical junction of Mr. Gates's force with Mr. Washington's might possibly decide the fate of the war; the failure of my junction with Sir Harry Clinton, or the loss of my retreat to Canada, could only be a partial misfortune.

Military logic, then, was compelling Gentleman Johnny to make a stand, even if he was compelled to stand alone. If he pulled out he might be destroyed on a retreat to Canada; even worse, he would leave Gates free to join Washington, and their combined armies would be strong enough to defeat Howe and end the war. By now Burgoyne had learned of Colonel Barry St. Leger's defection, and when he said his own troops might have to be devoted, he meant sacrificed. His one remaining hope of winning the decisive victory he still sought required the immediate, unequivocal commitment of Sir Henry Clinton.

On September 27 he sent an officer-courier with a verbal message to Clinton, and afraid the man might not be able to make his way through the enemy lines, he dispatched another with an identical message the following day. Fearful that the Americans might learn how weak he had become, he did not put these requests on paper. Gentleman Johnny failed to receive Clinton's reply, his messengers being unable to penetrate or circumvent the American positions, but Clinton's report to the War Office, called, "Conversation with Captain Campbell, Sent by General Burgoyne to Me," indicates the gravity of the situation faced by the Army of the North:

> He said he was desired by General Burgoyne to tell me that the General's whole army did not exceed 5,000 men; that the consequences of the battle on the 19th [the Battle of Freeman's Farm] were the loss of between 500 and 600 men; that the enemy were within a mile and a half of him; that he knew not their number for certain, but believed them to be 12,000 or 14,000 men; that there was besides that a considerable body in his rear. That he wished to receive my advice and opinion whether he should attack, or retreat to the lakes; that he had but provisions to the 20th of this month; and that he would not have given up his communications with Ticonderoga, had he not expected a co-operating army at Albany. That he wished to know my positive answer, as soon as possible, whether I could open a communication with Albany, when I should be there, and whether when there keep my

communication with New York; that if he did not hear from me by the 12th instant he should retire.

To which I returned the following answer by Captain Campbell, viz. That not having received any instructions from my commander-in-chief (General Howe) relative to the Northern Army, and being unacquainted even of his intentions concerning the operations of that army, excepting his wishes that they should get to Albany, Sir H. Clinton cannot presume to give any orders or advice to General Burgoyne. General Burgoyne could not suppose that Sir H. Clinton had an idea of penetrating to Albany with the small force he mentioned in his last letter. What he offered in that letter he has now undertaken: cannot by any means promise himself success, but hopes it will be at any rate serviceable to General Burgoyne, as General Burgoyne says in his letter answering the offer that "even the menace of an attack would be of use."

Clinton had tried to be helpful, but sensed what was ahead, and in his communication to London was trying to protect his own flanks. It was becoming increasingly clear to Burgoyne that the Army of the North stood alone, and he knew he would have to fight his way to Albany.

Approximately eight hundred of his men were hospitalized, some with wounds and some with illness, and the farm buildings being used for that purpose were so crowded that many who had been injured caught the ague and other diseases. The dead had been buried in shallow trench-graves, and the stench added to the soldiers' misery. Food rations were increasingly short, and Burgoyne set the example for his men by placing himself and his staff on a Spartan diet. Presumably his own supplies were still ample, but he refused to ask any sacrifice of his troops that he himself was unwilling to make. The ladies were housed in two of the sturdiest farmhouses available, so they suffered no privations, and Baroness von Riedesel set the tone for the group by demonstrating good cheer and confidence.

On October 4 General Burgoyne presided at a council of war attended by Phillips, Riedesel, and Fraser, and various options were discussed. The Baron favored a general retreat to Fort Edward and thereafter to Ticonderoga, where the decimated army could spend the winter, regain its strength and await the arrival of reinforcements from Canada. Fraser was inclined to agree, believing the army was incapable of doing anything else.

Burgoyne vetoed the suggestion on several grounds. The enemy would slash the retreating column to shreds, he said, and there were insufficient supplies at Ticonderoga to last through the winter. And he believed it unlikely that any reinforcements would be forthcoming either from England or from Canada. Experience had taught him to be skeptical.

Phillips refused to express an opinion of his own until he learned the commander's thinking.

General Burgoyne proposed a new plan, as daring as it was radical. He suggested that a tiny force of one hundred men be left to protect the camp and the ladies. The main body would sneak out at night, make a wide detour in order to avoid enemy patrols, and at dawn would attack the Americans in force, from the rear. The element of surprise, combined with a sustained infantry drive which would require maximum artillery support, might win the day.

Riedesel was afraid the army lacked the mobility to succeed in such an effort, principally because it would be difficult in the extreme to move the heavy artillery without the enemy's knowledge. Fraser again supported him, and Burgoyne was reluctant to insist in the face of his immediate subordinates' opposition, so nothing was done.

But inactivity was anathema to Gentleman Johnny. He felt that it would be folly to let his army continue to shrink and become weaker, and was convinced that only a bold stroke in the immediate future would offer him even a remote chance to achieve the victory he still craved, even though he had been abandoned by London and his colleagues in North America.

On the night of October 6 the entire army was served a double ration of rum, a sure sign to the veterans that a fight would follow in the morning. At dawn on October 7 Gentleman Johnny placed himself at the head of a mobile corps of light infantry, supported by ten cannon, and moved forward "to discover whether there were any possible means of forcing a passage should it be necessary to advance."

The Patriots had been keeping a close watch on the British and the movement was reported to Gates, who responded by ordering Morgan's riflemen to harass the enemy. Arnold disagreed, saying the Americans should counter in force, and his argument with Gates became so bitter that the deputy was ordered to return to his tent and remain there under a version of "house arrest."

Burgoyne's advancing infantry met Morgan's foot soldiers, and the final phase of the Battle of Saratoga was joined. Within a short time the entire bodies of both armies were engaged.

What makes the decisive battle astonishing is that Burgoyne, outnumbered three to one, his hungry troops limited in gunpowder and ammunition, came within a hair of winning.

The basic order of battle was simple. Burgoyne himself commanded the center and was flanked on the left by Fraser and on the right by Riedesel. They were supported, of course, by Phillips' artillery.

The Americans countered by giving Gates' own corps the center, minus Gates himself. In fact, the Patriot commander saw virtually no personal action. Morgan's riflemen were the key to the American tactics, but they couldn't be everywhere at once.

Forced to retreat because the British infantry held firm and Phillips' artillery laid down such a heavy barrage, the Americans fell back. They regained their momentum only when rallied by Benedict Arnold. The entire Patriot army surged forward irresistibly, following him across the field. Arnold was wounded, but by then the American drive could not be halted.

Brigadier Fraser was killed by a Patriot bullet in midmorning. Major Acland sustained wounds in both legs and was captured. Sir Francis Clark was seriously injured, dying later in the day, after he, too, was taken prisoner.

When Clark was identified he was taken to Horatio Gates' own tent, and there, with a maidservant in Gates' employ looking after him, he engaged in a debate on techniques of war with the American commander that lasted for hours. The dying Clark performed a greater service than would have been possible had he remained healthy and continued to fight: Gates became so engrossed in the discussion that he literally forgot about the battle still raging a short distance away.

Burgoyne's troops continued to press their advantage, and it appeared as though the Patriots would be pushed back and put to flight, thanks to inadequate leadership. But General Benedict Arnold, who had been pacing up and down outside his tent "like a wild beast," could tolerate the situation no longer. Mounting his horse, he rallied the faltering Continentals and militia, and personally led them in a headlong charge.

It has been said that Burgoyne and Arnold crossed swords at the climax of the battle, but no factual evidence supports this romantic claim. Whether the two generals actually saw each other on the field is debatable.

The drive by superior numbers could not be contained, and Burgoyne, who must have known the end was in sight, ordered a general retreat in the direction of his camp. Arnold pressed his advantage, leading the American infantry in a final lunge, and the outnumbered British and mercenary lines collapsed. In mid-afternoon the Battle of Saratoga, called by Sir Edward Creasy, in 1851, "one of the fifteen decisive battles of the world," ended in a total American victory.

The British had conducted themselves admirably, but the same could not be said of the Brunswickers and Hessians. Colonel Breymann was killed in action, and his men lost their cohesiveness, some units retiring to the British camp, while others, en masse, surrendered to the victors without continuing the fight.

Three bullets had passed through General Burgoyne's hat, others had ripped through his uniform, and his linen was blackened by gunpowder. He retired to his tent to change into a clean uniform so he would be presentable when he tendered his official surrender to the enemy. General Phillips is the authority for the statement that he wept, the only time in his adult life he was known to shed tears other than at the grave of his wife.

Even when suffering this supreme military mortification, however, he remained a gentleman. The woman who had attended Sir Francis Clark in his final hours came to the British with Clark's request, in writing, that she be paid for her services to him. Colonel Money, the British deputy quartermaster general and paymaster, obliged by handing her a wad of worthless paper dollars issued by the Continental Congress.

This fact was reported to General Burgoyne who lost his temper. He had long made it a practice never to reprimand a subordinate in the presence of others, but his nerves were so ragged that he lost control of himself, and had to be restrained. At his insistence Money paid the woman a second time, in British gold.

The account of the events that transpired on October 7 written by Frederica von Riedesel are more colorful than all of the official reports of the battle:

> I had just sat down with my husband in his quarters to breakfast. General Fraser and, I believe, General Burgoyne, were to have lunched with me on that same day. I observed some commotion among the troops. My husband told me there was to be a reconnaissance. On my way to the rear, I met some Indians in their war-paint, armed with guns. I asked where they were going, and they cried out, "War, war!"
>
> This upset me very much. When I got back I heard skirmishing and firing which grew louder and louder until there was a terrible noise. I was more dead than alive.
>
> About 3 o'clock in the afternoon instead of the guests who were to have food with me they brought poor General Fraser upon a litter, mortally wounded. The dining table all ready prepared was taken away

and a bed placed there for the General. I sat in a corner trembling.

The noise got louder and louder and I feared lest they should bring in my husband also wounded. The General said to the surgeon, "Do not hide anything from me. Am I going to die?" The bullet had gone through his bowels, just as in the case of Major Harnage. Unfortunately, the General had had a heavy breakfast, and his bowels were distended so that the bullet, the surgeon said, had not, as with Major Harnage, gone between them but through them.

I heard him often, between his groans, exclaim, "Oh bad ambition! Poor General Burgoyne! Poor Mistress Fraser!"

Prayers were read to him, and he sent a message to General Burgoyne asking that he might be buried on the top of a hill which was a kind of a redoubt.

Burgoyne wrote at length about the funeral of his colleague and friend:

About sun-set the corpse of General Fraser was brought up the hill, attended by the officers who had lived in his family. To arrive at the redoubt, it passed within view of the greater part of both armies. General Phillips, General Riedesel, and myself, who were standing together, were struck with the humility of the procession; they who were ignorant that privacy had been requested might construe it neglect. We could neither endure that reflection nor indeed restrain our natural propensity to pay our last attention to his remains. The incessant cannonade during the solemnity [guns that General Gates ordered fired as a gesture of respect]; the steady attitude and unaltered voice with which the chaplain officiated, though frequently covered with dust, which the shot threw up on all sides of him, the mute but expressive mixture of sensibility and indignation on every countenance; these objects will remain to the last of life upon the minds of every man who was present.

The growing duskiness added to the scenery, and the whole marked a character of that juncture that would make one of the finest subjects for the pencil of a master that the field ever exhibited. To the canvas and to the faithful page of a more important historian, gallant friend! There may thy talents, thy manly virtues, their progress and their period, find due distinction and long may they survive—long after the frail record of my pen shall be forgotten.

Gentleman Johnny, so sensitive that in the hour of his own greatest travail he thought his friend's funeral worthy of recording by an artist, mourned for the death of Brigadier Fraser, for the end of his own high hopes, and for the defeat that marked the beginning of a new era for the United States.

Creasy did not exaggerate when he wrote that Saratoga was one of the most decisive battles in history. Until October 7, 1777, the great powers of Europe did not take the aspirations of the rebellious British colonies seriously, but Saratoga changed all that. France and Spain, the former goaded by Benjamin Franklin, came to the assistance of the infant United States, and their money, supplies, and munitions, as well as the services rendered by the French war fleet, at that time the second most powerful in the world, enabled the new nation to win her independence. Great Britain was deprived of her most valuable overseas possession, and the nucleus of a future super-power came into being.

Saratoga was far more than a battle: the British loss of prestige was incalculable, and the myth that she was invincible was destroyed. Her rigid caste system was weakened, and it is no exaggeration to say that Saratoga, fought at a time when the Industrial Revolution was just beginning, led directly to the great reforms of the 1830s which shook Britain to the core and transformed her society.

According to every rule of politics and war that had been observed for centuries, Lieutenant-General John Burgoyne should have suffered permanent disgrace, even though the negligence and sloth of others were responsible for his defeat. But Gentleman Johnny was an extraordinary man, and it was no accident that he rose again, phoenix-like, from the ashes of Saratoga to create an extraordinary new life for himself, a life that would have won him permanent renown even if he had not been the man who lost America.

Twenty

Horatio Gates may have been incompetent as a general, but he was a gentleman. In the absence of Benedict Arnold, who was removed to the hospital in Albany for the treatment of his battle wounds, Gates not only accepted all of the credit for the great victory achieved by American arms, but did the necessary honors for the vanquished.

Lady Acland insisted on following her husband into captivity in the hope that she would be allowed to stay with him and nurse him back to health. The astounded Burgoyne could not dissuade her, so he wrote her a letter of introduction to General Gates, and she left the British camp on the night of October 7, escorted by a chaplain and her husband's orderly. Gates received her on the morning of the eighth, equally astonished to find the young and pretty daughter of an earl, far advanced in pregnancy, waiting outside his tent before he ate his breakfast. He showed her every courtesy, personally saw to it that she was reunited with Major Acland, and immediately sent off a letter to Burgoyne to tell him she was safe.

The last act of the great drama of Saratoga remained to be played, although it was anticlimactic. On the morning of October 8 Burgoyne wrote again to Gates, expressing his regret at the need to leave his wounded behind and commending them to the care of the Americans. The remaining British and mercenary effectives withdrew to the village of Schuylerville, where the commander of the shattered Army of the North occupied General Philip Schuyler's country house and raided his storage bins.

The American artillery continued to pound the British positions, and Burgoyne's guns answered in kind, although they were rapidly running short of ammunition and powder. The useless exchanges went on for the next five days, and for the final seventy-two hours the British starved, as did their horses. The inevitable end was in sight, but Burgoyne's honor did not permit him to surrender until, in desperation, he summoned a council of war on the night of the twelfth. Major-generals Phillips and Riedesel were in attendance, as was Brevet Brigadier Hamilton, who had replaced the fallen Fraser.

Never had Burgoyne been more of a gentleman. In a brief speech he made it clear that he was accepting full responsibility for any course of action taken, and he emphasized that he was merely asking his principal subordinates for their advice. He asked two questions, the first a query that placed Saratoga in historical perspective: had an army in similar circumstances ever surrendered? The generals replied in the affirmative.

The second question revealed the core of Gentleman Johnny's character: would a surrender be dishonorable, or could it be so construed? A surrender would not be dishonorable, the generals told him, nor could it be so construed.

On the morning of the thirteenth Burgoyne sat down to compose the most difficult letter he had ever written, and addressed it to General Gates. Only Gentleman Johnny could have held his head so high under excruciatingly painful circumstances:

> After having fought you twice, Lieutenant-General Burgoyne has waited for some days, in his present position, determined to try a third conflict against any force you could bring to attack him.
>
> He is apprised of the superiority of your numbers, and the disposition of your troops to impede his supplies, and render his retreat a scene of carnage on both sides. In this situation he is impelled by humanity, and thinks himself justifiable by established principles and precedents of state, and of war, to spare the lives of brave men upon honourable terms. Should Major-General Gates be inclined to treat upon that idea, General Burgoyne would propose a cessation of arms during the time necessary to communicate the preliminary terms by which, in any extremity, he and his army mean to abide.

The letter was delivered under a flag of truce by a Major Kingston of Burgoyne's staff, and while awaiting Gates' reply he chatted with Captain Wilkinson, the American commander's aide. The two young men discussed such matters as the beauty of Hudson River scenery and the extraordinarily lovely colors of leaves, now that the trees were turning.

Gates replied at length, naming his conditions, and Burgoyne objected vehemently to several. In one phrase the American referred to the British line of retreat having been cut, and Gentleman Johnny thundered, "Lieutenant-General Burgoyne's army, however reduced, will never admit that their retreat is cut off, while they have arms in their hands."

Gates devoted one complicated paragraph to the subject of officers' parole, and set terms for parole breakers. His conditions aroused Gentleman Johnny's ire to the breaking point, and he replied, "There being no officers in this army under, or capable of being under, the description of breaking parole, this article needs no answer."

One condition in particular threatened the entire agreement. Gates demanded that the Army of the North ground its arms, and that the men deliver themselves as prisoners of war, who would be marched under guard to Bennington. Burgoyne's sense of honor was violated, and he replied in a cold fury, "This article is inadmissable in any extremity. Sooner than this army will consent to ground their arms in their encampment, they will rush on the enemy determined to take no quarter."

Burgoyne's troops were starving, their munitions were exhausted, and they were almost literally incapable of fighting another battle, but Gentleman Johnny's strong stand was not a complete bluff. His intelligence force was still operating, and he had learned that the great part of Gates' army had already been detached for service elsewhere, so the two forces that still faced each other were more or less equal in size. Some of the problems separating the views of the two commanders were questions of semantics rather than substance, but many exchanges were required before an agreement satisfactory to both was reached. In the main, it was Gates who backed down, even though he still had the strength to destroy the enemy.

It was agreed that the British would march out of their camp and would be accorded full honors of war; the men would stack their arms on the orders of their own officers, who would keep their swords, carriages, horses, and private baggage, none of which would be searched. Free access to travel to England from Boston would be granted to all members of the Army of the North, on the condition that none participated again in the present war. In the event that prisoner exchanges were made prior to the departure of the British, members of the Army of the North could be so exchanged. The Army would march to Boston under the command of its own officers, with food supplies to be furnished by General Gates, and the officers and men would be given adequate quarters in Boston prior to their departure for home. The Canadians were permitted to return to their homes at once. All British officers would be placed on parole in Boston and would be permitted to carry their side arms there. And Burgoyne would be permitted to send sealed letters to Great Britain, to Sir Guy Carleton, and to Sir William Howe.

On the morning of October 17 the British marched out of their camp to surrender, with Burgoyne at the head of the column in his full-dress uniform. Bands of both armies played martial airs, and Horatio Gates awaited the vanquished at the head of his own forces. The two commanders exchanged salutes, and Burgoyne tendered Gates his dress sword, saying, "The fortune of war, General Gates, has made me your prisoner."

Gates, not to be outdone in courtliness, replied, "I shall always be ready to bear testimony that it has not been through any fault of your excellency." Making a great show of the gesture, he returned Burgoyne's dress sword.

The Redcoats and mercenaries stacked their arms, and the ceremonies having been completed, food was delivered to the vanquished. General Gates, meanwhile, entertained the general officers of both armies and their staffs at a banquet that even the fastidious Gentleman Johnny approved. The officers were served ham, goose, beef, and boiled mutton, along with "great platters overflowing with many vegetables." Large quantities of rum and hard cider were consumed, and as there were only two glasses on hand, these were reserved for Burgoyne and Gates. The others drank out of "small basons."

General Gates drank to the health of King George III, General Burgoyne proposed a toast to General Washington, and then every officer present offered a toast of his own. General Phillips' toast was apolitical and bawdy, which caused hearty laughter all around the table. Apparently it was strictly a soldiers' joke, and although those who wrote about the occasion referred to it, none quoted it.

On the seventeenth and eighteenth the Army of the North crossed the Hudson in preparation for the start of the march to Boston. The commissioned officers of both the victors and the vanquished mixed freely, but care was taken to keep the troops apart, the commanders wisely deciding not to run the risk of starting riots.

Baroness von Riedesel graphically describes the spirit that prevailed in the upper echelons:

In the passage through the American camp, I observed with great satisfaction, that no one cast at us scornful glances. On the contrary, they all greeted me, even showing compassion on their countenances at seeing a mother with her little children in such a situation. I confess that I feared to come into the enemy's camp, as the thing was so entirely new to me. When I approached the tents, a handsome man came toward me, took the children out of the wagon, embraced and kissed them, and then with tears in his eyes helped me also to alight. "You tremble," said he to me, "fear nothing." "No," replied I, "for you are so kind, and have been so tender toward my children, that it has inspired me with courage."

He then led me to the tent of General Gates, with whom I found Generals Burgoyne and Phillips, who were on an extremely friendly footing with him. Burgoyne said to me, "You may now dismiss all your apprehensions, for your sufferings are at an end." I answered him that I certainly should be acting very wrongly to have any more anxiety, when our chief had none, and especially when I saw him on such a friendly footing with General Gates. All of our Generals remained to dine with General Gates.

The man who had received me so kindly came up and said to me, "It may be embarrassing to you to dine with all these gentlemen; come now with your children into my tent, where I will give you, it is true, a frugal meal, but one that will be accompanied by the best of wishes."

"You are certainly," answered I, "a husband and a father, since you show me so much kindness."

I then learned that he was the American General Philip Schuyler. He entertained me with excellent smoked tongue, beef-steaks, potatoes, good bread and butter. Never have I more enjoyed a meal. I was content. I saw that all around me were so likewise. But that which rejoiced me more than everything was that my husband was out of all danger. As soon as we had finished, General Schuyler invited me to take up residence at his house, which was situated at Albany, and told me that General Burgoyne would be there also. I sent and asked my husband what I should do. He sent me word to accept the invitation; and as it was two days' journey from where we were, and already 5 o'clock in the afternoon, he advised me to set out in advance, and to stay over night at a place distant about three hours' ride.

Baron von Riedesel arrived with Burgoyne and Phillips to join the Baroness and their children, and the whole party received a hearty welcome from the hospitable Schuyler, his wife and their daughter, who would become the wife of Alexander Hamilton. The hospitality of the Schuylers was bountiful, and when Burgoyne apologized for burning the American's property at Schuylerville, his host replied with a shrug that the fortunes of war had been responsible.

During Burgoyne's stay at Albany he was taken by Schuyler to the hospital to visit his real conqueror, Benedict Arnold, who had suffered a severe leg wound in his last charge. Victor and vanquished entertained great professional respect for each other, and spent about a half-day together. General Schuyler was present for a portion of the time, but left the pair together while he went off to attend to private business.

Burgoyne and Arnold talked at length about the technical aspects of the battle they had fought against each other, and as their later correspondence with others revealed, in the privacy of the American's hospital room they were able to admit they had been the principals in the action at Saratoga, and that Horatio Gates had played a very minor role in the battle. They also discussed European versus American methods of warfare, and finally went on to find agreement on what Burgoyne called "the philosophy of war and the necessity for its avoidance."

The discussion was significant because it absorbed the attention of both the complete professional and the gifted amateur who had known nothing about waging war until his country had started its fight for independence. It was a tribute to the military acumen of Benedict Arnold that he could meet John Burgoyne as an equal.

But it is nonsense to assert, as some of Arnold's critics in the latter part of the eighteenth century claimed, that the seed for his defection to the British was planted during his private meeting with Burgoyne. Not only was Arnold not thinking of treason at that time, but Gentleman Johnny would not have tolerated any such talk. In fact, no one was more shocked than Burgoyne when Arnold tried to sell out the American garrison at West Point.

The two men came face to face again several years after the war, when Arnold was living on the half-pay of a retired British brigadier. They met in a London club, and Gentleman Johnny turned on his heel, stalking off without speaking. An officer who had betrayed his country had broken the soldier's sacred code of honor, and consequently was beyond the pale. Under no circumstances would the rigid sense of honor that Burgoyne accepted as a living principle have permitted him to even hint at the possibility of another's treason.

Certainly the Patriot for whom he felt the greatest respect was Philip Schuyler, whom he regarded as the most underrated general officer on the American side. General Phillips was also impressed by Schuyler, and the trio talked at length about the future of the war. Burgoyne appears to have been one of the first to realize that his defeat at Saratoga would lead to American independence, and he mentioned to Schuyler, in some detail, the possibility that the French would enter the war on the side of the rebels. The opportunity was too great to be ignored, and Gentleman Johnny realized that the French would not be slow to take advantage of the situation.

It is important to an understanding of Burgoyne's character to note that, even at this early date, he felt no personal sense of guilt. He had been defeated by a superior force for the simple reason that his fellow Englishmen had not contributed their share to his campaign. As yet he did not know whether Lord George

Germain or Sir William Howe was to blame, but he liked Howe and had ample cause to dislike and mistrust Germain, so he was inclined to suspect the latter of being at fault, even though he had not yet learned any details.

There can be no question that he believed he had done a first-rate job himself. Brigadier-General John Glover, whose amphibious fishermen-soldiers escorted the defeated Army of the North to Boston, had ample opportunity on the road to discuss every aspect of the catastrophic campaign with Burgoyne, and his correspondence indicates that Gentleman Johnny was convinced he had done everything that might have been expected of him. Glover himself shared that view, as did his superiors. George Washington not only felt sympathy for Burgoyne's plight, but regarded him as the most able and conscientious of the senior British general officers.

Burgoyne had no reason to hang his head. He had been defeated honorably, almost winning the battle in spite of the odds against him. He was wise enough in the ways of politics to know that Germain would try to make him the scapegoat, and, as will be seen, he took extraordinary precautions from the outset, protecting himself from frontal and flanking attacks in the letters he composed and was allowed to dispatch unopened to the men who would play major parts in the determination of his future. He had a strong case, and had no intention of permitting his good name to be blackened.

Twenty-One

Rumors of the Army of the North's defeat at Saratoga reached London about ten days before Burgoyne's official letter of confirmation was received, and the uneasiness spread rapidly. King George cancelled all audiences and public appearances, and went into seclusion at Whitehall, where he brooded behind the locked doors of his private suite. Even Lord North was turned away when he went to the palace on routine business, His Majesty sending word to his First Minister not to return until he could bring definite news of what was happening in America.

The first mention of the subject in Parliament was made in the House of Lords on November 18, when Lord Shelburne set the tone for other addresses to come. "The issue of Mr. Burgoyne's expedition is too melancholy to be made a subject of conversation," he said. "His army, by every appearance, is destroyed." But Shelburne went on to express full confidence in Burgoyne, whom he called one of the "ablest of the King's generals." He reserved his venom for Germain, launching an attack of almost unprecedented ferocity on him. Lord George, he said, was "a man who has so great a confidence in his own military talents as to think he can command an army and ensure a victory in his closet at three thousand miles' distance from the scene of action. His dismal record as a soldier, milords, proves to me that he is the last man in these islands who should have have been placed in the post of ultimate military trust. If we lose the Colonies, as it now appears we may, Germain alone must bear the full burden of blame."

The Duke of Richmond, who followed Shelburne, made an equally contemptuous speech. "Supposing, which is most improbable," he demanded, "that Mr. Burgoyne has got to New York, what has he effected? He has lost several thousand men! But he might have arrived at New York two years ago by sea without any loss at all. If he was directed by Germain to march overland, and it is not within our credence that Mr. Burgoyne would have made such a march without the approval of the Minister, why was another army not sent northward by land to meet him? Where, pray tell, is the army of Mr. Howe? Why is that army languishing elsewhere? And what troops does Mr. Clinton command? Where are they hiding? Perhaps from the enemy? This campaign appears to have been so ill-conceived that its stench offends our nostrils. And now, mark my words, milords, the Ministry will attempt to offer Mr. Burgoyne as a sacrificial lamb to be burned at the high altar of other, lesser men's ambitions!"

Germain made no reply to these assaults, and when questioned in Parliament insisted he would be in no position to discuss the matter until he received definite information regarding the fate of Burgoyne and his Army of the North. That word was received, at long last, by way of Quebec on December 2. Germain tried to soften the blow by coupling the announcement of Burgoyne's defeat with the news that Howe had captured Philadelphia. The Tory back-benchers cheered, but military men on both sides of the aisle were not fooled. Howe's line of communications, stretching from New York to Philadelphia, were too extended to be sustained for any long-term period, and it was inevitable that Philadelphia could not be held permanently while George Washington could still put an army in the field. Therefore Howe had been chasing a military will-o'-the-wisp when he should have coordinated his own activities with Burgoyne's march.

A retired Army colonel named Barré, now a Member of Parliament, opened the barrage in the House of Commons on December 3. "I am shocked," he said, "at the cool, easy manner in which the noble Lord has related the fate of the brave Burgoyne. No man can rightly claim that Mr. Burgoyne has failed through his own misconduct, military neglect or lack of courage. That possibility is too absurd to be borne. He was sent in pursuit of a wild goose, and sent alone! He was the victim of an inconsistent scheme, an impracticable one, unworthy of a British Minister of State, and if the truth be known, rather too absurd for an Indian chief."

The principal barrage was fired by Edmund Burke, and when it was learned that he intended to make an address on the subject on December 4, virtually every member of the Commons was in his seat and the visitors' galleries were filled. King George tried in vain to find out what the great orator intended to say, and Lord North made arrangements for messengers to bring him running accounts of the speech while it was in progress.

Burke minced no words. "Ignorance," he thundered, "stamped every step taken during the course of the expedition, but it was the ignorance of the Minister for the American department, not to be imputed to General Burgoyne, of whose good conduct, bravery and skill I do not entertain the shadow of a doubt." The fact that Burgoyne and Howe were to have met had become general knowledge now, and Burke touched the most sensitive of Germain's nerves when he declared, "The intended measure was a conjunction between Howe and Burgoyne, and it was to be produced in the strangest way I have ever heard. Oh, yes, the armies were to meet! Howe was traveling southward, and Burgoyne in the same direction! The Minister has found a new way for armies to meet, and must be congratulated upon having devised so infinitely clever a scheme!"

Charles James Fox had not been scheduled to make an address, but he leaped to his feet as soon as Burke finished speaking, and was even more contemptuous of Germain. "An army of ten thousand men destroyed through the ignorance, the obstinate, wilful ignorance and incapacity of the noble lord, calls loudly for vengeance," he said. "A gallant General sent like a victim to be slaughtered, where his own skill and personal bravery would have won him laurels, if he had not been under the direction of a blunderer, which circumstance alone was the cause of his disgrace, is too shocking a sight for humanity to bear unmoved. The General was imposed upon and deceived; this House has been imposed upon and deceived! Burgoyne's orders were to make his way to Albany, there to wait the orders of Sir William Howe and cooperate with him. But General Howe could have known nothing of this matter, for he was gone to a different country, and left the unhappy Burgoyne and his troops to make the best terms for themselves! If the Minister pursues the end of American independence, let him make peace terms with the Americans! Let him not sacrifice a great General and his courageous troops! Let him not make of this House and this nation a laughing-stock for the whole world to mock and deride!"

Germain, who had no legitimate defense, continued to maintain his stubborn silence in the face of the mounting criticism, and on December 5 the Earl of Chatham made it clear where his sentiments lay. Rising in the House of Lords, he paid a glowing tribute to "the zeal, courage and talents of General Burgoyne, as splendid a soldier as this once-proud nation has boasted in her long and glorious history." The fault for the defeat at Saratoga and the consequences of that loss had to be laid at the feet of Minister of State Germain, whose "plan of campaign was a most wild, uncombined and uncoordinated, mad project."

Chatham inspired Lord Shelburne to unburden himself again, and he made a speech in which he lashed out at "the Pall Mall planners of the campaign." He made the flat statement that if Burgoyne's instructions were placed before the House they would display "the incapacity of the King's ministers in the most glaring colors."

Germain still refused to rise to the bait, so Shelburne resumed his attack on December 11, saying, "Mr. Burgoyne is directed to march to New York to effect a junction with Mr. Howe. Mr. Howe goes aboard his ships and, after beating to the southward, gets on the other side of Philadelphia. If I do not hear full and sufficient reasons for this extraordinary conduct, I protest I think Mr. Howe would deserve to be brought home in chains. Yet I cannot in good conscience so condemn a man whose conduct throughout his lifetime has been honorable. The fault lies elsewhere. I accuse Lord George Germain, and I demand that he offer this House a full explanation for events too mystifying and disgraceful to be borne in silence."

The defenseless Germain, unable to admit he had totally forgotten to send Howe's orders to him, took temporary refuge behind a barrier of "military necessity." Events still in progress made it impossible for him to speak with candor as he might jeopardize military operations in which the government placed the highest hopes. When he could tell the whole story, he felt sure, even the most implacable of his foes would be forced to agree with the wisdom of the American policy, both political and military. His enemies did not believe his evasions, but he silenced them for the moment.

Meanwhile Gentleman Johnny Burgoyne was taking no unnecessary risks. He wrote a crisp dispatch to Germain in which he related what had happened at Saratoga, and enclosed a copy of the surrender treaty he and Gates had signed. He wrote at some length to generals Howe and Clinton, taking care not to attach any personal blame to either of his colleagues, and he began work on a detailed document covering his entire campaign. This volume, which would run several hundred pages, would form the core of his defense in the House of Commons inquiry that would take place after his return from England.

He also wrote several personal letters before leaving Albany on the march to Boston. One was sent to the young Earl of Derby, and he enclosed a copy of his dispatch to Germain, saying he was sending it "in order that it may be published by you in case that the Ministry should curtail or mangle any part of it in their Gazette." That one sentence summarizes the extent of Burgoyne's trust in his superior.

A second, longer letter went to an Army friend, Colonel Philippson, commander of the Third Dragoon Guards, and in it Burgoyne expressed his true sentiments regarding his defeat. Abandoning politeness, much less diplomacy, he held back nothing, setting the tone in his opening paragraph:

> Ministerial ingratitude will be displayed, as in all countries and at all times it is usual to remove the blame from the orders to the execution.

His defeat had been unavoidable, Burgoyne argued, in part because his orders had allowed him no alternatives. A sergeant who retreated in battle without authorization, claiming he would have been killed had he continued to advance, would be court-martialed and sent before a firing squad. Worse things happened to generals who disobeyed orders, Gentleman Johnny declared: they were made scapegoats for Ministers of State, and their reputations were destroyed for all time.

Until the very end, he wrote Philippson, he continued to hope he could win a victory, but that hope was forlorn because he had no substance on which to base it. Painting a picture as harsh as it was accurate, he wrote:

> This army has been diminished by scandalous desertions in the collateral parts, by the heavy drain of the garrison of Ticonderoga, and by great loss of blood. It has been totally unsupported by Sir William Howe.

His Canadians had shown no liking for combat, his Germans had been so dispirited he had been afraid they might surrender on the field of battle, and his Indians had proved treacherous. Only the courage and the gallant stand of his British regulars had enabled him to fight the Battle of Saratoga with honor. He did not neglect to pay tribute to the enemy, either, saying that the troops the Americans had sent against him were the equal of the best British units that had been sent to North America.

In a letter to Howe, written at Albany and dated October 20, Burgoyne was only a little more circumspect:

> Circumstances of a very melancholy nature, viz. a scandalous defection of the Indians, a desertion or timidity worse than desertion of provincials and Canadians, a very few individuals excepted, and a strong disposition in the Germans to be prisoners rather than endure hard blows . . . it was notorious that they meant to have given one fire and then have clubbed their arms.
>
> I think it not impossible that the persons who are most bound to vindicate me will be the first to attack my reputation; those for whom I cheerfully undertook a forlorn hope, and who would have crushed me had I remained inactive, I expect to find my accusers for rashness. These men know I have it in my power to justify my conduct, and it is a duty to myself and my profession not to be absent when occasion calls upon me to produce that justification.

Burgoyne best expressed his feelings in yet another letter, a simple note that he dashed off the same day to several of his late wife's nieces:

> I have been surrounded with enemies, ill-treated by pretended friends, abandoned by a considerable part of my own army, totally unassisted by Sir William Howe. I have been obliged to deliberate upon the most nice negotiations and political arrangements that required the most undisturbed reflection, and exhausted with laborious days and sixteen almost sleepless nights, without adequate change of clothes or other covering than the sky. I have been with my army within the jaws of famine; shot through my hat and

waistcoat; my nearest friends killed round me; and after these combined misfortunes and escapes I imagine I am reserved to stand a war with ministers who will always lay the blame upon the employed who miscarries.

In all these complicated anxieties, believe me, my dear girls, my heart has a large space filled with you; and I shall bring it home, when God shall so permit, as replete with affections as when I left you.

The march to Boston temporarily caused Burgoyne to forget his more important problems. The weather turned very cold, and the Army of the North, escorted by Glover's brigade, required two days to cross the Green Mountains. Many of the British soldiers were ill, suffering from "camp fever," or dysentery, and an American officer saved their lives by finding and boiling roots, then forcing them to drink the concoction. The best quarters available were reserved for General Burgoyne, but he was worn down by his ordeal, and ague forced him to go to bed for several days in Great Barrington at the house of Colonel Elijah Dwight. But he didn't want his men to think he had deserted them, and rejoined them in time to march into the town of Cambridge, six miles from Boston, at the head of the light infantry formation.

General Glover, a bluff Marblehead fisherman who had almost nothing in common with Gentleman Johnny, found him a delightful traveling companion. There was something of the chameleon in Burgoyne, and when in the company of men who would have felt ill at ease had he behaved like a character in a high comedy of London life, he could behave like the hearty soldier whose chief interests in life were the satisfaction of his physical needs.

What impressed Burgoyne most about the march to Boston, a fact corroborated by Glover in his report to General Gates, was the kindness of the American people toward the conquered Redcoats. Glover's men had been braced for trouble from the outset, fearing that civilians might try to abuse the prisoners, but the reverse proved to be true. Women, old men, and children came out of their homes to offer food to the captured British soldiers, few people jeered, and the officers, Burgoyne himself in particular, were treated with great courtesy.

Boston remembered John Burgoyne, and remembering the Battle of Bunker Hill and the long British occupation of the city, too, was expected to make trouble. But even the "cradle of rebellion" accepted the Army of the North pleasantly, albeit with a trace of true Bostonian reserve. General Glover was relieved when he could turn over responsibility for the prisoners to Major General William Heath, one of the founders of the Massachusetts Bay militia and an intimate friend of John Hancock.

In his *Memoirs* Heath related some of the many problems that rained on his shoulders. He had to find quarters for five thousand prisoners, and ramshackle barracks were built to house the men. Firewood was expensive, and Heath hoped to charge General Burgoyne for it, but Gentleman Johnny was too evasive, referring his captor to the surrender agreement with Gates.

Heath gave an "elegant dinner" for generals Burgoyne, Phillips, and Riedesel, which Glover also attended, and when the people of Boston learned that Gentleman Johnny had actually arrived in town, they filled the streets, hoping to see him. At the end of the dinner Heath offered his distinguished prisoner an escort to his own quarters, but Burgoyne refused. "I have nothing to fear from the good people of Boston," he said, and had the courage to ride alone, with Lord Petersham, his aide, a half-pace behind him. He was right: men removed their hats and bowed to him, ladies curtsied, and small children who darted out of the throngs to obtain a closer look were rewarded with smiles and showers of farthings and other small coins.

But Burgoyne did not enjoy his captivity, and took pains to let Heath know it. Gentleman Johnny and Will Phillips were forced to share a bedroom in an inn that was turned over to them and their staffs, and the sheets were changed too infrequently for his taste. He complained because his officers were crowded by the half-dozen into chambers meant to accommodate one or two, and he roared because the firewood for the enlisted men was inadequate. Unless these conditions were improved immediately, he said, he would be compelled to take up the issue with General Washington, who, as it happened, was spending the winter in far greater physical discomfort at Valley Forge.

Burgoyne was anxious to obtain immediate transportation for his corps to England, in accordance with the generous terms of his surrender agreement with Gates, who had promised the Army of the North free passage. But there were unaccountable delays, and although Gentleman Johnny did not know it for a long time, they were instigated by no less a personage than General Washington. The American commander-in-chief reasoned that the return of five thousand able-bodied professional soldiers to England would release an equal number there for combat duty in America. But he was uncertain that the Army of the North would actually sail to England. Some loophole in the surrender agreement might be found, and in that case nothing would prevent the troops from sailing to New York to reinforce Sir Henry Clinton's garrison there.

When Gentleman Johnny learned the reasons for the Americans' delaying tactics he was outraged. Claiming that the surrender terms had been dishonored, he opened a polite but firm correspondence with Washington, emphasizing that his own word of honor was at stake. Washington was equally polite, and completely absolved General Burgoyne, while at the same time indicating he had in his possession evidence indicating that Lord George Germain was entertaining other than honorable ideas.

History has vindicated Washington and justified the stand he took. Germain was indeed intending to find some way to send the Army of the North to New York so these units could reinforce Sir Henry Clinton. Germain was never one to let someone else's honor stand in the path of his own aims.

And John Burgoyne knew his superior sufficiently well to believe that Washington was telling him the truth. Unable to complain to the Americans that the surrender agreement was not being observed, he was compelled to wait until he could take up the matter with London. That was easier said than done, in part because it was difficult to send mail from the United States to England, and partly because Gentleman Johnny himself was in no physical condition to fight anyone. He had left his sickbed too soon and suffered a relapse, but he refused to take the rest his physicians said he needed. It was far more important, he felt, to visit his troops daily, listen to their complaints, and pass along their requests for improved housing and better food to General Heath. He felt he would have been derelict in his duty had he neglected his subordinates, and even as a prisoner of war Burgoyne's sense of honor was his primary consideration.

Twenty-Two

The winter of 1777–78 dragged on interminably. It was inevitable that members of the Army of the North, bored in captivity, should find outlets for their feelings. Most of them were young, and when they consumed quantities of strong ale and stronger rum, they quarreled with the young Patriots of Boston, many of whom frequented the same taverns. What is really surprising is that no one was killed or badly injured in some of the barroom brawls that broke the Boston peace, but those who lived in the eye of the storm didn't see things that way.

General Burgoyne repeatedly came to the defense of his men, claiming they were being harried and persecuted. The Continental Congress, always quick to take offence in order to hide its own inadequacies, charged that the Lobsterbacks were being menaces to the good people of Boston. General Heath, who was caught in the middle, tried in vain to pacify both sides. The untenable situation, for which neither the Army of the North nor the citizens of Boston could be blamed, was responsible. Five thousand fighting men defeated in battle should not have been lodged in the largest city of the United States and then be given the freedom of the town. The Continental Congress was asking for trouble, and it is to Burgoyne's credit that he and Phillips held their men in check as well as they did.

Gentleman Johnny had far more on his mind than the protection of his troops from the ire of their captors and the ill-will of the Congress. The longer he himself remained in America the greater the opportunity he was giving Lord George Germain to build up his own defenses. It was becoming obvious to every thinking man that, General Washington's army remaining intact, the war in the New World would sooner or later be won by the Americans. But Germain undoubtedly was thinking of his own future, and he could protect himself only at the expense of the general who had lost the Battle of Saratoga.

On February 11, 1778, Burgoyne sent a long letter to Horatio Gates, asking his official conquerer to use his influence in order to obtain a passport for a man "who will be miserable so long as his honour remains unvindicated." Gates promised to do what he could, but held out no real hope, so Burgoyne sent an even longer letter to Henry Laurens, the President of the Congress.

His health was indifferent, Gentleman Johnny wrote; in addition to the ague he was suffering from an attack of gout that only the healing waters of Bath could cure. He had complicated accounts to settle with the British Treasury, and would be bankrupted if he did not attend to them in the immediate future. Beyond all else, he said,

> By my detention in this country I am deprived of every possible means to give an account of my actions; and my character stands exposed after an intricate and unsuccessful campaign to all the aspersions and erroneous interpretations that the malevolent, the prejudiced or the misinformed may chuse to cast upon it.

The Continental Congress was so unsympathetic that Burgoyne wrote a second letter, saying he would return to America as a hostage for the good faith of his army, should that be desired. This desperate offer made by a desperate man won the support of the most powerful man in the United States, George Washington, who had troubles enough of his own with the Congress, and who sympathized with the captive British general. The American commander-in-chief wrote to Burgoyne from his Valley Forge headquarters, saying he was:

> ever ready to do justice to the gentleman and the soldier, and to esteem, wherever esteem is due, however the idea of a public enemy may interpose. You will not think it the language of unmeaning ceremony if I add that sentiments of personal respect, in the present instance, are reciprocal. Viewing you in the light of an officer contending against what I conceive to be the rights of my country, the reverses of fortune you experienced in the field cannot be unacceptable to me; but abstracted from consideration of national advantage, I can sincerely sympathize with your feelings as a soldier—the unavoidable difficulties of whose situation forbid his success; and as a man, whose lot combines the calamity of ill-health, the anxieties of captivity, and the painful sensibility for a reputation exposed, where he most values it, to the assaults of malice and detraction.

Washington used his own influence to obtain the release of his country's enemy, and at the end of February, 1778, it was Horatio Gates who wrote Burgoyne the good news:

> Your case I feel as I ever shall that of the unfortunate brave: if courage, perseverance and a faithful attachment to your Prince could have prevailed, I might have been your prisoner. The Chance of War has deter-

mined otherwise. The Congress now send the passports you desire, and I am happy to acquaint you that the Major and Lady Harriet Acland are in New York, and may possibly be in England as soon as, or very soon after, you.

On February 28 a fleet of British troop transports, escorted by a huge ship-of-the-line, the *H.M.S. Juno*, commanded by Captain Hugh Dalrymple, was sighted off the coast, and cast anchor off Cape Cod. Captain Dalrymple sent a message to General Burgoyne informing him that the vessels necessary to take him and the Army of the North home were at hand. This set off another flurry of correspondence between Gentleman Johnny and General Heath, it being the unhappy duty of the latter to announce that the Continental Congress refused to live up to the terms of the surrender agreement. Burgoyne could go home, but the Army of the North had to remain behind.

There was nothing that Burgoyne could do on behalf of his men by staying, so he decided to leave. Summoning his troops to a farewell meeting, he candidly explained the situation to them, but made it plain he was not abandoning them. He read them a draft of his pledge to the Continental Congress, in which he swore he would return to America as a hostage if an agreement on the release of his troops was not arranged by the time he attended to his own business in England. He left the meeting with the cheers of his men ringing in his ears, under the circumstances a rare tribute to an honest and honorable man.

On the day prior to his departure, Burgoyne wrote the final version of his pledge in his own hand:

I, John Burgoyne, Lieutenant-General and Commander-in-Chief of the British Troops under the restrictions of the Convention of Saratoga, do pledge my faith and sacred honour that I will go from here to Rhode Island, where I am to embark for Great Britain; that I will not during my continuance at Rhode Island, or in any other part of America, directly or indirectly, hold any communication with, or give intelligence to, any person or persons that may be injurious to the interest of the United States of America or either of them; that I do further pledge my faith and sacred honour that should the embarkation of the Troops of the Convention of Saratoga be by any means prolonged beyond the time apprehended I will return to America upon demand and due notice given by Congress, and will re-deliver myself into the power of The Congress of the United States of America, unless regularly exchanged.

General Phillips gave a farewell party in honor of his superior, and the affair was attended by all members of the Army of the North, along with General Heath and a number of other American guests. Although Gentleman Johnny's personal finances were precarious, thanks to the large sums he had spent on food and clothing for his men without the approval of the British Treasury, he privately gave Phillips most of his remaining cash for refreshments. The afternoon was raw and cold, so many of the athletic events planned for the day were cancelled, but that did not diminish the enthusiasm of the troops for the liquid refreshments provided for them.

The next day Gentleman Johnny sailed for home on a sloop-of-war, the *Grampus,* and although his quarters were cramped he did not mind, since there was no faster class of vessel that crossed the Atlantic. His health improved somewhat on the voyage, which lasted an unexpected six weeks, due to storms, and when he reached London on May 12, 1778, he went straight to the office of Lord George Germain, whom he presented with a formal, written demand for a court-martial, the trial to be held without delay.

Germain received Burgoyne with great cordiality, promised him that an immediate War Office inquiry would be held for the purpose of determining whether a formal court-martial board should be convened, and then suggested that until such time as his case was settled it might be improper for Burgoyne to call on

King George at Whitehall. Perhaps captivity or the long sea voyage had temporarily dulled Gentleman Johnny's political sensitivities; for whatever the reason he agreed to what appeared on the surface to be an honorable request, and completely failed to see that Germain was taking the first major step in an attempt to isolate him.

A Board of General Officers was convened on May 22 under the chairmanship of the judge advocate general, Charles Gould. Other members were General the Earl of Loudon, lieutenant-generals Robert Monckton and Thomas Gage, and major-generals William Amherst and Staats Morris. Burgoyne appeared confident that they would recommend a trial by court-martial so he could clear his name, and not until the Board announced its findings on May 23 did he begin to realize that he was being expertly maneuvered by Lord George Germain. The Board, acting without precedent, ruled that the British Army had no appropriate jurisdiction over Lieutenant-General Burgoyne because he was on a parole granted by the Continental Congress of the United States.

Judged on purely legal grounds the finding was gibberish, but Germain wasted no time in making it binding, and on May 25 King George issued a decree approving the ruling. Still moving at top speed, Germain tried to prove, through the attorney general, that Member of Parliament Burgoyne was not entitled to sit in the House of Commons because of his status as a paroled prisoner of war. This claim was so absurd that the effort failed, but the government was not yet done. Charles Jenkinson, the new war secretary, twice wrote to Burgoyne, ordering him to return without delay to Boston. A failure to comply, Jenkinson wrote, was "a neglect of duty and disobedience of orders."

It was obvious to everyone who learned of these efforts that the ministry of Lord North was making an extraordinary attempt to silence the man who could ruin Lord George Germain and make the entire government look ridiculous by testifying that Sir William Howe had marched in the wrong direction, thereby isolating the Army of the North and making the outcome of the Battle of Saratoga inevitable. John Burgoyne had no intention of being gagged, and his reply to Jenkinson indicated his outrage:

The time in which I am charged with neglect of duty has been employed to vindicate my own honour, the honour of the British troops and of those of His Majesty's allies, under my late command, from the most base and barbarous aspersions that ever were forged against innocent men by malignity supported by power.

I have been denied the court-martial that is my due on the questionable grounds that I am not amenable to the law, but *I am found amenable to the law* when it becomes convenient to stifle me by directing that I return to America. It has become apparent to all who love right and justice that my enemies are systematically desirous of burying my innocence and their guilt in the prisons of America, and of removing in my person to the other side of the Atlantic Ocean the means of renewing parliamentary proceedings which they have ample reason to fear and dread.

Not being permitted the court-martial that I desire and that the cause of true justice demands, I feel myself compelled to resign my appointment on the American staff, my colonelcy of the Queen's regiment of Light Dragoons and the governorship of Fort William. I shall, however, retain my rank of Lieutenant-General in the Army so that I might be amenable to a court-martial at a later date, and in order to fulfill my personal faith to return to America, should I be required by the enemy to do so.

The exchanges of correspondence, climaxed by Burgoyne's resignation of the honors he held at the king's pleasure, took place over a period of many months, and it was the autumn of 1779 when Jenkinson wrote that George III was pleased to accept the resignation of the various appointments. Burgoyne replied at once that he was still devoted to the Crown, although "I have reason to complain heavily of His Majesty's Ministers." Jenkinson had the last word, in mid-October, 1779, when he closed the correspondence by writing that under no circumstances would General Burgoyne be granted a court-martial.

By that time Gentleman Johnny had been home for a year and five months, and the decision in no way surprised him. During those seventeen months he was far from inactive.

Immediately after his return from America in May, 1778, Burgoyne held a long conference with Charles James Fox, who predicted what would happen to him. Gentleman Johnny needed little to convince him that his friend was not exaggerating, and as soon as the Board of General Officers refused his request for a court-martial he became an active member of the official opposition in the House of Commons.

In the early summer of 1778 a fellow Member of Parliament, Temple Luttrell, came to Burgoyne's defense in the Commons, and cast so many aspersions on Lord George Germain that the Minister challenged him to a duel. Luttrell accepted, naming Burgoyne as his second, and Germain, suffering a severe case of chilled feet, rescinded the challenge.

Thereafter the question of Burgoyne's conduct in the American campaign arose from time to time, and on one occasion he made a speech defending his use of Indians. But the Tory majority maneuvered adroitly to prevent a full-scale inquiry into the matter, and Gentleman Johnny was frustrated repeatedly.

During this long period he worked incessantly to clear his good name, but obviously did not devote all of his time to these efforts. His only income was his half-pay as a lieutenant-general, and he also received the token earned by Members of Parliament. His financial situation was desperate for a time, but the Treasury settled its account with him late in 1778, Germain and Lord North apparently being afraid of the repercussions if they denied him the money legitimately owed to him by the government.

The one-time man about town lived quietly in his Belgravia house. He dined with Fox and other friends at various London clubs from time to time, but he rarely attended the theater, never dropped in at the salons of prominent hostesses and at no time was seen at the gaming tables. He was fighting for his honor, his most precious possession, and had no heart for frivolity.

It was during the late summer of 1778, however, that he renewed his friendship with Susan Caulfield. Presumably it was Burgoyne who took the initiative, although few details are known. The young actress-singer appeared from time to time at Drury Lane in various plays, but Gentleman Johnny attended none of her performances and was not seen in the theater's green room. On the other hand, he did dine with her in public now and again, and the correspondence of various members of the Stanley family indicates that she sometimes accompanied him on visits to the young Earl of Derby's London house.

It is significant that the widower turned to Susan for friendship, comfort, and solace during the greatest period of stress he had ever known, and that he thought so highly of her that he did not hesitate to escort her to the home of his late wife's relatives. In all probability Susan did not become Gentleman Johnny's mistress at this time, however, if the talk of London gossips was accurate. A man of Burgoyne's prominence was always under the scrutiny of scandal-mongers, who would have been quick to pick up and pass along any juicy tidbit about him. But literally nothing was said in print or elsewhere about his relationship with Susan during this period.

It is safe to say that their affair did not begin until he completed the task of vindicating his honor, the longest and hardest battle he ever fought.

Twenty-Three

When it became evident to General Burgoyne in the autumn of 1779 that the government would never grant him a trial by court-martial and that he was being outmaneuvered in his attempts to win a hearing in the House of Commons, he adopted a new campaign strategy. Working in close concert with Fox and Burke, he started to write a document that told his complete story, and his friends agreed to present it in the Commons, which would be required to sit as a committee of the whole for the purpose. In other words, Gentleman Johnny's court-martial would take place as a civilian trial, and his fellow Members of Parliament would act as judges and jury.

The document, which he called *A State of the Expedition from Canada as Laid Before the House of Commons by Lieutenant-General Burgoyne and Verified by Evidence* was, in a sense, his master work. It consisted of the testimony, written and verbal, that he himself presented to the Commons, and in its published version also included the testimony of other members of Parliament who participated in his "trial." He had it printed at his own expense in 1780, and two thousand copies were distributed, enough to make certain that everyone of importance both in and out of the government would learn the full details of the expedition that had ended in disaster at Saratoga.

Beginning with a compliment to Sir Guy Carleton, "who did everything in his considerable power to expedite my requisitions and desires," Burgoyne relates that his initial force consisted of 3,724 British infantry and sappers, 473 artillerymen, 3,016 German mercenaries, approximately 250 Canadians and Loyalists, and perhaps 400 Indians. It had been estimated that he would have a Canadian force of 2,000 men, which he never received, and this serious deficiency was never overcome.

Pulling no punches, he denied that he marched with too much artillery, and explained that many of his heavier guns were left to protect forts Ticonderoga and George. He was frank in discussing the Bennington fiasco, criticized colonels Baume and Breymann, and admitted that he himself was to blame for placing his faith in as slender a reed as Major Skene.

The crux of his argument began with his crossing of the Hudson:

> My army was conscious of having the superiority and was eager to advance; I expected co-operation; no letters from Sir William Howe removed that expectation. . . . I read again my orders—I believe for an hundredth time—and I was decided. Had I retreated, I rightly would have received universal blame.

He claimed that he won the Battle of Freeman's Farm on September 19, but admitted that it was a victory "without any immediate advantages." And he was almost painfully candid in saying that he lost the decisive Battle of Saratoga on October 7 only because of the decisive, eleventh-hour leadership exerted by General Benedict Arnold.

A parade of witnesses appeared before the Commons, the first of them being Sir Guy Carleton. Cautious and wanting to offend no one, the diplomat-soldier said little that helped Burgoyne's cause. What would he have done had he been in Burgoyne's position? "Every man must decide for himself. What I would have done I really do not know." What was his opinion of Sir William Howe's failure to meet Burgoyne at Albany? "I took it for granted that Sir William Howe knew what he was about, and would do what he thought best for the public service."

Men who had served under Burgoyne in the campaign were far more blunt. The Earl of Balcarres, who embarrassed the Tories by paying glowing tributes to the qualities of Americans as fighting men, made it clear that every officer in the Army of the North anticipated the junction with Howe, and was astonished when he went off to Pennsylvania instead of marching up the Hudson River. The Earl of Harrington gave similar testimony, and in addition damned the Indians and Germans as unreliable.

Major Forbes of the 9th Regiment made the flat assertion that had Howe adhered to the original plan, as the entire Army of the North had so confidently anticipated, Saratoga would have been a great victory instead of a crushing defeat. Others echoed him, including a Captain Bloomfield, who had been a member of General Phillips' staff. Lieutenant-Colonel Kingston, recently promoted from the rank of major, was even more specific: "I looked upon our force not to be equal to the forcing our way to Albany without some co-operation. I expected, as did all of us, that such co-operation would come from New York, up the Hudson River, and would be given us by Generals Howe and Clinton. I am at a total loss to understand their failure to appear, as we believed, and still believe, that the union of forces from north and south formed the kernel of the grand military design to suppress the American rebellion."

From time to time throughout the hearings, which stretched over a period of many weeks, Burgoyne was not only the defendant but acted as his own chief prosecuting attorney. On one of these occasions, when he was reviewing the evidence presented to date, he asked for and received Sir Guy Carleton's permission to quote from the letter Carleton had written to him on November 12, 1777, in reply to his own message announcing the defeat at Saratoga:

> This unfortunate event, it is to be hoped, will in future prevent ministers from pretending to direct operations of war in a country at three thousand miles' distance, of which they have so little knowledge as not to be able to distinguish between good, bad or interested advices, or to give positive orders in matters which, from their nature, are ever upon the change, so that the expedience or propriety of a measure at one moment, may be totally inexpedient or improper in the next.

Gentleman Johnny also demonstrated conclusively that, when the occasion demanded, he could remove his gloves and wade into a fight. He read into the record a letter he had sent to Germain some months earlier, when the Minister had tried to muddle the issue by blaming Burgoyne for crossing the Hudson. One paragraph in particular caused Members on both sides of the aisle to forget their decorum and cheer.

> That a man, chief in authority, should take entirely upon himself a measure of doubtful consequence, and upon mere principle preclude himself from any future means of shifting or dividing the blame that might ensue, appears incredible at Whitehall: the greater part of that political school concluded the profession of such candour must be a finesse, and that, in fact, the General had not communicated with officers, because he knew opinions would be against him. When little minds think they have got a clue of littleness, with what zeal and dexterity they pursue and improve it. Correspondence and intelligence were not wanting; disappointed jobbers, discarded servants, dissatisfied fugitives of every sort, spies, tale-bearers and sycophants, whom

it is the honour of a General to have his enemies, and a disgrace to Office to encourage, abounded in town.

In his concluding testimony Burgoyne introduced evidence that proved his case against Germain. According to a letter he himself had recently received from Sir William Howe, no instructions from the Minister telling him to march north to effect a junction with the forces under Burgoyne's command had been received by Howe. The first he had learned of the plan, he declared, had been a reference in a letter from Germain that he had received on August 16, 1777, at which time he was so far south of the Hudson River that it would have been physically impossible for him to fight his way northward in time.

The case against Germain was so damning, so embarrassing to the government, that the Tories counterattacked. In May, 1779, with an almost certain vote of condemnation approaching in the Commons, one of Germain's Tory friends, an M.P. named Rigby, brought up the old, absurd charge that General Burgoyne had no right to sit in the House of Commons because he was still a paroled prisoner of war.

Charles James Fox answered the charge, and was scathing, saying that "sitting and voting in Parliament is no more a breach of a man's parole than getting his wife with child." Warming to his theme, Fox summarized the complaint against Germain: "No blame is imputable to the honourable General Burgoyne, and the miscarriage of the expedition from Canada was owing to the ignorance and incapacity of the Ministers who planned it, and not to the General entrusted with its execution."

Germain made one error that almost opened the lid of the Pandora's box on which he was sitting. Sir William Howe was relieved of his command in America and was replaced by Sir Henry Clinton. This meant that Howe was coming home to England, and if he testified in person before the House of Commons to the effect that he never received instructions from the Minister ordering him to cooperate with Burgoyne and effect a junction with him at Albany, the whole, sordid story of Lord George

Germain's criminal neglect of his duty would be verified beyond reasonable doubt.

Fortunately for Germain, however, Burgoyne did not know of Howe's relief, and neither did Fox or any of the others who were seeking the Minister's scalp. They were pressing for an immediate vote in the Commons, and the evidence already in hand, even without Howe's personal testimony, was so damning that there appeared to be no question regarding the outcome.

An official vote of censure was imminent, and not only would Germain be dismissed in disgrace, but it was virtually certain that Lord North's entire government would fall. King George shared the concern of the Cabinet that this would happen. The war was still being fought, the ministers were on congenial terms with the Crown, and if the Whigs came into office they would press for the ending of the war on terms favorable to the Americans.

This had to be avoided at all costs, so King George acted very suddenly, and Parliament was prorogued. By making it impossible for the committee of the Commons to report that Germain was guilty and then censure him, the King protected a former officer dismissed for misconduct and cowardice in the field and denied Burgoyne his ultimate vindication. This trickery infuriated Burgoyne and angered his friends, who were still in the minority.

Gentleman Johnny would not be denied his voice, however, and as the publication of the proceedings in the Commons would take several months, he found another, more rapid way to lay his case before the British public. He wrote a letter to his constituents, addressing it to "the gentlemen, clergy and other voters of the town of Preston," but in actuality it was intended for the consumption of all of the people of Great Britain.

In it he reviewed his entire career as a soldier and as a politician, and he bore down hard on the subject of the conspiracy against him: a new etiquette was invented to make it impossible for him to have a private meeting with King George. Lies were spread regarding the strength of his army and that of the Americans he faced at Saratoga. He was charged, falsely, with being dilatory and even cowardly. Now his friends in the Army were being denied promotions they deserved, and he himself was being subjected to insults that were intolerable.

Tens of thousands of copies of the letter were printed, and they flooded the British Isles. Germain could not hope to counter this stroke of propaganda warfare without revealing more than he wanted known about his own activities, so he retreated into a dignified silence. King George made his own feelings known by promoting him in the peerage, and the reward was so ill-received that there was a noticeable decline in the monarch's already shaky personal popularity. The beginning of the end was at hand for Lord North's ministry, too, although it would continue to survive on an unstable basis for many months.

The publication of Burgoyne's voluminous report of the inquiry made by the Commons into his affairs in February, 1780, made Gentleman Johnny a public hero. He had lost a battle, it was true, and it was becoming increasingly obvious that, as a result, America was lost. But people finally realized that Lieutenant-General Burgoyne was in no way responsible. It finally dawned on the public that he was being made the scapegoat for the inadequacies and failures of the Government itself, and he became a symbol, a gallant soldier who had fought against impossible odds, first at Saratoga and then in London. Certainly Gentleman Johnny's vigorous defense of his own honor was one of the causes of the reversal of public sentiment that would sweep Lord North and his ministry out of office.

Crowds cheered Burgoyne whenever he rode through the streets, hundreds gathered outside his house to catch a glimpse of him, and when it was rumored that he was dining in a public place, the constabulary had to summon reserves in order to clear the street in front of the inn or tavern.

The government was tempted to insist that Burgoyne return to America, but his friends were too clever. Edmund Burke wrote a letter to his old friend, Benjamin Franklin, who was in Paris coaxing still more aid for the United States from France, and the old man, by far the most popular and still the most influential of Americans, took appropriate action. Letters to various leaders of the Continental Congress were all the situation required, and Burgoyne was officially exchanged for a group of about fifteen hundred Americans who were being held as prisoners by the British. And, at long last, steps were taken to permit the long-suffering troops of the Army of the North to end their enforced sojourn in America as prisoners.

The sudden increase in Gentleman Johnny's popularity, combined with his release from parole, had a tonic effect on him. Almost overnight he became one of London's popular men about town again. He was seen frequently at the theater, and when Susan Caulfield was a member of the cast it was inevitable that he should make an appearance in the green room after the performance, then escort her to supper. He renewed his friendship with playwright Sheridan and others in the theater, and he began to frequent the salons of the wealthy and fashionable again.

He continued to absent himself from the gaming tables, however, presumably because he could not afford the sport. During this period, when his income was curtailed, he had to watch his expenditures carefully, and he did not play cards again until he enjoyed a sudden, dramatic improvement in his fortunes in 1782. The fact that he did reappear at the whist table indicates that he had never lost his liking for cards.

Another major change in his style of living was his lack of interest in London's many young women. He was attracted only to Susan Caulfield, and by the autumn of 1780 the couple gave the gossips of the town something substantial to discuss. How long Susan had been Gentleman Johnny's mistress is unknown, but they made no secret of their relationship now, and before the year ended she moved into the house in Belgravia, where she acted as her lover's hostess at small dinner parties for prominent Whigs, members of the nobility, and theater people.

Perhaps the greatest mystery in the life of John Burgoyne, unsolved down to the present day, is why he and Susan Caulfield never married. They lived together openly for a decade and a half, Susan bore Gentleman Johnny four children, to whom he gave his name, and when he died he left his estate to her, so for all practical purposes she was his wife.

Early in the nineteenth century it was said that the differences in their ages was responsible, Gentleman Johnny being fifty-eight in 1780, while Susan was not yet out of her twenties. This argument is illogical, however, and appears irrelevant, since they lived together as man and wife, reared their children together, and were faithful to each other.

It may be that Burgoyne was too conscious of his standing as a gentleman to make Susan the legal successor to Lady Charlotte Stanley. Members of the gentry did not marry actresses, no matter how lovely and refined they might be, and the few who broke this unwritten rule created scandals that deprived them of the company of their peers. What makes the situation of Gentleman Johnny and Susan particularly intriguing is that both continued to enjoy a close relationship with the Stanley family, exchanging frequent visits with the Earl of Derby and with Lady Charlotte's other nephews and nieces.

Whatever the reasons for the couple's failure to marry, Susan was satisfied with her status, and Gentleman Johnny settled down with her in a comfortable domesticity that had been lacking since the death of his wife. He was happy with his mistress, and she not only shared in the triumph that restored his reputation as a soldier, but her own interest in the theater was partly responsible for the career that occupied him during the last years of his life.

Twenty-Four

John Burgoyne's dramatic muse tapped insistently on his shoulder in 1781, and he began to write a new musical play, composing the music as well as doing the libretto and lyrics, and it is not surprising that the leading feminine role was tailored to fit the talents of Susan Caulfield. But Gentleman Johnny was not yet ready to return to the theater. He was still a lieutenant-general on half-pay, and although he had succeeded in vindicating himself, he would not be satisfied until he could return to active duty in a high position of trust, thereby making it plain to the world that he enjoyed the confidence of England's rulers.

There was no chance he would be recalled while Lord North remained in office, to be sure, but Charles James Fox, Edmund Burke, the Earl of Shelburne, and other Whig friends felt confident that North's days in office were numbered. The war in America was going badly, much to the disgust of the British people, who believed the government had bungled, and the war with France and Spain was equally unpopular. Ireland was demanding a greater measure of self-rule, which Lord North refused to grant, and it seemed probable that another full-scale rebellion would break out at any time. Ample opportunities for employment awaited a general officer temporarily on the retired list, provided he could exercise patience.

Lord North and his ministers suffered from a myopia that made it impossible for them to see what the rest of Britain already knew, that the war in America was lost, and in the autumn of 1781 the Prime Minister actually prepared several drafts of a speech he intended to make when Parliament reconvened. In it he had the temerity to claim that the rebellion in the Colonies would be completely crushed within a short time and that all America soon would be restored to Crown control.

Then, in November, 1781, word was received to the effect that General Lord Cornwallis had lost the Battle of Yorktown to General George Washington, surrendering his entire force to the Americans. This defeat sealed the verdict: America had won her independence.

The British public demanded Lord North's head, and even he knew that Parliament would waste no time in voting his government out of office, so he resigned before the Lords and Commons could be called into session. A new era, for which John Burgoyne had been waiting, was about to begin.

King George was forced to offer the Prime Ministership to Charles Watson-Wentworth, Marquess of Rockingham, the leader of the Whig opposition, who was strongly supported by Shelburne, Burke, and Fox. Rockingham accepted the task of forming a new government, took office in March, 1782, and immediately opened peace negotiations with the United States, called a halt to the war with France and Spain, and announced that the Irish Parliament would be granted complete freedom in that country's internal affairs.

One of Rockingham's first acts was the recall to active duty of Lieutenant-General John Burgoyne, who was made commander-in-chief of the Army in Ireland, a post that would require as much diplomatic as military skill. But that was only the beginning. Gentleman Johnny was also made a Privy Councilor, an honor that made him one of a small group of official advisors to King George III, whom he had not seen since his return from America. And, as a final touch, he was also given the title of Master General for the Foreign Forces in Canada, a post that required him to perform no duties but paid him a full, additional salary.

Burgoyne's rehabilitation was now complete. The reputation of Sir Henry Clinton, who was remaining in New York until the conclusion of peace negotiations, was on the decline, the good name of Lord Cornwallis was ruined, and of all the senior officers who had served in the New World and were still in active service, only Burgoyne and Sir William Howe emerged with their standing unimpaired. Saratoga was not forgotten, certainly, but Gentleman Johnny's new double appointment, combined with the honor of being made a member of the Privy Council, destroyed the last vestiges of disgrace that still clung to him. His sacred honor was untarnished, thanks to the efforts of Shelburne and Burke, the most influential members of the new government.

The Irish command was welcome, but the appointment was made at an unfortunate time in Gentleman Johnny's private life. At the age of sixty he was about to become a father for the first time, and Susan was too far advanced in pregnancy to accompany him to Dublin. So he was forced to leave her behind in the care of the Stanley family's competent physicians.

A Royal Navy frigate was provided to carry him across the Irish Sea, and he traveled in his usual style, accompanied by two aides-de-camp and three personal orderlies. He had gained weight in the past two years, since he and Susan had been living together, and consequently had been forced to order a new set of uniforms, which filled a number of leather boxes. Not trusting the wines he would find available in Ireland, he brought his own supply, but apparently did not find it necessary to carry any special foods with him.

A large mansion in Dublin became his home as well as his

headquarters, he had several blooded horses in his stable, and he settled down comfortably, enjoying his post in spite of his concern over Susan. The new government's policy had defused the Irish bomb, peace was restored almost overnight, and the principal functions performed by the Army in Ireland were largely ceremonial. The eight thousand Redcoats of Burgoyne's command enjoyed an unprecedented popularity, which the commander-in-chief shared.

Every Saturday a different division passed in review, with General Burgoyne and Lord Temple, the Lord Lieutenant for Ireland, taking the salute. Dubliners by the thousands came to watch the military show, and men who had been in active rebellion a few weeks earlier cheered as the soldiers paraded.

Occasionally small units were sent out into the countryside to persuade rebels who had not yet laid down their arms to return in peace to their homes. But no shots were fired in anger by anyone, and General Burgoyne's principal problem was that of finding enough to keep his men occupied.

He himself had little to do. He took brisk canters mornings and evenings, he read a great many books and he wrote scores of letters to Susan, whom he called, "My Dearest Girl," urging her to obey the physicians and let nothing injure her health. Lord Temple's correspondence in the late spring and early summer of 1782 indicates that General Burgoyne was restless and frequently wished aloud that he were in London.

Late in July Gentleman Johnny received a short letter from Susan, informing him that on the twenty-fourth she had given birth to a son, "perfect in face and form," and that both she and the infant were fine. Two weeks later she came to Dublin with the baby, escorted in style by one of Burgoyne's aides and a platoon of light infantry who formed a guard of honor.

The child was named John Fox Burgoyne, after his father and Gentleman Johnny's close friend, and was baptized with due pomp, Lord and Lady Temple attending the ceremony along with a number of other high-ranking British officials and the leaders of the Irish Parliament.

The child was the first of four Susan would bear between

1782 and 1788, and was the only boy. The elated Gentleman Johnny proved to be a sensible father, and refusing to indulge his son, directed him almost from birth toward a military career. John Fox was educated at Eton and the Royal Military Academy at Woolwich, and was commissioned a lieutenant in 1798, two years after his father's death.

Serving in the wars with Napoleon, the younger Burgoyne enjoyed a military career as distinguished as his father's. He was subjected to severe criticism for errors in judgment made during the Crimean War, but in spite of these difficulties he was made a baronet in 1856. After the Crimean War Sir John was given the honorary post of Constable of the Tower of London, and in 1868, three years before his own death, he was promoted to the rank of field marshal.

Tragedy struck during the last year of Field Marshal Sir John Burgoyne's life when his only son, Captain Hugh Burgoyne of the Royal Navy, died during the sinking of the experimental warship he was commanding. The line died out with Hugh Burgoyne.

There appears to have been no question in Gentleman Johnny's mind regarding the future of his son. He entered the baby at Eton only a month after his birth, and his letters to Fox and other friends in England predicted a brilliant future for the child.

But life in Dublin was proving dull, and both Gentleman Johnny and Susan wanted to return to London. Burgoyne wrote a number of letters to Lord Shelburne, strongly hinting that he would appreciate a recall and suggesting that he would not be averse to an appointment as Lieutenant General of Ordnance, a post that would make it possible for him to live in town, although on active duty and full pay. The duties were more than honorary, but were far from onerous or exacting, and Gentleman Johnny apparently hoped he could end his career as a soldier pleasantly and at home. Unfortunately for his ambitions, however, Sir William Howe also had Whig connections, and was on the London scene where he could promote his own interests. He had put in a prior claim, and was made Lieutenant-General of Ordnance late in 1782.

But fresh honors were still in store for Gentleman Johnny. King George tried to make amends for his previous treatment of an old friend he had deserted by making him colonel of the 4th Regiment of Foot, which gave Burgoyne yet another salary and put more of a gloss on his refurbished reputation.

A change in the command at Gibraltar was imminent late in 1782 and the first part of 1783, and Burgoyne was offered the important post, but declined. He had grown weary of military life, Susan was pregnant again, and the couple wanted to go home to their London house. Politics gave them the opportunity. Fox was sponsoring a bill so severely restricting the East India Company that, for all practical purposes, the crippled giant would be totally destroyed. And Burgoyne wanted to vote in favor of his friend's measure.

Reaching the Commons on the day the vote was scheduled, he displayed his usual flair for drama by announcing that he had come "directly from a country in which I have the honour to hold a high post, I have crossed the sea and traveled three hundred miles overland" in order to cast his ballot.

He remained in London for the better part of two months, writing frequently on political matters to the new Lord Lieutenant, Lord Northington. During this period John Fox Burgoyne was baptized a second time, at St. Anne's Church, Soho, the highly unorthodox ceremony being held, apparently, so Charles James Fox could participate as godfather. The Earl of Derby was also present on this occasion, and thereafter took a great interest in the boy, who, as he grew older, spent some of his holidays at the Derby mansion in Grosvenor Square.

Gentleman Johnny, Susan, and their son spent Christmas under their own roof in Belgravia, and three days later their second child was born and was named Susan. The birth of their first daughter may have influenced Burgoyne's decision to remain in England, and he resigned his Dublin post, writing a letter that proved he had lost none of his flair for pomposity:

> At my age, and with a temper that finds no terror
> in the loss of income, there may be little merit, but

there will be solid comfort, in laying up for the close of life this reflection, that at a juncture which I thought a crisis in the fate of my country I took a decided part, and voluntarily, without a complaint of hardship or anger against any man or power, relinquished a splendid, a profitable, and in many respects a pleasing professional station, to pursue my parliamentary duty in connection with those men, and in support of those principles, by which alone I believed my country would be redeemed.

King George was pleased to accept the resignation, and on January 18, 1784, a few days before his sixty-second birthday, Lieutenant-General John Burgoyne formally retired from the British Army after enjoying a career that had spanned forty years. Had he been offered a place in the peerage he would have accepted it, but no such offer was forthcoming, and it is unlikely that Gentleman Johnny expected the honor, his relations with the monarch having soured since his return to England from America.

It was his intention to devote the rest of his days to writing plays, but old habits were hard to break, and he remained active in both politics and military affairs. An election was held in 1784, and Gentleman Johnny became a candidate to succeed himself as a Member of Parliament from Preston. He was so popular there that his election was taken more or less for granted, and his opponent, a man named Elton, tried to win support by publicly taunting the general.

Elton was sitting in an inn with several of his friends when Burgoyne's servant entered the place. In an attempt to entertain the crowd and make a name for himself, Elton handed the servant a valuable watch, telling him to take it to Burgoyne and ask him "if he could tell the time of day."

The manservant went straight to his master, and Gentleman Johnny was not amused. He placed the watch on a tray, together with a pair of duelling pistols, and with the servant carrying the tray, he marched to the inn. The crowd fell silent when he entered, and he asked in a loud, firm voice to whom the watch belonged.

A duel with a retired lieutenant-general who was still an expert shot had not been part of Elton's plan, and he remained silent.

Burgoyne's manner changed, and smiling pleasantly, he said, "Since the watch belongs to none of you gentlemen it remains my property."

The story of the incident spread quickly, and the delighted citizens of Preston sent General Burgoyne back to Parliament by an overwhelming majority.

In 1785 Gentleman Johnny was unexpectedly recalled to active military duty for several weeks when he was one of twenty-three prominent officers appointed by the Crown to a commission given the task of "considering the Defenses of the Country Against a Possible Foreign Invasion." The Duke of Richmond was the chairman, and the group visited a number of seaports, large meals being consumed at each stop.

The majority favored the building of forts on the Channel coast and elsewhere, but Burgoyne, ably supported by Lord Percy, was opposed to the scheme. Not only would the building of the forts place a heavy burden on taxpayers, he argued, but these bastions would be useless in the event of an invasion since an enemy would be safe if he landed beyond the range of permanently emplaced cannon. The Royal Navy, he insisted, offered England her best means of defense.

Outvoted by the majority, Burgoyne managed, as always, to have the last word. A pamphlet appeared in London, entitled *A Short Essay on the Modes of Defence Best Adapted to the Situation and Circumstances of This Island*. It was published anonymously "by an officer," but no one doubted its authorship, and the style of writing was easily identified as Burgoyne's. He presented his arguments capably, and ended with the rhetorical flourish that had become his trademark: "When the rage of innovation and novelty seizes on the imagination of a projector, reason is sacrificed to fancy, love of country to vanity, and utility to whim."

The report of the majority was submitted to the Commons, and as the debate opened, copies of the "anonymous" pamphlet were distributed. Burgoyne led the opposition to the report, and a measure recommending the building of the forts was defeated by a narrow margin. That vote enabled Gentleman Johnny to win his last military victory. But his greatest triumphs were still to come in his second profession, the theater.

Twenty-Five

The house in Belgravia was far too small to accommodate a household that now consisted of Gentleman Johnny and Susan, two small children, a governess, a cook, a valet, a lady's maid and a maid-of-all-work. So Burgoyne sold the place in 1784 and bought a larger house in Hertford Street, Mayfair, a short distance from Piccadilly. His tastes, as always, far exceeded his purse, and he had to borrow more than two thousand pounds to complete the purchase and furnish the new dwelling.

The need for funds spurred his efforts as a dramatist, and Gentleman Johnny buckled down in earnest to complete his musical play, which he called *The Lord of the Manor*. Recognizing his inadequacy as a composer and aware, too, of the need for the play's success, he discarded his score and arranged for another to be written by an exceptionally competent professional musician, William Jackson, who had achieved his own success in the medium.

The plot of *The Lord of the Manor* was as artificial as the stories of virtually all comedies of the period, but the lines were witty, the characterizations were strong, and the play contained some of Burgoyne's best poetry. The leading role, that of a sweet young woman named Anna, was played by Susan, the part having been written for her; she was fortunate to be between pregnancies when it was presented at Drury Lane in February, 1785.

The playbill announcing the production did not mention the name of the author, and the curious were informed, without explanation, that he preferred to remain anonymous. Thanks to the quality of the work the dramatist was presumed to be Richard Brinsley Sheridan, a compliment to author Burgoyne. The reason for Gentleman Johnny's reticence was as real as it was delicate, Susan's appearance in the starring role making it necessary for him to conceal his own identity so that audiences would not jump to the conclusion that she had been assigned the part because of their relationship.

In the published version, which appeared in the autumn of 1785, Burgoyne admitted that he was the author. And in a preface he paid a graceful compliment to Sheridan, saying, "As an author he is above my encomium; as a friend it is my pride to think we are exactly upon a level."

The theme of *The Lord of the Manor* was a subject which the author knew more about than any other dramatist in the history of the English theater: life in the British Army in war and in peace. The two leading roles were stereotypes, and neither Anna nor the lieutenant who loved her was in any way memorable. But some of the lyrics they sang were first-rate, and one of the lieutenant's songs became the hit of the day:

> Encompassed in an angel's frame
> An angel's virtues lay;
> Too soon did Heaven assert the claim
> And call its own away.

My Anna's worth, my Anna's charms
Must never more return!
What now shall fill these widow'd arms?
Ah, me! My Anna's urn!

The Lord of the Manor was a resounding success, its popularity due to three original, comic characters. One was a French valet, a second was a recruiting officer, and the third was a tough, hard-drinking battle-ax of a soldier's wife, Moll Flagon, the role being played by an actor rather than an actress.

The recruiting officer, Captain Trepan, offered Burgoyne some of his greatest fun. One of his posters asking for recruits, which he pins to a tree in a village green, contains a caricature of a maharajah, who is throwing handfuls of diamonds to young soldiers so they can enjoy a game of marbles. In one scene the conscientious Captain Trepan declares: "I never run the same recruit through more than three regiments, and that only when we have been hard pressed for a review."

Moll Flagon is best described by her costume: "a soldier's coat over her petticoat, she carries a gin bottle by her side and a short pipe in her mouth." She is a veteran pillager, and has the eye of an expert when she enters a captured town in the wake of the regiment she follows. When she is widowed, which happens frequently, she promptly marries another soldier, always a member of the same regiment, in which she takes great pride. One of her songs was also a hit:

Sing and quaff,
Dance and laugh,
A fig for care and sorrow;
Kiss and drink,
But never think:
'Tis all the same tomorrow.

The French valet was more of a stereotype, but Burgoyne took advantage of the character to ridicule the habits of upper-class Englishmen through the man, whose description of his master's daily toilet preparations convulsed audiences familiar with the ways of beaux who primped for hours before being seen in public.

The Lord of the Manor played one performance per week over a period of twenty-five weeks, setting a record for the age that was only bettered by the hardy *Beggars' Opera*. Gentleman Johnny not only enhanced his reputation as a playwright, causing theater managers to offer him large sums for the right to present his next work, but he also managed to repay one thousand pounds of his debts while continuing to live in the high style to which he was accustomed and to which Susan and their children quickly became acclimated.

His credit having been restored, Burgoyne once again could be seen at the whist table, where he spent a pleasant and profitable hour every afternoon. He allowed neither his pleasures nor his duties in Parliament to interfere with his work on a new play, however, and he was convinced from the time he began to write it that *The Heiress* would be his greatest success. Some of his contemporaries claimed that Sheridan worked on the script with him, but the assertion does neither man credit. Sheridan, like Burgoyne, was a professional playwright, and not only was he occupied with his own theatrical efforts, but he would have demanded a percentage of the author's royalties had he collaborated on it.

The Heiress, generally regarded as the best high comedy of the period after Sheridan's *School for Scandal*, opened at Drury Lane—the only theater Burgoyne considered for the play—on January 14, 1786, and the thunderous applause of the opening night audience acclaimed it as a spectacular success. Not only was it a solid, amusing, and cultivated dramatic work, but the starring role was played by the leading actress of the day, Elizabeth Farren.

Miss Farren was the daughter of a surgeon from Cork who fell on evil days and became the manager of a troupe of traveling players. Reared in the theater, Elizabeth displayed an extraordinary talent for portraying highborn ladies, and from the time of her first appearance in London at the age of eighteen she had been a star, the mainstay of both Drury Lane and the Haymarket.

She was Susan Caulfield's closest friend, and consequently had been close to Gentleman Johnny for a number of years. Thanks to that relationship she met the Earl of Derby, who had been separated from his wife for some time, and became his mistress. After Lady Derby's death the widowed Earl caused the gossips of London to murmur in furious, shocked tones when he made Elizabeth the new Countess of Derby, and she retired from the stage at the zenith of her fame.

It appears curious, at first glance, that Derby could marry the actress with whom he was living, but that John Burgoyne could not, or believed he could not, which was more or less the same thing. The difference, however, is easy enough to discern: the Earl of Derby was one of England's wealthiest and most powerful nobles, so he could do as he pleased without fear of censure, but John Burgoyne, soldier and dramatist, was far more vulnerable to criticism than was his late wife's nephew.

The Heiress was written at the Earl of Derby's country seat near London, Knowsley, to which Gentleman Johnny retired for several days each week in order to commune with his muse in an atmosphere free of small, noisy children. The grateful author dedicated the published version of the play to the patron who had enabled him to work in solitude.

It may or may not be true that Burgoyne wrote the part of Lady Emily for Elizabeth Farren, but the question is academic and becomes trivial because, as soon as the play took shape, there was no doubt in the playwright's mind regarding the actress he wanted for the role, nor did Miss Farren hesitate after she read the play. The blending of their talents made *The Heiress* the delight of the decade, duplicating the success of the *School for Scandal* nine years earlier. Even Horace Walpole, the inveterate letter-writer of the century, who strongly disliked Burgoyne, called it "the genteelest play I have ever seen."

Gentleman Johnny and a radiant Susan sat with the Earl of Derby in a stage-side box on the night of the opening performance, and it was obvious before the curtain fell at the end of the first act that the play would be a tremendous success. A few moments before the final curtain descended the author vanished from his seat, and was nowhere to be seen when the audience demanded that he appear on stage to take a bow. A sense of false modesty was not one of Gentleman Johnny's personality defects, so his contemporaries, Walpole among them, were somewhat bewildered by his attitude, but his conduct is not difficult to understand. He had no desire to dim the glory of Miss Farren and the other members of the cast.

The Heiress was played thirty times in its first season, more frequently than any other play in the Drury Lane repertory, and thereafter it was seen at least twenty-five times each season for the rest of the century. Always selling out, it earned the author approximately fifty pounds per performance, and gave General Burgoyne a larger income in the last years of his life than he had ever before enjoyed. In fact, The Heiress made Susan Caulfield solvent after his death and paid for the education of her children.

The plot of the play was slight, and was built on a series of contrived misunderstandings that strain the credulity of an audience. But the characterizations were masterful, the writing itself witty, urbane, and civilized. John Burgoyne's whole career as an author had been pointed toward the writing of The Heiress, and it is no exaggeration to say that his entire life had been a preparation for the comedy. The authenticity of the characters was striking: these were the ladies and gentlemen he had known and with whom he had associated, and after observing them for a lifetime he knew them thoroughly.

Lady Emily was the "compleat" aristocrat, a young woman of great beauty, charm, and artifice, whose high-society airs concealed a native intelligence, warmth, and compassion. The two male leads, Lord Gayville and Mr. Clifford, were something of a composite of the author's own personality, their mannerisms and occasional pomposity partly hiding their intellect, humanity, and desire to help the underdog. Susan thought that the heiress of the title, Miss Alston, who turns out to be Mr. Clifford's long-lost sister, was based on her own character.

To an extent the sustained success of the play was due to

the inclusion of a relatively minor character, Mr. Alscrip, an elderly attorney and roué. Audiences howled at his attempts, always foiled, to seduce Lady Emily and Miss Alston, and through him Burgoyne mocked the morals of the age, including his own acceptance of current standards.

The author's wry description of a gentleman, as voiced by Lord Gayville, is worthy of note. He is "one of those beings peculiar to this town who assume the name of gentleman, upon the sole credentials of a boot, a switch, and a round hat—the *things* that escape from counters and writing-desks to disturb public places, insult foreigners, and put modest women out of countenance." It was no mean feat for a man universally known as Gentleman Johnny to laugh at himself in public.

The play's most popular speech was delivered by Mr. Alscrip:

> What a change have I made to please my unpleasable daughter! Instead of my regular meal at Furnivall's Inn, here I am transported to Berkley Square, to fast at Alscrip House, till my fine company come from their morning ride two hours after dark. Nay, it's worse if I am carried among my great neighbors in Miss Alscrip's suite, as she calls it. My Lady looks over me, my Lord walks over me, and sits me in a little, tottering cane chair, at the cold corner of the table—though I have a mortgage upon the house and furniture and arrears due of the whole interest. It's pleasant though to be well dressed. Lord! The tightness of my wig and stiffness of my cape give me the sense of the pillory—plaguey scanty about the hips, too, and the breast something of a merry-thought reversed.

One little scene, in which Lady Emily gives instruction in manners and deportment to Miss Alscrip, the lawyer's old-maid sister, is significant because it contains a phrase, invented by the author, that immediately caught the public favor and became a part of the language for the better part of a century:

Lady Emily: My dear Miss Alscrip, what are you doing? I must correct you as I love you. Sure you must have observed the drop of the underlip is exploded since Lady Simpermode broke a tooth. (*Sets her mouth affectedly*) I am preparing the cast of the lips for the ensuing winter —it is to be called the Paphian mimp.

Miss Alscrip (Imitating): I swear I think it pretty—I must try to get it.

Lady Emily: Nothing so easy. It is done by one cabalistic word, like a metamorphosis in the fairy tales. You have only, when before your glass, to keep pronouncing to yourself Nimini-primini—the lips can not fail of taking their plie.

Miss Alscrip: Nimini-primini, imini, nimini. Oh! It's delightfully infantine! And so innocent, to be kissing one's own lips.

Lady Emily: You have it to a charm.

Everyone in London who was anyone began to say, "Nimini-primini," and the phrase was picked up by people who had never heard of Burgoyne or the play. No less an authority than Sheridan remarked that nimini-primini played a large part in the enduring success of *The Heiress*.

Certainly Gentleman Johnny's feat carried him to new heights of popularity. Never had an age so admired versatility, and he was so many things to so many people: a soldier who, by his own efforts, had risen to the rank of lieutenant-general, his standing as a strategist in no way impaired by his misfortune in losing the Battle of Saratoga; a Member of Parliament associated in the public mind with his long fight against the evil octopus of the period, the East India Company; a handsome rake who defied convention by living openly with his mistress and giving his name to their children; and finally, the author of a play that sold out at every performance and won the respect of even the most diligent theatrical critics.

Recognized wherever he went, the portly, handsomely attired Gentleman Johnny became "the chief ornament of the town," according to Walpole, who paid him a grudging tribute by commenting that *The Heiress* continued to be the delight of the theater and would be remembered long after General Burgoyne's battles and speeches were forgotten. He was right about the speeches, but like many eighteenth-century Englishmen, he failed to grasp the long-range significance of Saratoga.

England took the loss of her North American colonies in stride; her empire was still expanding, and the Royal Navy was the most powerful on the world's seas. Gentleman Johnny knew better than most that his reputation would decline through the coming decades, thanks to Saratoga, and tried to change the tide of history by delivering another long defense of his conduct in a House of Commons speech in March, 1786.

It is curious that he elected to make the address at a time when the independence of the United States had not only won universal acceptance but was being taken for granted. The loss of America was no longer an issue, and other matters were occupying the attention of Great Britain's politicians. But Gentleman Johnny could not forget that he had been the general in command of the British Army of the North, and that his defeat had made that of Cornwallis at the Battle of Yorktown inevitable.

So, at a time when he was winning renown on all sides for *The Heiress*, whose financial success permanently ended the money problems that had plagued him intermittently throughout his life, he elected to worry about posterity's opinion of him. There was nothing new in his Commons speech, which appears to have been made extemporaneously. Studded with classical references, it was long, dull, and repetitious, causing more than one critic to suggest that he might have fared better had he devoted the care to its writing that he had lavished on *The Heiress*.

Certainly Charles James Fox understood why a man of sixty-four, in his hour of triumph, should be concerned about a blot on his record that was due to no fault of his own. After Burgoyne resumed his seat, his fellow-members politely stifling their yawns, Fox stood and delivered a succinct speech on the same subject, summarizing the reasons Saratoga had been lost and placing the full blame where it belonged, on the plump shoulders of Lord Sackville, previously Lord George Germain.

Gentleman Johnny appears to have been satisfied with his own efforts and those of his friend to protect his good name. In April, 1786, the children and their governess were taken into the Derby house on Grosvenor Square, and the playwright-general-politician and Susan went off to the Continent for a holiday, a trip that was to bear unexpected fruit.

Twenty-Six

Traveling in their usual style with more than forty pieces of luggage and accompanied by a valet and lady's maid, Gentleman Johnny and Susan landed at Calais on April 12, 1786, after a crossing from Dover. They hired a private carriage and set out on a leisurely journey to Paris, where they took a large hotel suite, went shopping, dined in the best restaurants, and spent their evenings at the theater. During this holiday they attended a performance of an opera, *Richard-Coeur-de-Lion*, with a book and lyrics by Michel Sedaine and music by André Grétry, first produced two years earlier, which had won Sedaine election to the Académie Française a month or two earlier. That evening changed John Burgoyne's life and ambitions.

Richard was the product of an author who had written a number of light operas in the John Gay tradition, and then had gradually moved into a more serious field. *Richard*, his best work to date, showed only a few traces of the operetta style he was weaving into the grand opera form, and was a study of the life and character of King Richard I of England, a son of the difficult Henry II. A romantic warrior who established a reputation as a soldier early in life, Richard was one of the greatest of Christian generals who won glory in the Crusades. Kidnapped and held a prisoner while en route home, he was released only when England paid an enormous ransom for him, and thereafter he returned to the wars with his energy unimpaired.

As seen through the eyes of Sedaine, King Richard was a courtly, ferocious gentleman, a brilliant general, a soldier of great courage, yet endowed with a poetic sensitivity rarely seen in monarchs and even less frequently in generals. The character fascinated John Burgoyne, who may have seen something of himself in Sedaine's King Richard. One facet of the king's personality, his homosexuality, was not considered appropriate for the eighteenth-century stage, and consequently was ignored.

Gentleman Johnny and Susan saw the opera a second time, and the enthusiasm of the English playwright-soldier became even greater. He made it his business to meet Sedaine through mutual friends in the theater, and cancelled a projected trip to Bordeaux so he could hold uninterrupted talks with the French writer. Within a very short time Burgoyne revealed his own goal: he wanted to translate *Richard* for production in London.

Others had approached Sedaine for the same purpose over a period of two years, but he had refused to grant any of them the right. In Burgoyne he found a kindred spirit, someone who not only understood and appreciated his poetry, but saw Richard of England as he did. An agreement was reached, and Gentleman Johnny and Susan were invited to spend a week at Sedaine's country house outside Paris. There the two men discussed the opera, while Susan wandered in the flower gardens.

Returning to England after curtailing the holiday, Burgoyne started to work on the project, the most exacting writing chore he had yet attempted. He had agreed that the music would be left intact, without the changing of a single note, but Sedaine had given him permission to adapt the libretto and lyrics as·he saw fit. He bought a piano, locked himself up with it, and spent long hours at his labors. Susan was forced to reject all social engagements in the summer and autumn of 1786, but could not tell people the reason, Gentleman Johnny having decreed that the project had to be kept secret until he learned whether he could make the translation-adaptation to his own satisfaction. Friends wondered why he had become a virtual recluse, and it was rumored that he was suffering from an incurable disease, but he kept his own counsel, offering no explanation.

In February, 1787, Susan gave birth to Gentleman Johnny's third child, a daughter whom the couple named Maria, and later that same month the proud father announced a birth of his own, the completion of an English version of *Richard*. News of the latter created the greater stir.

Ordinarily no grand operas were included in the repertory of Drury Lane, but the management wanted to present *Richard*, so the author loyally agreed, although every theater in town would have been delighted to produce a new work by the author of *The Heiress*. The opera went into rehearsal in March, with a minor but difficult tenor role being sung by a newcomer with a promising future, Charles Caulfield. He happened to be Susan's younger brother, and thanks to the help he received at the beginning of his professional career by his not-quite brother-in-law, he went on to stardom.

The French composer and librettist came to London for the final week of rehearsals, with the former agreeing to conduct the pit orchestra on the opening night. *Richard* opened on April 9, almost a full year after Gentleman Johnny had been enchanted by the original French version. The English *Richard-Coeur-de-Lion* achieved a financial and critical success, playing to sold-out audiences for eighteen performances during its first season and coming close to that mark in succeeding years. Burgoyne earned thirty pounds per performance as his share of the royalties, so his already bulging purse was fattened still more, and he had no legitimate cause for complaint.

All the same, he was deeply disappointed, and with seemingly good cause. He had done the adaptation-translation because he had sought to establish a name for himself in yet another field. He had wanted recognition as a serious poet, but Sedaine was already so well established, with his membership in the Académie putting the seal of authority on his reputation, that he was given credit for Burgoyne's achievements.

Gentleman Johnny and Susan went to Bath for their annual visit soon after the opening of *Richard*, and there they read the newspaper and magazine reviews of the opera, all of them hailing Sedaine for the duplication of his Paris triumph. Burgoyne sent a bitter letter to one of Lady Charlotte's nieces, raking the critics for what he considered their unfairness. But posterity has taken a view less prejudiced than Gentleman Johnny's, and it must be admitted that the critics were right.

The only effective, first-rate poetry in *Richard* was Sedaine's, and every time Gentleman Johnny departed from the original and branched out on his own he turned out pedestrian work. He was as adept at writing light verse and high comedy as he was at commanding troops, but serious poetry was beyond his grasp, even though he reached as far as he could in an attempt to win yet another laurel wreath.

When he and Susan returned to London and their three children he had to console himself with the knowledge that he could support his growing family without strain. One of the songs from the opera, "O Richard! O my King!" duplicated its French success, and became enormously popular in England. It was played and sung everywhere, which did nothing to diminish the financial success of *Richard*, but Gentleman Johnny's cup of triumph was a bitter brew. Sedaine was given full credit everywhere, and only professional theatrical people remembered that John Burgoyne had translated and adapted the work.

Displaying artistic temperament for the first time in his sixty-five years, Gentleman Johnny brooded until he fell ill. His physicians bled him, after the custom of the time, in order to rid him of the "foul & evil humours" which afflicted him, but he showed no improvement and might have been bled to death, as was also common, had he not called a halt to the proceedings.

In the summer of 1787 the Earl of Derby gave the Burgoyne family the exclusive use of one of his estates, near the Scottish border, and there Gentleman Johnny regained his physical health and mental equilibrium. He especially enjoyed the company of his small son, took the boy riding every morning, taught him to handle firearms, and even had a small-sized fowling piece made for him so they could hunt together. Susan revealed in her letters to her brother that Gentleman Johnny was also an expert swimmer, and she said she felt no concern for the safety of John Fox when his father took him for a dip in a small lake located on the estate. Inasmuch as she did not swim herself, it did not occur to her that, even in midsummer, the waters of a lake near the Scottish border were chilly, and that father and son alike might have come down with the ague.

That summer was the most carefree that Gentleman Johnny had ever known. He played at length with all three of his children, ignoring the custom that prohibited eighteenth-century aristocrats from recognizing the presence of their children under their roofs. He read extensively, he went out alone for a long, hard ride every day before sundown, and he spent his evenings quietly with Susan, who was pregnant again by the time the family returned to London in September.

Burgoyne continued to enjoy his well-earned sabbatical, did no work, and spent several hours each day in the company of various friends, among them Fox, Burke, Sheridan, and Sir Joshua Reynolds, who was also on close terms with Burke. Occasionally he sat down for a drink at one of his clubs with such men as Lord Percy, who had fought at Bunker Hill, but in the main he saw little of fellow soldiers. He had put his military career behind him, his interests lay elsewhere, and he made few efforts to keep up old Army friendships. It was rumored that he avoided other retired generals and colonels, but the gossip lacks foundation. Lieutenant-General John Burgoyne, retired, simply didn't bother to seek the company of others who had also worn their country's uniform.

Perhaps it was because they were living in the past, while he himself was still actively pursuing his career in the theater. In addition he had a young semi-wife, there were three small children in his house, with a fourth on the way, and he had neither the time nor the inclination to sit before a fire in a club for gentlemen and reminisce about past battles, triumphs, and defeats.

He remained faithful to his political obligations, to his constituents, and when Parliament was in session he spent at least an hour or two each day at the House of Commons. Aside from maintaining his high level of attendance, however, he paid only surface attention to the issues of the day, which he found minor and irritating. He voted consistently with the Whigs, and on occasion he stood to unburden himself of a few remarks, but he made few of the long-winded speeches that had enlightened his fellow Members of Parliament in the past. It might be said that he was still active in politics, but that the interest failed to absorb him. He could still converse fluently on issues that came before the Commons, but did not become involved in them.

The failure of *Richard* to win him recognition as a major poet still rankled, and a new ambition was forming in Burgoyne's mind that, he hoped, would correct society's oversight. He was not yet ready to undertake another major writing project, however, so he continued to enjoy his daily rounds. And out of his social life he formed yet another ambition, one which coincided with his desire to win a name for himself as a poet of consequence.

He was already a member of several clubs for gentlemen, including White's, one of the most prestigious, but he wanted membership in yet another, which called itself The Club. Founded informally in 1764 by Sir Joshua Reynolds, the organization had grown, solidified, and taken on a far more formal, rigid cast. It was made up exclusively of men who had attained intellectual stature in the arts, and even Sheridan, the first-ranking writer of high comedy, had not been admitted. Its members were accused of trying to build an organization that would become an English version of the French Academy, and to an extent the charge contained an element of truth.

Never lacking self-confidence, never failing to appreciate his own talents, Burgoyne thought his poetry the equal of anything written by Oliver Goldsmith, virtually a charter member of The Club, whom he had long known but not admired. So he thought it was his due to be admitted.

According to the tradition of the organization, always observed even though The Club was not yet a quarter of a century old, newcomers did not ask to be admitted, but were invited to join. No such invitation had as yet been extended to Gentleman Johnny, in spite of his close and enduring personal friendship with the founding father, Sir Joshua. Whether Burgoyne hinted that he wanted to be admitted, and whether Reynolds replied that his ambition was premature is not known. James Boswell, the critic and gossip, who had been somewhat at loose ends since the death a few years earlier of the literary deity he had worshipped, Dr. Samuel Johnson, hinted in his own writing that this was the case, but Boswell's veracity could not always be trusted, even though he himself was an admirer of Burgoyne.

Whatever may have happened, Burgoyne had to be content to wait, and frittered away the autumn of 1787. A bill to provide the wife and sons of Sir Guy Carleton with a pension came before the Commons, and Gentleman Johnny not only supported the measure with vigor, reminding Parliament in a long address of the help Carleton had given him, but he took over active management of the measure and did not rest until it was passed by an almost unanimous vote. The activity won him the undying gratitude of Lady Carleton.

In the winter of 1787–88 trouble arose with Spain, which had the temerity to think she had a right to join in the tea trade with China and India. For a time it appeared that a new war threatened, and Gentleman Johnny promptly remembered he was a lieutenant-general. He offered his services to the Crown, even though he had celebrated his sixty-sixth birthday a few days earlier, and his letter proved he had not lost his knack for pomposity when writing on official subjects:

> I hope it will not be construed a professional rant,
> or appear in any degree a forced sentiment of an old
> soldier to say that should his period in the destination

of Providence be near, he would rather meet it in the duties of the field than amidst the sorrows and afflictions of a sick bed.

Spain backed down when she saw that Great Britain was prepared to go to war over the issue, the crisis came to a swift end, and Gentleman Johnny's offer was declined with thanks.

The affairs of the East India Company called themselves to his attention again, and he rejoined forces with Fox and Burke to fight his old enemy. He had lost none of his zest for the battle, but confined his attacks on Warren Hastings, who currently sat in Clive's hot seat, to brief remarks. He was beginning to exert his efforts as an author in another direction, and did not feel inclined to write long speeches about the evils of the East India Company when others could perform the task with greater efficiency and effect.

Two military matters aroused his sharp interest in the Commons. Burgoyne was one of four sponsors of a bill that proposed the appointment of a military commander-in-chief. Arguing in favor of the measure, Gentleman Johnny unnecessarily reminded the Commons of his own background as a soldier, and then went on to describe the bill as one intended to "bring military merit to the foot of the throne and to draw it forth from the places where ministers now never look for it—the field of actual service." Parliament, fearing the rise of a dictator if a military man was given too much power, rejected the bill.

The other bill, which he sponsored alone, was equally sensible. Army recruiting was lagging, which always happened in a time of peace, and the ranks of many regiments were unfilled. General Burgoyne, long the defender and friend of the common soldier, knew how to solve the problem, and submitted a bill that, to the horror of both Houses of Parliament, would have doubled the pay of the Army private.

He made his longest, most impassioned speech in five years, dwelling at length on the hardships suffered by the soldier, his risks, and his inability to support himself. Declaring that the profession would never be regarded as truly honorable until a soldier earned enough to keep himself and his family, General Burgoyne was far ahead of his time. "We err when we ask the soldier to make financial sacrifices in the sacred name of patriotism. It is enough that we ask him to risk life and limb out of his love for the Crown. If we take pride in him we must pay him wages that are his due, and in that manner enable him to take pride in himself."

Not satisfied with his pleas for the enlisted man, Burgoyne also supported an increase in pay for junior officers, saying, "I only wish that the Commons would take under consideration the situation of the subaltern officers at this same time: they are still obliged to subsist on their scanty pittance, although every article of subsistence is at least thirty percent dearer than when their pay was originally settled. Today's subaltern is tomorrow's general officer, and if we fail to give the junior the right to earn wages commensurate with his talents, only the wealthy, rather than the talented, will rise to the posts of responsibility. Shall we entrust the future of our armies to men whose sole qualification is their ability to pay their debts out of their own purses?"

The proposal was so revolutionary that both Whigs and Tories refused to countenance it. After a brief debate it was rejected by a bipartisan vote so overwhelming that many years passed before any M.P. with sensible, humanitarian feelings had the courage to submit a similar measure.

In the winter and early spring of 1788 Gentleman Johnny was devoting a great deal of his time and energy to a secret literary project. He referred to it briefly in a letter he sent to Susan when he went alone to Bath for a few days, assuring her that his work on it was uninterrupted in spite of the change in his daily regimen there. He also mentioned it briefly in a letter to James Boswell, who appeared to know something of what he was doing. Unfortunately, Burgoyne did not identify the work, so the subject is as much of a mystery today as it was in his own time.

He was forced to abandon it, at least temporarily, because of a personal crisis, and when he returned to his project it no longer satisfied him, so he destroyed the manuscript. The reason for his inability to concentrate was Susan's illness. Her frequent pregnancies had sapped her strength, and the alarmed Burgoyne summoned the physicians who were taking care of her.

They held a consultation after examining her, then informed Burgoyne that her health was indeed precarious. Forgetting that he was a gentleman, he brandished a pistol and threatened to shoot all three physicians if Susan died. As he later wrote Lord Derby, he instructed them to save her, regardless of what happened to the infant, and he so alarmed them that they confined Susan to her bed, ordering her not to leave it under any circumstances.

She remained there for the last eleven weeks of her pregnancy. Gentleman Johnny cancelled all of his engagements during that time to remain at her bedside, where he nursed her, read to her, and encouraged her flagging spirits with his liveliest conversation. According to Boswell he was a "model of husbandly virtues," and attended no sessions of Parliament, refused invitations to the theater, and was not seen at any of his clubs.

On May 23, 1788, Susan Caulfield gave birth to John Burgoyne's fourth child and third daughter, who was named Caroline Anna after her grandmothers. Both mother and child survived, but Susan was so exhausted by her ordeal that she remained in bed for an additional month. As soon as she was able to travel, in late June, the family went up to the Derby estate near the Scottish border for the summer. It was there that Gentleman Johnny conceived of a project that he hoped would gain him a place in the ranks of poets equal to those he had won as a playwright, a soldier, and a Member of Parliament.

Twenty-Seven

John Burgoyne's plan to win enduring literary renown was as bold, outrageous, and daring as any military strategy he had ever concocted. Now sixty-six years of age, he realized his talents might have limits, and certainly he knew he was no tragedian. So he made up his mind to work in the field of high comedy, in which he had already made his mark.

His idea was basically simple: he would translate a play by William Shakespeare into the idiom of his own time. Audiences sometimes complained that the plays of Shakespeare were too abstruse, and the masses were unable to understand their wording, so he would rewrite one in the language of his own era. He spent the better part of the summer of 1788 experimenting, when he was not riding with his son, playing with his daughters, or strolling in the gardens of the estate with Susan. He spent several hours in seclusion at his desk each day, and when visitors became curious he would only tell them that he was trying his hand at a type of writing that was new to him.

By the time the family returned to London in September, Gentleman Johnny had made his final decision and set his new goal: he would write a modern adaptation of *As You Like It*.

The revelation made sense to members of the theatrical community, and they accepted it with equanimity. *As You Like It* had been the most popular of Shakespeare's plays for a number of years, and three or four theaters included several performances every season, so Burgoyne's effort made good business sense. Literary society, on the other hand, was horrified, and called it an outrage that a man whose only claim to fame had been a handful of light comedies and a translation of an opera should tamper with the immortal work of the man Dr. Johnson had called the greatest of all playwrights.

Gentleman Johnny had expected the storm, and kept his composure, even though a number of acquaintances tried to quarrel with him when he dined with friends at one or another of his clubs. His self-confidence was unimpaired, and he spent about four hours at his desk each day, working steadily.

His schedule was less pressing than it had been when he had done his previous writing, and he found time for visits with friends, attendance at the Commons when Parliament was in session, and most evenings he escorted Susan to the theater. His life was full, he had no financial problems, and he appears to have been a more attentive and devoted father than most upper-class men of the era.

Then, in the winter of 1788–89, his timetable suffered a severe setback when he fell ill. At first his condition was not regarded as serious, although he was confined to his bed, but his condition deteriorated gradually. The door of his bedchamber was closed to the many visitors who came to see him, several physicians were in daily attendance, and the newspapers printed the rumor that he was lying at death's door. The nature of his ailment was not announced, but from the comments of Boswell and others it may be deduced that he had contracted pneumonia.

Susan nursed him with the same unflagging love he had shown her in reverse circumstances, and by the early spring of 1789 Burgoyne was sufficiently recovered to go off with her for a period of convalescence at Brighton, which was just becoming a fashionable resort. The couple did not return to London until June, and Gentleman Johnny did not return to work on *As You Like It* until the latter part of July.

He finally completed his adaptation in November, at about the same time that he began to be seen in public again. Playbills advertising the production appeared at Drury Lane in December, and no one connected with the theater was surprised to learn that Elizabeth Farren would play the role of Rosalind. She had made few appearances in Shakespeare's plays, partly because she preferred contemporary works and partly because she herself was not regarded as a classical actress. But her ties with Burgoyne were so close it was only natural that he wanted her for the role, and she was a woman who could not ignore or reject a challenge.

The John Burgoyne version of *As You Like It* opened on January 15, 1790, and the audience that filled Drury Lane accorded the star and the author ovations. Gentleman Johnny, sitting in a box with Susan and the Earl of Derby, was less bashful than he had been when *The Heiress* had opened, and went to the stage to accept his accolade. The critics were less enthusiastic, and although they admitted he had written a lively, amusing play, it was the consensus of the reviewers' opinions that the absence of Shakespeare's poetry was an irrevocable loss.

Gentleman Johnny was angry and hurt, but should have known how the critics would react. He had invited comparison with Shakespeare, and it had been inevitable from the outset that he would lose the contest. Had his *As You Like It* been judged exclusively on its own merits, it might have elicited higher praise.

Posterity has made its own judgment of his play. It was presented at Drury Lane for an average of nine or ten performances per season over the period of a decade, and then was quietly dropped. During that time it earned substantial sums, however, and after Burgoyne's death it continued to bring welcome income to Susan and their children.

Certainly Gentleman Johnny proved to the conclusive satisfaction of others that he could not be regarded as a poet of the first rank. A single stanza from one of Rosalind's songs, which reads suspiciously like doggerel, even though witty, suffices as an illustration:

> To be honest and fair is too much for our share
>   Impartially nature replies,
> Ere that Phoenix I make, let me see for his sake
>   A man that's deserving the prize!

All the same, his effort was marked by good humor and had a verve of its own. His hunting song, for example, enjoyed a widespread popularity for several years, so it can be argued that he succeeded in achieving at least one of his goals, that of bringing a modern version of Shakespeare to those who lacked the education to gain a full appreciation of the original. Even today, in spite of its obvious faults, it is not totally lacking in amusement or merit:

> Ah! the dappled fool is stricken,
> See him tremble—see him sicken,
> All his worldly comrades flying,
> See him bleeding, panting, dying.
> From his eyelids wan and hollow
> How the big tears follow—follow,
> Down his face in piteous chace,
> How they follow, follow, follow
> Without stop, drop by drop,
> How they follow, drop by drop!

The lukewarm critical reception accorded the Burgoyne *As You Like It* hurt neither Gentleman Johnny's reputation nor his purse, and after recovering from his initial disappointment he appears to have accepted the stature he had actually won for himself in the world. He knew now that he would never be regarded as a major poet, but there were few men in his own or any other time who had won as many laurels in as many fields.

In the summer of 1790 the sixty-eight-year-old playwright-general-politician went off again to the Derby estate near the border of Scotland with Susan and their four children. John Fox was eight years old now and growing rapidly, so he may have inspired his father's contemplation of his own mortality. Little is known about Gentleman Johnny's activities that summer other than the fact that he wrote his will.

It was a simple document, devoid of the bombast that usually was so evident in his prose writing. Referring repeatedly to Susan as "my dearest Sue," he left his entire estate to her, including his home, his accumulated funds, his papers, documents, and personal belongings—and his future royalties from his plays. He also specified that, after her own death, forty per cent of whatever remained was to got to John Fox, with each of his daughters to receive twenty per cent. The Earl of Derby was named as the sole trustee and executor. One portion of the will was sealed, and Burgoyne gave written instructions that it was not to be opened until his death.

An incident that occurred late in 1790 was an unfortunate aftermath of the critical failure of the Burgoyne *As You Like It*. Boswell nominated Gentleman Johnny for membership in The Club, and Sir Joshua Reynolds, who was ill, submitted a seconding in writing; it appeared that at least one of the ambitions of Burgoyne's later years would be fulfilled. He was shocked and deeply embarrassed when he was blackballed. The votes of members were supposedly secret, but Boswell made it his business to find out who had hurt his friend, and no one was more expert in the art of ferreting out information. He later wrote that two blackballs had been cast, one by George Steevens, an authority on Shakespeare, whose reasons are obvious, and the other by Sir Joseph Banks, a scientist, whose dislike for Burgoyne has never been explained.

In 1791 Gentleman Johnny was in his seventieth year, and gradually settled into genuine retirement. Susan and his children were of paramount importance to him, and he spent most of his time with them. His appearances in the House of Commons became less frequent, and he dined with various friends at his clubs no more than one or two days each week. By now he had lost interest in whist and no longer sat at the gaming tables.

That summer the family paid a final visit to the Derby estate, and the weeks passed serenely. Gentleman Johnny made no new attempts to write plays, and was content to spend his days riding, reading, and watching Susan work in her garden.

His interest in the theater remained unabated, however, and he and Susan attended performances several nights each week after their return to London in the autumn. By this time Susan's life was full, too, and she did not try to revive her own theatrical career. Gentleman Johnny spent the last year of life quietly, in the company of those he loved most and who loved him in return.

By the summer of 1792 Burgoyne's health was less robust, so the family decided to remain in London. On the night of August 3 Gentleman Johnny and Susan attended the Haymarket Theatre, then returned home for a supper of "pepper soup, poached sea-fish, a cold joint, Italian salad and tarts." Later in the night the gourmet suffered from what he believed to be indigestion, but by morning his condition grew worse, and a physician was summoned.

Before the doctor arrived, however, Burgoyne dropped off to sleep, and a few moments later he died. Susan, who stood at his bedside, saw his breathing falter and stop.

The secret clause of his will was opened that same day, and in it he expressed the wish to be buried privately. The man who had been so fond of flamboyance and glitter all of his life had realized how little these things meant. He also specified that he wanted to be buried in the cloisters of Westminster Abbey, near the spot where Lady Charlotte was buried. But, a gentleman to the last, he requested, out of deference to Susan Caulfield, that his grave not be placed adjacent to that of his late wife.

According to the *Gentleman's Magazine*, the funeral was strictly private. Only one coach drove up, and in it were Lord

Derby and three other men. One lady "was likewise present, whose convulsive agitation showed her to have that within which passeth show."

In the years that followed Burgoyne's death Susan continued to live quietly with her children in the house on Hertford Street. The marriage of Elizabeth Farren to the Earl of Derby solidified her own relationship with the Stanley family, and Lord Derby not only managed her business affairs, making certain she received the royalties that were her due from the plays Gentlemen Johnny had written, but he played an increasingly active role in the lives of the Burgoyne children, who came to regard him as something of a foster-father. Susan remained in retirement, occasionally attending the theater that she and Gentleman Johnny had loved.

In 1799 a bill was introduced in Parliament authorizing the expenditure of funds to erect a statue in honor of Lieutenant-General John Burgoyne. But the wars with Napoleon caused the Commons to devote itself to more pressing matters, and the measure was forgotten as new generals, few of them Members of Parliament and none of them playwrights, seized the center of the stage and captured the hearts and imagination of the public.

The last of the eighteenth century's renaissance men was virtually forgotten after his death. There is not one statue of Burgoyne to be found in a monument-filled London, nor one theater plaque to commemorate his literary achievements.

It remained for an Irishman, George Bernard Shaw, to make Burgoyne immortal. "Gentlemanly Johnny," as G. B. S. refers to him, steals the show in one of Shaw's most popular plays, *The Devil's Disciple*. In his notes about the play Shaw renders a judgment on his character that will last as long as men can read:

> Burgoyne fell a victim . . . in two ways. Not only was he thrown over, in spite of his high character and distinguished services, to screen a court favorite who had actually been cashiered for cowardice and misconduct in the field fifteen years before; but his peculiar

critical temperament and talent, artistic, satirical, rather histrionic, and his fastidious delicacy of sentiment, his fine spirit and humanity, were just the qualities to make him disliked by stupid people because of their dread of ironic criticism. Long after his death, Thackeray, who had an intense sense of human character, but was typically stupid in valuing and interpreting it, instinctively sneered at him and exulted in his defeat. That sneer represents the common English attitude towards the Burgoyne type. Every instance in which the critical genius is defeated, and the stupid genius (for both temperaments have their genius) "muddles through all right," is popular in England. But Burgoyne's failure was not the work of his own temperament, but of the stupid temperament. What man could do under the circumstances he did, and did handsomely and loftily. He fell, and his ideal empire was dismembered, not through his own misconduct, but because Lord George Germain overestimated the importance of his Kentish holiday, and underestimated the difficulty of conquering those remote and inferior creatures, the colonists. And King George and the rest of the nation agreed, on the whole, with Germain. It is a significant point that in America, where Burgoyne was an enemy and an invader, he was admired and praised. The climate there is no doubt more favorable to intellectual vivacity.

Principal Bibliography

ADAMS, C. F., *Studies, Military and Diplomatic*, London, 1911.

ALMON, J., *The Parliamentary Register, 1766–1800.* London, 1766.

ANDERSON, TROYER S., *The Command of the Howe Brothers during the Revolution*, New York, 1936.

BAXTER, J. P., *The British Invasion from the North*, London, 1887.

BEER, GEORGE L., *British Colonial Policy*, New York, 1907.

BURGOYNE, JOHN, *A Letter to His Constituents*, London, 1779.

———, *A State of the Expedition from Canada*, London, 1780.

———, *Orderly Book*, London, 1860.

———, *Dramatic and Poetical Works*, London, 1808, 2 vols.

Cambridge History of the British Empire, J. Holland Rose, ed., London, 1936, 8 vols.

CARRINGTON, H. B., *Battles of the American Revolution, 1775–1781*, London, 1877.

CHANNING, EDWARD, *History of the United States*, New York, 1905–1925, 8 vols.

COBURN, F. W. *History of the Battle of Bennington*, New York, 1912.

COMMAGER, HENRY STEELE, *Documents of American History*, New York, 1934, 2 vols.

DEANE, C., *Lieutenant-General J. Burgoyne*, London, 1877.

DRAKE, S. A., *Burgoyne's Invasion of 1777*, New York, 1889.

EELKING, M. V., *German Allied Troops in the North American War of Independence*, London, 1893.

FISHER, S. G., *True History of the American Revolution*, Philadelphia, 1902.

────── ,*The Struggle for American Independence*, Philadelphia, 1908, 2 vols.

FORTESCUE, SIR J. W., *A History of the British Army*, London, 1899.

HADDEN, J. M., *Journal in Canada and on Burgoyne's Campaign, 1776–77*, London, 1884.

HEATH, WILLIAM, *Heath's Memoirs of the American War*, Boston, 1904.

HOCKETT, HOMER C., *Political and Social Growth of the American People*, New York, 1941.

HUDLESTON, F. J., *Gentleman Johnny Burgoyne*, Indianapolis, 1929.

LANCASTER, BRUCE, *From Lexington to Liberty*, New York, 1955.

LOWELL, E. J., *The Hessians in the Revolutionary War*, Boston, 1884.

NEILSON, C., *Burgoyne's Campaign*, New York, 1849.

NEVINS, ALLAN, *The American States during and after the Revolution*, New York, 1925.

RIEDESEL, F. C. L. BARONESS VON, *Letters and Journals Relating to the American War of the Revolution*, Translated by W. L. Stone, New York, 1867.

SCHUYLER, ROBERT L., *Parliament and the British Empire*, New York, 1929.

STEDMAN, C., *History of the Origin, Progress and Termination of the American War*, London, 1794.

STONE, W. L., *The Campaign of Lieutenant-General John Burgoyne*, London, 1877.

TILLEY, A. W., *British North America*, London, 1911.

WALPOLE, HORACE, *Letters on the American War of Independence*, London, 1908.

WINSOR, JUSTIN, *History of America*, Boston, 1891, vols. 5 and 6.

WHITTON, F. E., *The American War of Independence*, New York, 1931.

WRONG, GEORGE M., *Canada and the American Revolution*, New York, 1935.

Index